Japanese Journalism and the Japanese Newspaper

Japanese Journalism and the Japanese Newspaper

A Supplemental Reader

EDITED BY
Anthony S. Rausch

AMHERST, NEW YORK

Copyright 2014 Teneo Press

All rights reserved
Printed in the United States of America

No part of this publication may be reproduced, stored in or introduced into a retrieval system, or transmitted, in any form, or by any means (electronic, mechanical, photocopying, recording, or otherwise), without the prior permission of the publisher.

Requests for permission should be directed to:
permissions@teneopress.com, or mailed to:
Teneo Press
University Corporate Centre
100 Corporate Parkway
Suite 128
Amherst, NY 14226

Library of Congress Control Number: 2014960261

Rausch, Anthony S.
Japanese Journalism and the Japanese Newspaper: .
p. cm.
Includes bibliographical references and index.
ISBN 978-1-934844-70-0 (alk. paper).

TABLE OF CONTENTS

Conventions vii

Introduction ix

Section One: Japanese Print Media Present, Past and Future 1

Chapter One: New Journalism in Interwar Japan
            Shiho Maeshima 3

Chapter Two: Rebalancing Japanese Newspaper Coverage
            Sachiyo Kanzaki 31

Chapter Three: New Journalism in Japan
            Akihiro Ogawa 55

Section Two: Japanese Journalism and Social Discourse 75

Chapter Four: The Ambiguity of Memory in East Asian
            Newspapers
            Choonghee Han 77

Chapter Five: Japanese Newpaper's Influence on Societal
            Discourse and Governmental Policy toward North
            Korea, 1998-2006
            Seung Hyok Lee 105

Chapter Six: Reporting of the World's Biggest Single Plane Crash
            Christopher Hood 131

Chapter Seven: Japanese Journalistic Communities
            Keizo Nanri 153

Section Three: Japanese Journalism and the Great East Japan
            Disaster 177

Chapter Eight: The Media, the Government, and the Tripartite
  Disaster of 2011
  Mary M. McCarthy 179

Chapter Nine: The Local Press in Japan and Discourses of
  National Sacrifice
  Ann Sherif 197

Chapter Ten: Local Newspapers and the Post-Earthquake and
  Tsunami Reconstruction in Iwate Prefecture
  Shunichi Takekawa 217

Chapter Eleven: From News to Memory Creation
  Anthony Rausch 241

Conclusion 265

Appendix ....

Index 275

Contributors 279

Conventions

1. Following Japanese practice, Japanese names will be provided family name first, given name second.
2. Rendering Japanese in the English alphabet can be problematic; a case in point is *"shimbun"* versus *"shinbun"* for the word "newspaper." *"Shimbun"* will be used in the romanized names for Japanese newspapers, except when there are compelling reasons to use *"shinbun."*
3. The research herein is that of the respective contributors. Any language errors that remain are a product of the editing of the text and are therefore the responsibility of the editor.

Introduction

Japanese Journalism and Japanese Newspapers

The aim of this reader is to introduce Japanese journalism and print media in Japan, focusing on Japanese newspapers and the journalism that produces it. The chapters present research that has either focused on journalistic practice and product as research topic or has used journalism and newspapers as an information source in social science research. In this sense, the contents both describe and evaluate Japanese journalism and its newspapers, while also highlighting the contribution such research has made to the field of Japanese Studies. At a broader level, the contents offer exploratory viewpoints, outline methodological approaches, and present empirical case studies, highlighting not only how journalistic practice and the news it produces constitute a meaningful research area, but also how use of journalism and the newspaper as source can contribute to research across a range of diverse themes.

Journalism and the Newspaper

Some say print is dead. Yet, the newspaper has a number of specific qualities that continue to make it relevant and meaningful. Most general-interest newspapers are published daily, and arrive for most readers on the doorstep each morning by virtue of a paid subscription and a local delivery system. Alternatively, one can find a range of national and local newspapers available at newsstands, convenience stores and most stations and airports. Newspapers generally cost little more than a vending machine beverage and are organized and written with the average adult reader in mind.

Newspapers cover an impressive range of content on an everyday basis. National and regional newspapers offer timely news on governance, economics and politics both international and domestic, along with editorials outlining the viewpoint of the newspaper as well as guest opinions reflecting a range of views. Most large newspapers also offer sports, a lifestyle section, and local news. Local newspapers, with limited resources and a more restrained mandate, focus on their locale, providing local business or agricultural news, local weather and and sports, and local obituaries, along with the local television and radio listings. To sum up, the average newspaper is accessible on the basis of availability, price, and readability, and both extensive and intensive in terms of content, interest and news value. As such, the print-on-paper newspaper continues to be a dependable, one-stop news and information source that is mobile yet disposable, tangible yet recyclable, and provide for much of the content we need in our day-to-day lives.

The journalism that has produced this newspaper likewise reflects a number of meaningful qualities. The institutional gravitas of the industry, together with the process of gathering, writing and editing content that constitutes journalism, has meant that newspapers were deemed authoritative, comprehensive and relevant. Journalistic authority originated in its access to power and information, while the writing and editing that have always been inherent in traditional newspaper publishing reflected professional practices that ensured comprehensive content and important context. The journalistic endeavor not only ensured that important issues were covered, but that the issues that were covered were important, and that there was something of value for each reader in each paper.

The demise of the newspaper is generally seen as an outcome of advancing information technology and changing social dynamics, whether in relation to the gathering of the news, the process of production and dissemination, or the eventual consumption by reader. Reporters don't "work a beat" as in the past; content is now made available through press conferences or purchased through wire services. Electronic "publications" don't require costly brick and mortar infrastructure; rather, fierce competition demands portability, appealing formats, and interactivity, all while also providing constant updates, with social media replacing the traditional opinion-editoral column. In this sense, print journalism's future authority, comprehensiveness and relevance in this high stakes, high tech media environment will be increasingly important. Authority will likely be seen less in the trappings of name value and links with political power than in diligence toward neutrality based in truth. Comprehensiveness will likely come less with institutional reach and thematic coverage than with journalism working to counter the polarization of special interests though accommodation of the multi-dimensional interactions, connections and viewpoints that characterize modern controversy. And finally, journalistic relevance will come less with traditional agenda setting than with journalism's contribution to an informed citizenry, thereby furthering the public good.

While the fate of journalism within the trajectory of overall media evolution is still being negotiated in a mutually-deterministic relationship between producer and consumer, the daily newspaper still maintains a prominent place in contemporary society, and therefore consideration of its function, its impact, and its trajectory remains meaningful.

Japanese Journalism and the Japanese Newspaper

According to *"Geographies of the World's Knowledge"* (Oxford Internet Institute, 2011), the Japanese newspaper *Yomiuri Shimbun* is the most read newspaper in the world, claiming a circulation of well over ten million daily readers. The *Yomiuri* is followed in the second spot by the *Asahi Shimbun*, with around eight million readers, and by the *Mainichi Shimbun* in the third, with around five million readers. Next in line are two more Japanese newspapers, the *Nihon Keizai Shimbun* (number 4) and the *Chunichi Shimbun* (number 5), with the *Sankei Shimbun* number nine out of the top ten.

Such global prominence is meaningful to note in that contemporary newspapers around the world are experiencing clearly different fates. According to the World Association of Newspapers and News Publishers (WAN-IFRA), whereas the most recent five-year trends in newspaper circulations have shown declines in North America (-13%), Western and Eastern Europe (-25%) and Latin America (-1%), growth has been the trend in Asia (+10%), the Middle East and North Africa (+10%) and Australia and New Zealand (+1%). Likewise, newspaper-advertising revenues have declined over the past five years in North America (-42%) and Western and Eastern Europe (-25%), as well as the Middle East and Africa (-23%), and Australia and New Zealand (-25%), while increasing in Asia (+6%) and Latin America (+37%) (WAN-IFRA, 2 June 2013).

Such strong numbers for the Asian newspaper media as a whole aside, the industry within Japan is facing what Hayashi (2013) called the "calm before the storm." While circulations have declined slowly, from 53 million in 2000 to 47 million in 2013, total newspaper revenue in Japan has fallen by 20% over the past 15 years, with that decline clearly due to a dramatic drop in advertising revenue. Accounting for roughly one-third of total revenues in 1997, advertising revenue is now approximately half what it once was, while the 60% of revenue gained from circulation has remained largely steady. Industry data reveals subscriptions to both morning and evening editions numbered 12.4 million 2013, with morning

Introduction   xiii

only subscriptions numbering 33.5 million, yielding a home delivery rate of 0.86 per household in 2013, but down from a level of 1.13 in 2000. Accordingly, the total number of newspapers operating in Japan has also seen a decrease, dropping from 122 in 2000 to 117 as of 2013 (Japan Newspaper Publishers and Editors Association, undated; cited from Hayashi, 2013).

There are three characteristics of the Japanese newspaper industry that account for its state of "calm"—high issue and subscription price, ubiquity of home (and business) subscriptions, and *chirashi* advertising—and one that portends the "storm," demographics. Japanese newspapers, while generally affordable, have a relatively high price, meaning that the industry is partially immune to the decline in advertising revenue from described above. The price resiliency of Japanese newspapers is in part explained by the high rate of subscription delivery by both residents and businesses. What drives the subscription rate? For businesses, it is the practice of providing, both for employees and customers, a daily paper. For homes, it is inclusion of the *chirashi* advertising copy that accompanies home delivery of every newspaper. *Chirashi* is separate from the newspaper itself and typically includes supermarket sales information, notices of retail sales, real estate advertising, and pachinko-gaming house fliers. Most readers appreciate the informational value and convenience of this advertising, and expect it as a part of their newspaper. In sum, *chirashi* advertising contributing to high rates of home delivery and businesses' sense of obligation in providing newspapers for their employees and customers work in combination to relieve the newspapers from overrelying on advertising revenue and therefore allow them to maintain their current business models. The demographic "storm" that Hayashi referred to is, however, clear and near. Readership data for 2005 and 2010 show clearly that the male over-50 age group reads the print newspaper at twice the rate they use the Internet. For cohorts under 50, the pattern is reversed, and increasingly stark with descending age-groups, to where print newspaper reading rates are approximately 5% for the 20-29 age group with Internet use more than doubling over the period

(NHK Broadcasting Culture Research Institute, 2010; cited in Hayashi, 2013). The question that will determine the fate of newspapers in Japan is which pattern will prevail: the continued allure of the Internet as the dominant medium of information access for these young consumers even as they age or the value-added draw of home delivery that accompanies a newspaper for a increasingly domicled readership.

Turning from circulation and revenues to the newspapers themselves, these national, regional and local newspapers combine to constitute a three-layer highly regional industry structure. The first layer is composed of the five national dailies—the *Yomiuri Shimbun*, the *Asahi Shimbun*, the *Mainichi Shimbun*, the *Sankei Shimbun*, and the *Nihon Keizai Shimbun*— that are distributed and read throughout the nation. These newspapers are, in fact, pieces of massive corporate entities. The *Yomiuri Shimbun* is part of Yomiuri Shimbun Holdings, which includes a major publishing company and the Nippon Television Network Corporation along with the Yomiuri Giants professional baseball team. The *Asahi* can claim as part of its company group Nikkan Sports and TV Asahi, the Asahi Broadcasting Corporation and Nippon News Network. The *Sankei Shimbun*, literally the "industrial and economic newspaper," is part of the Fuji Sankei Communications Group and is partly owned by Fuji TV.

The second and third layers contain what can be defined variously as regional (also referred to as block), and, more locally, prefectural or local newspapers, depending on the character and geographic range of a particular paper. Regionally geographical in identity, the block newspapers are based in a large regional-center city and have circulations that cover a regional block of Japan: the *Chūnichi Shimbun*, which is Japan's largest block newspaper, covering the Nagoya area, and its sister publication the *Tokyo Shimbun*, published in Tokyo, for example. Virtually identical in content, their combined circulation nearly matches that of the national-level *Mainichi*. The other two dominant block newspapers are the *Hokkaido Shimbun* and the Kyushu-based *Nishi-Nippon Shimbun*. Under the block newspapers in size and prestige are the prefectural newspapers.

Introduction xv

As the name implies, prefectural newspapers cover a namesake prefecture, with 26 adopting the name of their host prefecture, as in *The Iwate Shimpō* of Iwate Prefecture and *The Nagasaki Shimbun* of Nagasaki Prefecture to name just two. Conversely, there are "prefectural newspapers" that do not take the name of the prefecture, seen in examples such as the *Tōōnippō* of Aomori Prefecture and the *Nihonkai Shimbun* of Tottori Prefecture. Finally, constituting the bottom layer, there are many small and local newspapers that are supported by their locales, in both the urban centers of Japan and throughout the outlying areas. This has yielded an interesting array of monopoly markets, areas with only one prefectural newspaper, versus competive markets, where prefectural-level newspapers have to compete with other local papers (Rausch, 2012). As for Japanese journalism, the content herein will provide ample substance for readers to come to their own conclusions.

The Present Book

With this foundation in mind, we return to the aim of this book: to introduce Japanese journalism and Japanese newspapers through a series of academic research works. The content includes eleven case studies reflecting research undertaken by researchers with varied disciplinary backgrounds and differeing research objectives. Some of the chapters reflect research in which a specific research question was posed, for which journalism or a newspaper emerged as the primary research component to answer that question. Other chapters present research in which the media itself presented a socially meaningful research theme, in grounded approaches emerging out of long-term and systematic reading of a newspaper or newspapers. Some of the research utilizes themes examained elsewhere: the Japanese Press Club, the Yasukuni Shrine visits, the crash of JAL flight 123. Other work focuses on more recent themes and events: print media's response to advancing digital technology, the interaction between media and consumer consciousness, and, of course, the Great East Japan Disaster of 3.11. The chapters are all different in style: some vaguely autobiographical, others rigorously academic. Some of the research is historical, some contemporary; some is ethnographic, some empirical. Some of the work is offered by Japanese researchers viewing their own society; other work is the product of non-Japanese academics looking inward to further understand Japan.

The first section focuses on Japanese print media in the past, the present and the future. The first chapter, *New Journalism in Interwar Japan: Cautionary Notes for Researching Japanese Print Media* by Shiho Maeshima, identifies insights that can be gained from historical studies of print media. Examining the emergence of "new journalism" in early 20th century Japan, the focus is the relationships between nation-state, publishing industry, social milleau, and writer, article, and reader. Through this analysis, Maeshima identifies historical continuities and transitions that account for common media representations while also highlighting points for the researcher to be aware of when working with historical media.

Sachiyo Kanzaki, in the second chapter, *Rebalancing Japanese Newspaper Coverage: National and Kansai Newspapers in the Digital Age,* looks at regional characteristics of the print media environment in Japan while also considering how increasing digitalization of print media can accommodate not just regionalism, but more significantly, localism. Centralisation on Tokyo as a Japanese national phenomenon has long been problematic. Although significant in the early history of Japanese print media, newspapers of the Kansai area today are suffering from this centralisation as well. However, an opposite tendency can be observed in parallel to this concentration: diversification of print media through the Internet. Based on a historical review and extensive interviews with Kansai journalists, Kanzaki outlines these contrasting phenomena, pointing to the value of the local journalism made possible through advancing information technology.

In the third chapter, *New Journalism in Japan: Using Independent Digital Sources for Social Research,* Akihiro Ogawa considers new forms of independent journalism in Japan and what these can mean for researchers who

Introduction   xvii

look to journalism sources in their research. To present his case, Ogawa focuses on how independent Internet-based news services covered the post-2011 disaster anti-nuclear demonstrations of summer 2012, sources that provide unedited media data, allowing researchers to independently judge the news for its veracity, viewpoint and value. Finally, with five years experience as a staff reporter at a major Japanese wire service in Japan, the suthor also offers valuable personal reflections on the practice of journalism in Japan.

The second section takes up Japanese journalism and its influence on social discourse through consideration of four highly specific cases. The first chapter, *The Ambiguity of Memory in East Asian Newspapers: Journalistic Representations of War Memories,* contributed by Choonghee Han, takes up print media's influence on social memory. The chapter explores the discursive constructions of memories relating to the Asia-Pacific War that appeared in three newspapers, one each from China, South Korea, and Japan, on the basis of three fundamental disputes playing between Japan and its neighbors: politicians' visits to Yasukuni Shrine, history textbook revisions, and the "Comfort Women" issue. Critical discourse analysis, together with interpretive policy analysis, show that the construction of memory occurred in different ways in different newspapers, a reflection of ambiguity, reification, naturalization, exclusion, and appropriation of memory.

The second chapter, *Japanese Newspaper's Influence on Societal Discourse and Governmental Policy toward North Korea, 1998-2006,* takes up Japan's foreign policy toward North Korea. Noting how Japanese policy evolved between 1998 and 2006, Seung Hyok Lee focuses on the role of national Japanese newspapers in framing Japanese social discourse toward its neighbor. The research contends that comprehensive coverage of North Korean threats to Japan in newspaper editorials changed the views of ordinary Japanese citizens, and that this shift of social opinion in turn influenced policy decision-making at government levels. Lee's conclusion speaks to the influence that Japan's journalism community, by generating changes in societal discourses, had on national policy determinations.

In a chapter titled *Reporting of the World's Biggest Single Plane Crash*, Christopher Hood takes up the journalistic treatment of the Japan Air Lines (JAL) flight JL123 crash, which occured in the mountains northwest of Tokyo on 12 August 1985. As a media frenzy enveloped the crash, the way in which the event was reported on varied greatly between national and local newspapers. The chapter highlights the importance of various media levels in gaining an understanding of a particular topic, taking into account different social viewpoints, news objectives and operational constraints between levels of media coverage.

In the last chapter of the section, Keizo Nanri provides an important contribution to the debate regarding Japanese media as lacking opinion diversity and accommodating content conformity. The chapter, *Japanese Journalistic Communities: Politics, the Newspaper and Nico Nico Dōga*, is based on analysis of 40 national, regional, and local Japanese newspapers together with political videos uploaded to the video streaming website *Nico Nico Dōga*. The research examines coverage related to the TransPacific Trade Partnership, Abenomics, and national security issues. Extensive in coverage and detailed in analysis, the research focuses on diversity and conformity in Japanese journalism, offering timely conclusions on the intersection of politics, media and public political consciousness as a function of journalism and news source.

The third section focuses on Japanese journalism in its treatment of the 3.11 Great East Japan Disaster. The first chapter of this section takes up an examination of journalism as related to panic, leadership, transparency and cooperation in the aftermath of a disaster. After outlining the role of media in a time of crisis, Mary M. McCarthy, in a chapter titled *The Media, the Government, and the Tripartite Disaster of 2011*, uses "print media content analysis" to outline how the government and the media interacted in these four realms. The research finds that editorialization of the event in the *Yomiuri Shimbun* was highly nuanced, being both quiescent to

Introduction   xix

a government agenda that sought to create a sense of calm, while also bringing up critical questions about political leadership, cooperation and transparency as well as journalistic access to information.

In a chapter titled *The Local Press in Japan and Discourses of National Sacrifice,* Ann Sherif examines the *Chūgoku Shimbun's* journalistic treatment of the 3.11-related nuclear disaster, focusing particularly on image versus reality and the government's handling of the evacuee-returnee situation against the backdrop of radiation concerns. The chapter reveals the ways that the local press in Japan operates in forming public opinion and how newspapers provide a means for researching opinion formation on timely issues, demonstrating the importance of monitoring a newspaper's single-issue coverage over time as a means of uncovering the ideological and ethical assumptions that guide a newspaper in its investigative activities and coverage.

In the third chapter, Shunichi Takekawa looks at local newspaper reporting in a chapter titled *Local Newspapers and the Post Earthquake and Tsunami Reconstruction in Iwate Prefecture.* After the 3.11 earthquake and tsunami disasters, the *Iwate Nippo,* a major newspaper of Iwate prefecture, together with a more local community newspaper in one of the tsunami damaged areas in Iwate, the *Tokai Shimpō,* both worked to record the struggles of the residents and the recovery of the region. Takekawa categorizes serialized content of these papers in five functional categories: fact recording, collective memory creation, public policy, human bond promotion and future / local wishes. Looking at this quantitatively as well as qualitatively, Takekawa outlines the functional objectives of newspapers in post-disaster coverage, not just in terms of reporting facts, but as importantly in creating and consolidating solidarity among community members at one level and prefectural residents at another.

The fourth chapter also takes up local newspaper coverage of the 3.11 disaster, focusing in detail on how journalism practice contributed to creation of long-term memories of the disaster. In a chapter titled *From News to Memory Creation: Regional Newspaper Coverage of the Great*

East Japan Disaster, 2011, Anthony Rausch examines post-disaster local newspaper coverage in its role in public memory creation of the event. On the basis of a long-term multi-dimensional examination of three Tohoku-disaster area newspapers and a wire service column, the research identifies a transition from multiple "news" themes to a variety of thematic frames that are presented and developed in long-running newspaper columns. The research contributes to better understanding of both media response to large-scale disasters and proposes a new understanding of the newspaper in post-event public memory construction through the form of newspaper columns.

REFERENCES

Hayashi, K. (2013). Japan's Newspaper Industry: Calm Before the Storm. nippon.com (6 November 2013). Available online: www.nippon.com/en/currents/d00097/.

Oxford Internet Institute. (2011). Geographies of the World's Knowledge. Available online: www.oii.ox.ac.uk/.../convoco_geographies_en.pdf.

Rausch, A. S. (2012). *Japan's Local Newspapers: Chihōshi and Revitalization Journalism*. London: Routledge.

World Association of Newspapers and News Publishers. (2013). World Press Trends. Available online: www.wan-ifra.org/microsites/world-press-trends.

Japanese Journalism and the Japanese Newspaper

Section One

Japanese Print Media
Present, Past and Future

Chapter One

New Journalism in Interwar Japan

Cautionary Notes for Researching Japanese Print Media

Shiho Maeshima

Introduction

In the interwar period, Japanese women's magazines dominated Japanese print media, their popularity in the 1930s described by Nii (1931) as follows:

> Most women's magazines in today's Japan . . . enjoy an extraordinary level of circulation, which is said not only to exceed those of all the other kinds of magazines, but also to surpass those of withering newspapers. (p. 267)

Annual circulation figures from Tōkyōdō subscription agent, show that women's magazines were the most popular magazine genre from 1929 until 1934 (Tōkyōdō Tōkeibu, 1935), and Hashimoto (1964) wrote that the top three selling magazines at the time were women's magazines, each with double the circulation of *Chūō Kōron,* a top intellectual magazine.

This chapter will examine the characteristics of interwar Japanese women's magazines in the context of print culture in modern Japan, considering the development of gendered magazines in modern Japan and the impact of the women's magazine in the early 20th century. The chapter will conclude by outlining what lessons relevant to the study of present-day journalism can be taken from historical studies of periodicals.

Rethinking Popular Women's Magazines in Interwar Japan

Ōya Sōichi, a leading early 20th century journalist, observed that women's magazines brought about an "industrial revolution" in Japanese publishing culture. Distinct from the reading public that existed at the time, what he termed an "advanced, civilized intelligentsia," women's magazines brought about "the discovery of a cultural colony" of female readers in the new Japanese middle class. This new reading public, he explained, appeared after the First World War, thanks to the spread of education, rising interest in cultural affairs, increased disposable income, and expanded demand for mass-market print media by middle class women (1959/1934).

Interestingly however, the readers of interwar women's magazines, *fujin-zasshi*, were neither just middle class nor women. Not only did women from lower classes also became avid readers of popular women's magazines, these "women's magazines" were also read by men (Nagamine, 1997). Moreover, comments on interwar women's magazines at the time also suggest that their editorial and promotional influence on journalism in general was notable. A June 24, 1933 article appearing in the *Asahi Shimbun* pointed out:

Generally speaking, in terms of capitalistic production, no sector made progress as drastic as women's magazines did. One could say that magazine culture was led by women's magazines to an extraordinary stage. ... [E]ven major general magazines and newspapers have adopted methods used by women's magazines to one degree or another. (Aono, 1933, p. 9)

MARGINALIZED RESEARCH

Despite the powerful role the women's magazine played in the early history of print publication in Japan, study in this area has largely been marginalized in academia. Pre-Second World War Japanese mass-market women's magazines, such as *Fujokai* (The World of Women and Girls, 1910–1952), *Shufu no Tomo* (Housewife's Friend, 1917–2008), and *Fujin Kurabu* (Women's Club, 1920–1988), have been studied on the basis of either the history of print culture or women's history. In the former, the work has focused largely on the flashy popularization of print-culture (Hashimoto, 1964; Ishikawa, 1959; Ogawa, 1962; Okano, 1957; Shimizu and Kobayashi, 1979). Early studies based on women's history regarded interwar women's magazines as "insignificant" or "vulgar," particularly when compared with the "sophisticated" or "more stylish" women's magazines such as *Seitō* (Blue Stockings, 1911-1916), *Fujin Kōron* (Women's Review, 1916-), and *Fujin Gahō* (Women's Pictorial, 1905-). These magazines were viewed as intellectual and served as archival sources from which one could retrieve "women's voices" (Kindai Joseibunkashi Kenkyūkai, 2001; Oka, 1981; Watashitachi no Rekishi o Tsuzuru Kai, 1987). While recent scholarship has been more nuanced, the focus has been on socio-historical analysis of the construction of modern discourses or practices concerning women's subjectivity, using such themes as the housewife or the modern girl, consumer culture, and new lifestyles (Ishida, 1998, 2001, 2003, 2004; Kimura, 1989, 1992, 2004, 2006a, 2006b; Koyama, 1991, 1999; Muta, 1996; Wakakuwa, 1995; Yomo, 1995). Some researchers have insisted that attention should be paid to the crucial role that women's magazines played in the modernization of Japanese publishing, on the basis either of the genre itself (Nagamine

1997; Satō, T., 2002) or a particular element of the genre such as serialized novels or advertising styles (Kitada 1998; Maeda, 1973/2001). It is with this background in mind, that analytical attention to women's magazines *per se* as a cultural product in the context of the development of print media in Japan is justified.

Gendered Development of the Modern Japanese Magazine

Early Magazines in Japan

The first magazine published in Japan in the "modern" sense, which is to say in the form of a periodical featuring a variety of content connecting past reportage and commentary with present "news," was *Seiyō Zasshi* (Western [or European] Magazine), founded by Yanagawa Shunzō in 1867 and continuing until 1869. As the title suggests, this monthly was modeled after European magazines of the time, and consisted of translated academic articles, ranging from natural sciences to history.

Strictly speaking, however, it was not until the 1870s that the magazine as a regular periodical was established in Japan, with the publication of *Meiroku Zasshi* (*Meiroku Magazine*) in 1873. Various others followed: *Eisai Shinshi* (*New Magazine for Geniuses*, founded in 1877), *Tokyo Keizai Zasshi* (*Tokyo Economics Magazine*, 1879), *Seirisōdan* (*Magazine of Political Theories*, 1882), *Jogaku Zasshi* (*Magazine of Women's Learning*, originally founded as *Jogaku Shinshi* or *New Magazine of Women's Learning* in 1883 and relaunched in 1884), *Chūō Kōron* (*Central Review*, originally launched as *Hanseikai Zasshi* in 1887, and renamed *Hansei Zasshi* in 1892 and *Chūō Kōron* in 1899), *Kokumin no Tomo* (*The Nation's Friend*, 1887), two versions of *Katei Zasshi* (*Home Magazine*, one in 1892 and the second in 1903), and others like these. These early magazines targeted mainly intellectuals and contributed greatly to the introduction of Western ideas and trends, both social and cultural, into Japan.

Reflecting this, early periodicals in Japan were not categorized according to the gender or age of their target readers. While some titles included words such as *jogaku* (women's learning) and *katei* (home), appearing to indicate that they were published especially for women and edited differently from magazines for men, until the turn of the century Japanese magazines had been, both thematically and formally, undifferentiated in terms of gender. Analyzing various magazines in the 1880s and 1890s, historian Muta (1996) concluded that, up until around 1890, so-called "general magazines" included articles concerning family, love-based marriage, domestic chores and the like, themes that later came to be known as "women's matters." Moreover, most articles in these 19th century periodicals, except for creative essays that offered a venue for experimentation in colloquial writing styles, were rendered in a literary writing style called Meiji general style (*Meiji futsūbun*).

Indeed, these magazines were read by all intellectuals, male and female. Although originating with an aim in "enlightening" Japanese women, *Jogaku Zasshi* was actually viewed as a general magazine aimed at intellectuals and was a venue for progressive writers offering new writing styles (Yamamoto, 1981). Thus, magazines that came to be categorized as "women's magazines" functioned early on as general intellectual magazines for male and female alike.

Content Diversification and Gendered Differentiation
The late 1880s to the early 1900s saw trends toward content diversification in publishing in Japan, with big publishers issuing a range of monthlies. Hakubunkan formed its own "publishing kingdom" on the basis of general magazines such as *Taiyō* (*The Sun*, launched in 1894), *Bungei Kurabu* (*Literature Club*, 1895), *Shōnen Sekai* (*Boy's World*, 1895), *Jogaku Sekai* (*Female Students' World*, 1901), and *Shōjo Sekai* (*Girls' World*, 1908). Jitsugyō no Tomosha also published a diversified range of thematic magazines such as *Jitsugyō no Nihon* (*Japan Business*, founded in 1896), *Fujin Sekai* (*Woman's World*, 1906), *Nihon Shōnen* (*Japan Boy*, 1906), *Shōjo no Tomo* (*Girls' Friend*, 1908).

With this diversification, periodical publication in Japan experienced a dramatic discursive configurative shift, as magazine genres at the turn of the century gradually became differentiated by age, gender, and education level or class of their target readers, both in terms of their content and their form. First, thematic distinctions began to appear between magazines for men and those for women. Gradually, anything related to "family" or "everyday life," namely, things belonging to "the domestic sphere," came to appear only in women's magazines, however social or philosophical the actual content or intention might have been. Considering the gravity of the gendered thematic division among magazines emerging around 1890, Muta called this phenomenon "feminization/privatization of domesticity" (1996, p. 54).

The feminine/masculine dichotomy of print culture was also apparent in the adoption of different writing styles, where orality as a style was pioneered by women's magazines. After decades of struggling to create new writing styles based on everyday utterances, two colloquial writing styles (the "*desu/masu*" style and the less formal "*da/de aru*" style) were officially established with government-designated textbooks compiled in 1903–1904 (Yamamoto, 1981). Soon after that, in 1906, *Fujin Sekai* was launched as one of the first periodicals in Japan that was completely based on a colloquial writing style, preceding the first "national" magazine to do so, *Taiyō*, by a few years, and the major newspapers by a decade. While magazines for women, youths, and children overall had adopted the "*desu/masu*" style by 1910 (Iwata, 1997), magazines for male intellectuals and major newspapers maintained a formal literary writing style. Even in the 1910s, around 10% of bylined articles in *Taiyō* used the formal "*nari/tari*" language (or *Meiji futsūbun*) (Suzuki, 1996). For newspapers, it was only in the 1920s that there was a gradual shift in their writing style to the "*da/de aru*" style (Mainichi Shinbun Shashi Hensan Iinkai, 1972; Shashi Hensan Iinkai, 1952).

Therefore, women's magazines were said to be filled with "conversations" (*danwa*), while articles in "general" magazines and newspapers were regarded as more objective and scientific. In fact, many of the articles in women's magazines were talks dictated by magazine writers (Satō, S., 1931; Tsugawa, 1992/1930). In this way, the gendered development of magazine genres was also related to formation of a modern hierarchy among periodicals, as this shift put off male readers who began to see women's magazines as "too feminine" and "too unsophistocated," offering nothing for educated men to read (Kimura, 1930/1933). Designation of magazines for male intellectuals as "general-interest magazines (*sōgō zasshi*)" positioned them as "norm" or "standard" periodicals, implicitly marking magazines for women as marginal.

Women's magazines and "general" magazines were visually marked as well. While the front covers of women's magazines after the turn of the century were often colorfully illustrated with various images, those of general magazines for male intellectuals carried only the magazine title on a plain background. Thus, even at first glance on bookstore shelves, their appearance was clearly gendered. At the same time, more illustrations and photos came to be included in women's magazines, while magazines for male intellectuals maintained their text-oriented style. In this way, by around 1910, magazine genres became divided by target gender in terms of content, editing and format, and the women's magazine as we understand it today came into being, a shift termed the "feminization of women's magazines" (Maeshima, 2009a, 2013a).

Innovations in Interwar Women's Magazine

A Variety of Colloquial Article Genres
Specific traits marking mass-market women's magazines were furthered during the interwar period. Making the most of the colloquial writing style, mass-market women's magazines appearing in the 1910s further expanded their range of content and developed a variety of new article genres; these included practical how-to articles (*jissai kiji*), confessional essays (*kokuhaku kiji*), reports by special correspondents (*tokuha kiji*),

interviews (*taidan* or *hōmonki*), round-table discussions (*zadankai*), and serialized novels by popular writers. Often, this content diversification was intentional; it was the policy of Ishikawa Takeyoshi (also known as Ishikawa Takemi), founder of *Shufu no Tomo*, to include as many diverse components as possible in each issue so as to survive the competitive market of the times (Ishii, 1940; Shufu no Tomosha, 1967).

These articles not only deployed the colloquial style; they also relied heavily on direct quotation, which gave a more phonetically pseudo-mimetic or realistic, and thus vivid tone, to the content (Maeshima, 2011). This was important for the interview-based content, where interviewees ranged from celebrities to mid-level bureaucrats and even factory workers and farmers. Observing the rise of such content as confessional writings, interviews, and round-table discussions, social critics claimed that the age of fact-based literature had arrived (Satō, S., 1931). The colloquial style and inclusion of fewer editorial columns, together with the practice of adding phonetic reading guides (*furigana* or *rubi*) to the printed texts, especially those with complicated Chinese characters, made the magazines more accessible, serving to expand their reach beyond their existing readership and appeal to less educated readers as well.

In addition, women's magazines encouraged active participation, by including content, not only in "from the readers" columns but also full-length stories, from those who read the magazines (Tsugawa, 1930). Readers were also invited to participate in various events introduced through the magazines, such as round-table talks, exhibitions, workshops, competitions, and the like. In this way, the magazines promoted a seemingly intimate yet egalitarian relationship between their readers and the professional writers and editors.

In addition, magazine content provided entertainment content, in the form of serialized novels, humorous stories, short quizzes, comic strips, movie digests in reconstructed photo stories, interviews featuring movie stars or singers, and so on. Content directed toward practical "life information" was cast as entertainment as well. Colorful illustrations or photographs added visual pleasure to otherwise "practical articles" primarily intended to instruct readers regarding how to cook, sew, raise children, entertain guests, or prepare for marriage, the New Year, and the like. Supplements to women's magazines also offered useful everyday information in an entertaining manner to readers by including items such as illustrated recipe cards, sewing patterns, social manner books, or fashion catalogues, along with gender-free items such as calendars, game books, travel guides, and reproductions of famous paintings, as well as picture books for children. After *Shufu no Tomo* started appending a separate-volume supplement in 1918, all mass-market magazines followed suit. The competition was so intense that the January 'New Year' 1934 issues of *Shufu no Tomo* and *Fujinkurabu* presented their readers with fifteen kinds of supplements; the *Shufu no Tomo* issue sold so well it was reprinted twice (Shufu no Tomosha, 1967). Tosaka (1937) asserted that almost all popular magazines in the 1930s, but especially mass-market women's magazines, attempted to please readers with this type of entertainment-related content.

Technology, Visuals, and Commercialization

The publishers of women's magazines were always the first to use new techniques, technologies and systems for editing, printing, binding, distribution, and marketing. Women's magazines were the first to adopt the commission-based selling system in 1909, wherein retail dealers could return unsold items to publishers, rather than following the old system in which retailers had to buy periodicals outright, risking loss in unsold stock. (Kōdansha Shashi Henshū Iinkai, 2001; Shimizu and Kobayashi, 1979). *Shufu no Tomo* adopted a "one-coin" sales policy in 1922, wherein the magazine could be bought for a single 50-sen (0.5 yen) coin. This sales approach stabilized the price of magazines, and was soon adopted by the industry at large (Ishii, 1940; Matsuda 1965; Shashi Hensan Iinkai, 1959a, 1959b).

Popular women's magazines were the first magazine genre in Japan to utilize more flexible and dynamic layouts, made possible by adopting new and internationally standardized printing technologies (Shufu no Tomosha, 1967). These technological advances allowed for attractive covers, front and back, and virtually all articles were accompanied by some visual imagery. In the 1920s, as major publishers such as Shufu no Tomosha and Kōdansha created their own photographic departments, they were able to use original photos without borrowing from press agencies and could replace pictorial cuts with photo images (Shashi Hensan Iinkai, 1959; Shufu no Tomosha, 1967). Indeed, the most impacting change that mass-market women's magazines brought about in Japanese magazine culture was the transformation of the photographic section into a feature of the magazine (Maeshima, 2007, 2009b). Modern Japanese magazines had included pictorial sections since the late 19th century (Hasegawa, 1987; Kaneko, 1999), usually in the opening pages, which were called *kuchi-e* (frontispieces) and which were followed by an exclusive text section, the *honbun* (main text). The most popular women's magazine of the time, *Shufu no Tomo*, gradually expanded the pictorial section in the 1920s from several pages to about 50; by the 1930s, photos accounted for 80-90 pages of every issue, approximately 20% of the magazine total, thereby deconstructing the domianant dual-section magazine format.

The interwar women's magazine created new modes of expression for photos as well, which, in turn, changed the relationship between readers and the people featured in the photo articles. Originally, the modern Japanese photo article employed a "detached" or "objective style," using mostly static photos, with a short accompanying descriptive text. From the late 1920s, popular women's magazines started developing what can be called an "intimate" photo article style, consisting of multiple chronologically ordered photos and several accompanying long textual units. While the photos extensively employed new photographic techniques such as the close-up, straight photo, and snap shots, and were printed full-color, the texts were usually written in a conversational style, which often included direct quotes of the featured persons' speech and inner thoughts. With this style, readers came to feel a deeper affinity with the people represented in these articles (Maeshima 2007, 2009b). This photo narrative style, popularized by *Shufu no Tomo*, spread among Japanese popular magazines in the 1930s, disciplining the readers' eyes and presenting to them lively reports on people in Japan and modern life styles, likely contributing to the discursive formation of modernity (Maeshima, forthcoming).

Women's magazines also underwent extensive commercialization during the interwar period, deploying advertisements in order to promote sales. Until the emergence of the mass-market women's magazine, newspapers had offered the flashiest, most eye-catching advertisements in Japan (Kitada, 1998). However, "design-oriented ads sections" (*ishōkōkokuran*), together with advertising techniques such as direct mail, flyers, colorful ad posters placed on power poles, and inserts in newspapers and magazines became common in the women's magazine industry at this time (Tsugawa, 1930). Another signature promotion strategy among mass-market women's magazines was the distribution of free gifts. The leader again was *Shufu no Tomo*; to commemorate becoming "No. 1 in circulation in the East" in 1921, the magazine presented new two-year subscribers with a removable summer kimono collar (*han'eri*) "made of refined silk with hand-stitched embroidery that would cost 2.5 or 3 yen at market" (Shufu no Tomosha, 1967, p. 90). While this first attempt was severely criticized by its rivals and intellectuals for its commercialism (Takashima, 1922), free gifts soon became common among popular women's magazines.

In order to obtain advertising revenue and propel various commercialized collaboration projects, women's magazines were also keen to advertise products of their business partners in other industries. Pages of advertisements were inserted in women's magazines, sometimes in exactly the same formats as magazine articles, which blurred the distinction between the articles and the ads (Kitada, 1998). With its May 1922 issue, *Shufu no Tomo* even started reserving a page solely for advertisements, separate from any other content, a practice again followed by other women's magazines and common even today.

The introduction of a mail-order system by *Fujin no Tomo* in 1905, which was followed by other popular magazines such as *Shufu no Tomo*, *Fujokai*, and *Fujin Kurabu*, also illustrates the commercial innovativeness of mass-market women's magazines (Fujin no Tomosha, 2003). Each magazine included a catalogue and advertisements of its own "sales agent" (*dairibu*). In addition, the regular articles functioned as a kind of mail-order catalogue, featuring items that were for sale. Thus, it was mainly through women's magazines that purchasing by mail-order became common practice in Japan. Popular women's magazines not only sold goods in collaboration with trading partners; they also developed and marketed their own original products. There were health-building tablets, a variety of unique kimonos, and original hair care products offered by *Shufu no Tomo*, summer kimonos and cosmetics by *Fujin Kōron*, and kimonos and healthy soft drink by the magazines of Kōdansha, to name a few. With articles on fashion, cooking, medicines, cosmetics, and seasonal or life events, the mail-order selling system connected readers' everyday lives with various traders and department stores, inviting them to a materially affluent lifestyle (Maeshima, 2013b).

Building on the overwhelming popularity of these magazines, publishers developed a media-mixing strategy, whereby plays, movies, and records were produced based on the content of popular women's magazines such as popular serialized novels (Shashi Hensan Iinkai, 1959b; Shufu no Tomosha, 1967, 1996; Tsugawa, 1930). Criticism emerged, as magazines mixed content and commercialism (Akita 1927; Chiba et al. 1928, 101; Satō, S., 1931). Ōya Sōichi, a media critic of the time, wrote: "Not only is the entire women's magazine itself a department store, but every single novel appearing within it constitutes a department store in the same way" (Ōya, 1959/1934, 193-194).

Increasing Range of Readership during the Interwar Period

Increasing Circulation

As women's magazines developed innovative and reader-friendly editorial styles and took up sophisticated promotional strategies, their audiences expanded, reaching a wide range of people across age, class, marital status, and even gender variation. From the turn of the century to the interwar period, women's magazines grew to be the most read type of magazine in Japan. During a time when the average magazine circulation was between 2,000 and 3,000, *Jogaku Sekai* claimed a circulation of 70,000 to 80,000 (Suzuki, 2001, p. 7) and the more daily life–oriented *Fujin Sekai* had a circulation of about 300,000 to 400,000 (Kōdansha Shashi Hensan Iinkai, 2001, p. 75). Considering that *Taiyō*, the most popular "general magazine" of the time, had a circulation of approximately 100,000, the popularity of women's magazine was undeniable.

Moreover, the genre was stable in its circulation. Statistics compiled by the Bureau of Police and Public Security at the Ministry of Home Affairs reported *Kingu's* 1927 circulation at 300,000 issues, followed by *Shufu no Tomo* at 200,000, *Fujokai* at 155,000, and *Fujin Kurabu* at 120,000 in the same year (Naimushō keihokyoku, 1927/1979). Market competition intensified in the following years, but as of 1931, *Shufu no Tomo's* monthly circulation had increased to 600,000, *Fujin Kurabu's* to 550,000, and *Fujokai's* to 350,000 (Nagashima, 1951, p. 33).

A Wide Range of Readership, Female and Male

With the rise of mass-market women's magazines, the divisions among readers according to their education level, class, and gender became increasingly blurred. Indeed, as is often mentioned in histories of Japanese publishing, women's magazines first boosted their sales among middle-class housewives of urban white-collar families, together with wealthier farmers and merchants from all over the country (Maeda, 1968; Yamamoto,

1981). However, thanks to innovations in editing toward more accessible style and modern layout, together with practical how-to articles, increased entertainment content, and reader-oriented policies, the magazines grew in appeal to lower-middle-class women and unmarried young women as well, both in the cities and the countryside (Ariyama, 1984; Kimura, 1989a; Kitada, 1998; Nagamine, 1997; 2001; Yomo, 1995).

For example, Nagamine (1977) concluded that from around 1921 *Shufu no Tomo* rapidly increased its popularity not only among female factory workers, but also, according to an area-by-area survey, among women across the range of socio-economic variables. If one were to include the less well-off readers who rented magazines or circulated them in groups, purchased discounted second-hand issues at street stalls, or browsed periodicals at libraries, readers of mass-market women's magazines amounted to even more than what surveys suggested (Chiba et al., 1928; Hayasaka, 1930; Nagamine, 2001; Nii, 1931; Satō, S., 1931). Thus, unlike in previous decades, the readership of magazines was no longer neatly divided according to educational level or social class, but rather cut across class, education, age, and marriage status.

Likewise, it is noteworthy that mass-market women's magazines had a considerable number and variety of male readers as well. Male readers, however, were not enticed solely by the sexually sensational stories and news of love affairs, romances, and celebrity scandals that were common to women's magazines. Male media critics at the time attested to enjoying content such as serialized novels, practical how-to articles, advice columns, human-interest stories, and various features on entertainment (Chiba et al., 1928; Hirano, 1930; Hiratsuka, 1928; Kimura, 1930/1933; Komaki, 1927; Nakamura, 1928a, 1928b; Sugiyama, 1934/1935a; Tosaka, 1937). Media critics Komaki and Nakamura wrote that they enjoyed reading practical articles on fashion, food, child rearing, washing, and seasonal diseases for both pleasure and erudition. Nakamura even confessed that women's magazines were far more enjoyable than those for male intellectuals, including such titles as *Kaizō* or *Chūō Kōron*.

This indicates the degree to which women's magazines cut across genre boundaries, being both an "entertainment media" that also introduced important information in interwar Japan.

Socio-cultural Background: Education, Systematization and Interest in Home Life

In considering the factors behind the enormous popularity of mass-market women's magazines at the time, one has to consider the socio-historical context that made large circulation, especially that of these popular women's magazines, possible. One of the factors that led to the expansion of readership of mass-market women's magazines was the increase in literacy brought about by compulsory education. The Fundamental Code of Education of 1872 required all children, both boys and girls, to attend school for four years. In 1907, the period of compulsory attendance was raised to six years and by 1910, almost all children were completing the state-mandated education (Hunter, 1984). In 1873, 15% of girls were enrolled in elementary school, a statistic that jumped to 59% in 1899, and 91% in 1904 (Monbushō chōsakyoku, 1962). Similarly, the number of women educated in secondary schools after elementary schools also grew; there were 2,363 students at girls' high schools in 1887, 8,857 in 1899, and 40,273 in 1907 (Miki, 1989). These figures clearly point to a rapid increase in literacy among women over this period.

Growing interest in "home life" and "home culture" represents another factor contributing to the spread of women's magazines. The transition from Meiji era (1868-1912) to Taishō era (1912-1926) represented a societal shift from "public" to "private" (Minami et al., 1965). The Taishō era was also a time when practices related to the Western-style "home life" started to emerge among the new middle class (Inuzuka, 1989; Koyama 1991, 1999). Various movements and trends to "improve" or "refine" home life and home culture appeared during Taishō and early Shōwa era, including exhibitions related to the modern home life and child rearing (Jinno 1994; Koresawa, 2008; Kurihara 2003; Minami et al., 1965; Nakamura, 1997, 1998; Ōshima 2002, 2007; Sukenari 2003). Articles in women's magazines concerning home life appealed directly to such trends. The social ardor for home life, therefore, drew back even male readers to women's magazines, who had once stepped away from them when these magazines were deemed "feminized" in style and content.

A final factor that contributed to the popularity of mass-market women's magazines was industry systemization and industrialization of the publishing industry. In the 1920s, wholesale booksellers were merging and by 1924, all the magazine-selling associations of Japan had merged into a single national organization, the Nihon Zasshi Kyōkai (Japan Magazine Association). Together with advances in the paper industry, such developments as advancements in printing technologies and systematization of the industry and adverting through print media no doubt contributed to mass print culture (Hashimoto, 1964; Satō, T., 2002; Shimizu and Kobayashi, 1979).

Impact of Popular Women's Magazines on Interwar Periodical Journalism

Still, such socio-cultural background factors alone cannot fully explain the popularity of mass-market women's magazines specifically in interwar Japan. In addition to the above-mentioned factors, the astonishing popularity of these magazines derived from the fact that there was no comparably comprehensive, egalitarian, and entertaining periodical at that time. This is clear when one compares this magazine genre with other kinds of periodicals, which were greatly influenced by the practices of women's magazines. As Aono (1933) pointed out,

> [Recently,] through their commercialism, and accompanying sensational stimulation, entertaining and 'practical' characteristics, [women's magazines'] have come to have the power to lead magazine culture. (p. 9)

Influences on other "Serious" Periodicals
As the above quotation implies, strategies used in women's magazines affected even "general magazines" for intellectuals. Newspapers adopted women's magazines' editing strategies and included a focus on domestic or private matters. Starting in the late 1920s, national newspapers such as the present-day *Yomiuri, Asahi,* and *Mainichi,* expanded their "home" or "women's" sections. "General" magazines of time followed the practice of women's magazines in sponsoring large-scale events. From the mid-1930s, "general interest" magazines such as *Chūō Kōron* and *Kaizō* started to sponsor lectures and round-table talks (*zadankai*) featuring internationally famous faces, with a follow-up supplements including abundant visuals published in the magazine. A noted critic, Tosaka (1937), observed that, "the round-table talk is rampant among all the magazines and the newspapers;" media critic Sugiyama lamented:

> One can see "special peices" and "supplements" as usual matter. [...] [E]ven so-called "quality magazines" such as *Chūō Kōron* and *Kaizō* seem unable to resist using them. (1934/1935a, p. 11)

In 1935, critic Ōya Sōichi saw in this a shift in "the hegemony of the publishing world" from the "high-quality magazine" to these "popular magazines" (1959/1935, pp. 248-249). Observing this phenomenon, Sugiyama took "the fact that it is the women's magazine that has the largest circulation in Japan today" to be the epitome of "the extraordinary expansion of the power of women in journalism."

The Interwar Japanese Mass-Market Women's Magazine as a New Medium
Thus, by the end of the 1920s the mass-market women's magazine had developed into a distinctive magazine genre. With extensive visuals, an inclination toward human-interest stories, heavy emphasis on orality in writing styles, intensive commercialization, and an orientation toward entertainment and diverse multifunctional components, popular women's magazines provided readers with an innovative and unprecedented

reading experience. In a sense, these mass-market women's magazines were a new form of media for people in interwar Japan.

Accordingly, the form and content of women's magazines affected their readers' reading habits. In the case of "general magazines," one needed to read each article attentively in order to understand the content. By contrast, in the case of women's magazines, while readers could still find content that demanded attentive reading, they could also enjoy the miscellaneous stories and pictorial articles as a leisure activity, or even as a way to kill time. Critics in the 1920s and 1930s witnessed this shift in readers' habits, and described it as a change from "reading" to "seeing" (Chiba et.al., 1928, pp. 105-106). From the late 1910s through the 1930s, numerous intellectuals of both sexes criticized this new trend in periodicals for being "low-taste" or "degrading." The controversial status of popular women's magazine at the time can be understood as an attempt by the intellectual class to maintain the existing hierarchy of print and reading culture that valued the "general magazines" intended for male intellectuals and the exclusivity of the related reading habits as the "norm" of print culture (Maeshima, 2009a).

Conclusion

The Interwar Women's Magazine: Trailblazer of New Journalism in Japan

In this way, during the 1920s, women's magazines evolved their own magazine style separate from other magazine genres, contradicting completely the standard format of the so-called "general magazine" in all aspects. While they shared certain entertainment characteristics with other popular magazine genres, it was the women's magazines that most intensively utilized and developed these features. Thus, in addition to new accessible editing styles and commercialized promotional strategies, developments in printing technology, the systematization of publishing related industries, increasing literacy, as well as the craze for a "home" with cultural life, all in combination contributed to the enormous popularity of mass-market women's magazines involving avid male and female readers.

In fact, these elements comprise what is referred to in media studies as "new journalism" or "tabloidization," and are considered to be the direct origin of today's editing and promotional strategies in mass communication. The emergence of an increasingly literate readership, especially women, led to an increasing democratization of print culture occurring simultaneously around the world between the 1880s and the 1920s. To expand their circulation, periodicals adopted more accessible and entertaining editing styles together with inclusion of high quality visuals and publishers used new promotional strategies such as reader invitations to sponsored events in order to increase the diffusion of print media (Becker 1992; Bird 1992; Conboy 2002, 2006; Gripsrud 1992; Hayashi 2000; Sparks and Tulluch, 2000; Tulloch 2000; Zelizer, 2009).

In early 20th century Japan, democratization of print culture was led by women's magazines, rather than the existing ungendered "male" periodicals. As shown, it was popular women's magazines that most extensively used and developed new accessible editorial techniques as well as promotional strategies, that in principle appealed to everyone in society, regardless of age, class, gender, or marital status, while at the same time maintaining their conventional façade as periodicals for women. While tabloidization could be observed in a variety of print media in the interwar period in Japan, it was most aggressively realized by mass-market women's magazines, which, as the genre name openly proclaimed, were regarded as media essentially for female readers—in other words, this "female" media expanded its readership to men. These popular women's magazines not only deployed the most extensive democratic editorial and promotional strategies; they also turned into the first truly national magazines by including male readers across classes among their avid fans, and, moreover, they were to become the prototype of periodicals in the following decades.

Cautionary Notes for Researching Modern Japanese Print Media

Historical investigation of modern Japanese periodicals alerts researchers of Japanese journalism to the following points: First, one should not approach Japanese periodicals through extension of present-day periodical categorization in Japan or in other regions. Categorization and characteristics of periodicals have never been static and always differed from area to area and from period to period. While caution against cultural or national essentialization is necessary, historical, social, and cultural contextualization is also extremely important in journalism studies. Second, and related to this, one should conduct studies of journalism by taking into consideration its relationship with other institutions and industries, such as politics, economics, technologies, and business strategies. Third, as British journalism studies scholar Conboy points out (2011), in situating Japanese periodicals within socio-historical as well as cultural contexts, one should not assume a linear historical development or project European or American historical developments onto the Japanese case. In considering journalism or the publication of periodicals, it is also crucial to pay close attention to the interaction between different periodical genres, especially between newspapers and magazines. By extension, journalism studies should not ignore the mutual influences among different media, such as radio, film, and television, since any medium develops through mutual relations with other diverse media. Last but not least, the transitions in modes of expression remind us of the importance of attentiveness to the mediatedness of representations appearing in periodicals. As Marshall McLuhan famously insisted, "the medium is the message" (1964): how news materials are presented affects their meaning, as well as the communication styles or relationships between readers/audience, writers, editors, and the issues being reported and people being featured.

References

Akita, U. (1927, March). Zasshikisha no jikaku to kyōryoku o nozomu. *Kaiō*, 69-70.

Aono, S. (1933, June 24). Zasshi bunka no hensen 4: fujin zasshi no koto. *Tōkyō Asahi Shimbun*, pp. 9.

Ariyama, T. (1984). 192, 30-nendai no media fukyū jōtai: Kyūryō seikatsusha, rōdōsha o chūshin ni. *Shuppan Kenkyū*, 15, 30-58.

Becker,K. (1992). Photojournalism and the Tabloid Press. In P. Dahlgren and C. Sparks (Eds.) *Journalism and Popular Culture* (pp. 130-153). London: Sage.

Bird, E. (1992). *For Enquiring Minds: A Cultural Study of Supermarket Tabloids*. Knoxville: University of Tennessee Press.

Chiba, K., Miwada, M., Miyake, Y., Nakamura M., Nii, I., Satō, H., Tokuda S., Yamakawa, K. (1928, June). Fujinzasshi no hihankai. *Shinchō*, 98-123.

Conboy, M. (2002). *The Press and Popular Culture*. London: Sage, 2002.

Conboy, M. (2006). *Tabloid Britain; Constructing a Community through Language*. Abingdon: Routledge.

Conboy, M. (2011). *Journalism in Britain: A Historical Introduction*. London: Sage.

Fujin no Tomosha. (2003). *Fujin no tomosha kengyō 100 shūnen kinen: Dokusha to ayunda isseiki ten*. Tokyo: Fujin no Tomosha.

Gripsrud, J. (1992). The Aesthetics and Politics of Melodrama. In P. Dahlgren and C. Sparks. (Eds.). *Journalism and Popular Culture* (pp. 84-95). London: Sage.

Hasegawa A., (1987). Sensō to hōdō shashin. In K. Kuwabara (Ed.) *Nihon shashin zenshū*. (pp. 161-164). Tokyo: Shōgakukan.

Hashimoto, M. (1964). *Nihon shuppan hanbaishi (History of Japanese Publishing and Distribution)*. Tokyo: Kōdansha.

Hayasaka, J. (1930, November). Gendai goraku zasshiron. *Keisaiōrai*, 115-119.

Hayashi, K. (2000). The 'Home and Family Section' in Japanese Newspapers. In J. Tulloch & C. Sparks (Eds.), *Tabloid Tales. Global Debates over Media Standards* (pp. 147-162). Lanham: Rowman and Littlefield.

Hirano, M. (1930). Fujinmen no henshū nit suite. In T. Atsurō (Ed.) *Sōgō jānarizumu kōza II* (pp. 1-16). Tokyo: Naigai shuppan.

Hiratsuka, R. (1928, June). Fujin zasshi no aku keikō nitsuite. *Chūōkōron,* 82-84.

Hunter, J. Ed., (1984). *Concise Dictionary of Modern Japanese History.* Berkeley: University of California Press.

Inuzuka, I. (1989). Meiji chūki no 'hōmu' ron ni miru kateikan to kaseikan: Meiji 18 – 26nen no Jogakuzassi o chūshin ni. *Kazoku kaseigaku,* 18, 15-20.

Ishii, M. (1940). *Takumashiki kensetsu: Shufu no tomo shachō Ishikawa Takemi shi no shin'nen to so no jigyō.* Tokyo: Kyōbunkan.

Ishikawa, S. (Ed.). (1959). *Shuppan hanbai shōshi.* Tokyo: Tōkyō Shuppan Hanbai Kabushiki Gaisha.

Iwata, K. (1997). Meiji kōki ni okeru shōnen no shoji bunka no tenkai: Shōnensekai no tōkōbun o chūshin ni. *Kyōikugaku kenkyū,* 64 (4), 417-426.

Jinno, Y. (1994). *Shumi no tanjō: Hyakkaten ga tsukutta teisuto.* Tokyo: Keisōshobō.

Kaneko, R. (1999). Insatsu bunka no naka no shashin: sono hajimari kara kakuritsu made. *Kokubungaku.* Tokyo: Gakutōsha.

Kimura K. (1930/1933). Nihon zasshi hattatsu-shi. In *Gendai jānarizumu kenkyū* (pp. 155-212). Tokyo: Kōjin shobō.

Kimura, R. (1989). Fujinzasshi ni miru atarashi'i josei no tōjō to sono hen'yō: Taishō demokurasii kara haisen made. *Kyōikugaku kenky Ōsakadaigaku kyōiku shakaigaku, kyōiku keikakuron kenkyū shūroku* 56 (4), 331-341.

Kimura, R. (1992). Fujinzasshi no jōhōkūkan to josei taishū dokusha no seiritsu: kindai nihon no shufu yakuwari no keisei tono kanren de. *Shisō* 812, 231-252.

Kimura, R. (2004). 'On'na ga yomu shōsetsu' no tanjō: 1920-30 nendai tsūzoku shōsetsu no hatten. *Ningen kankei ronshū,* 21, 93-107.

Kimura, R. (2006a). Kindai katei ni okeru 'shufu' to 'otto' no amai seikatsu: senzen no taishū fujinzasshi no shimen bunseki kara. *Joseigaku kenkyū*, 13, 1-32.

Kimura, R. (2006b). 'On'na ga yomu shōsetsu' ni yoru yokubō no hensei: 1920-30 nendai 'tsūzoku shōsetsu' no sekai. *Ōsakadaigaku daigakuin ningenkagaku kenkyūka kiyō*, 32, 145-170.

Kindai Joseibunkashi Kenkyūkai. (2001). *Sensō to joseizasshi: 1931-1945*. Tokyo: Domesu Shuppan.

Kitada, A. (1998). 'Shiteki na kōkyōkūkan' o megutte: 1920-30 nendai 'fujinzasshi' no dokusho kūkan. *Tōkyōdaigaku shakaijōhō kenkūjo kiyō*, 56, 155-179.

Kōdansha Shashi Henshū Iinkai (Ed.). (2001). *Kuronikku: Kōdansha no 90-nen*. Tokyo: Kōdansha.

Komaki, O. (1927, March). Fujin zasshi wa doko e yuku. *Kaizō*, 67-70.

Koresawa Y. (2008). Taishō-ki ni okeru Mitsukoshi jidō hakurankai no tenkai. *Tōkyō kaseidaigaku hakubutsukan kiyō*, 13, 39-46.

Koyama, S. (1991). *Ryōsai kenbo toiu kihan*. Tokyo: Keiō Shobō.

Koyama, S. (1999). *Katei no seisei to josei no kokuminka*. Tokyo: Keiōshobō.

Kurihara, Y. (2003, Mar.) 'Sumai' to 'katei' shisō: Meiji kōhanki kara Taishōki o chūshin ni shite. *Tagen bunka*, 3, 147-160.

Maeda, A. (2001). Taishōkōki tsūzoku shōsetsu no tenkai: fujinzassi no dokusha sō (pp. 211-284). *Kindai dokusha no seiritsu*. Tokyo: Iwanamishoten.

Maeshima, S. (2007). 'Gahōran' no jidai: Zasshi shashin no hensen to Shōwa shoki no *Shufu no tomo*. *Hikaku Bungaku Kenkyu*, 90, 47-67.

Maeshima, S. (2009a). Rethinking Women's Magazines: The Impact of Mass-Market Women's Magazines on Reading Culture in Interwar Japan. *Windows on Comparative Literature*, 4-5, 50-65.

Maeshima, S. (2009b). Just Like Motion Pictures: Transformations of Illustrated Articles in Pre-World War II Japanese Magazines. *Windows on Comparative Literature*, 4-5, 125-137.

Maeshima, S. (2011). Melodramatized Experiences: Textual Appeal of the Confessional Story in Interwar Japanese Popular Periodicals and Its

Socio-Historical Implications. *Windows on Comparative Literature*, 6–7, 9-17.

Maeshima, S. (2013a). Print Culture and Gender: Toward a Comparative Study of Modern Print Media. *Proceedings of the ICLA 2010 Seoul Congress*, 354-363.

Maeshima, S. (2013b). Constructed/Constructing Bodies in the Age of the New Middle Class: Representations of Modern Everyday Life Style in the Japanese Interwar Women's Magazine. *Proceedings of the Japan Studies Association of Canada*.

Maeshima, S. (forthcoming). Representing the Empire: Technological Advancements and the Emergence of "Transparent" Photo Stories in Interwar Japanese Popular Print Media. *Proceedings of Association for Japanese Literary Studies*.

Mainichi shinbun hyakunenshi kankō i'inkai (Ed.). (1972). *Mainichi shinbun hyakunenshi: 1872-1972*. Tokyo: Mainichi Shinbunsha.

McLuhan, M. (1964/1994). *Understanding Media*. Cambridge, MA: MIT Press.

Miki, H., (1989). Meiji fujin zasshi no kiseki. In Kindai josei bunkashi kenkyūkai (Ed.). *Fujin zassi no yoake*. Tokyo: Ōzorasha.

Minami, H. & Shakai Shin'ri Kenkyūjo (Eds.). (1965). *Taishō Bunka: 1905-1927*. Tokyo: Keisōshobō.

Monbushō chōsakyoku (Ed.) (1962). Zu roku: Danjo betsu no gimukyōiku shūgakuritsu no sui'I [Figure]. *Nihon no seichō to kyōiku: Kyōiku no tenkai to keizai no hatten* (p. 32). Tokyo: Ministry of Education.

Muta, K. (1996). *Senryaku toshite no kazoku: kindai nihon no kokumin kokka keisei to josei*. Tokyo: Shin'yōsha.

Nagamine, S. (1997). *Zasshi to dokusha no kindai*. Tokyo: Nihon Editā Sukūru Shuppanbu.

Nagamine, S. (2001). *Modan toshi no dokusho kūkan*. Tokyo: Nihon Editā Sukūru Shuppanbu.

Naimushō keihokyoku. (1979). Shinbun zasshi tsūshinsha ni kansuru shirabe. Naimushō keihokyoku. *Shinbun zasshisha tokuhi chōsa*. Tokyo: Taishō shuppan,

New Journalism in Interwar Japan 27

Nakamura, K. (1997). Kindai Nihon ni okeru <kodomo> imēji to kodomo hakurankai: Mitsukoshi ni okeru kodomo hakurankai no ranshō. *Bijutsu kyōikugaku: Daigakubijutsu kyōiku kenkyū*, 18, 215-225.

Nakamura, K. (1998). Kindai Nihon ni okeru <kodomo> imēji to kodomo hakurankai 2: Kodomo hakurankai no tancho ni tsuite. *Bijutsu kyōikugaku: Daigakubijutsu kyōiku kenkyū*, 19, 223-235.

Nakamura, M. (1928a, July). Fujin zasshiron. *Shinchō*, 9-17.

Nakamura, M. (1928b, August). Fujin zasshiron. *Shinchō*, 5-15.

Nagashima, K. (Ed.) (1951). *Zasshikigyō no rekishi to genjō*. Tokyo: Asahi shinbunsha.

Nii, I. (1931). Fujinzasshiron. In Tachibana A. (Ed.). *Sōgō jānarizumu kōza* Vol. VII (pp. 267-278). Tokyo: Naigaishuppan.

Ogawa, K. (1962). *Nihon shuppankai no ayumi*. Tokyo: Seibundō Shinkōsya.

Oka, M. (1981). *Fujinzasshi jānarizumu: josei kaihō no rekishi to tomoni*. Tokyo: Gendai Jānarizumus Shuppankai.

Okano, T. (1957). *Nihon shuppan bunka shi*. Tokyo: Shunpodō.

Ōshima, S. (2002). Media to shite no hakurankai: *Mitsukoshi taimusu* ni miru 'bunka no tenjijō' Mitsukoshi hakurankai. *Shinbungaku*,18, 43-66.

Ōshima, S. (2007). Shinbunsha no kigyōka to kodomo bunka jigyō: Ōsaka mainichi shinbunsha no kodomo hakurankai to Nikkan kodomo shinbun tanjō o chūshin ni. *Masu komunikēshon kenkyū*, 70, 177-194.

Ōya, S. (1929, April/1959). Heibon no haikan to taishū zasshi no shōrai. *Ōya Sōichi Senshū*, 7 (pp. 189-190). Tokyo: Chikuma shobō.

Ōya, S. (1934, July/1959). Fujin zasshi no shuppan kakumei. *Ōya Sōichi Senshū*, 7 (pp. 191-194). Tokyo: Chikuma shobō.

Ōya, S. (1935/1959). Gendai jānarizumu chōkanzu. *Ōya Sōichi Senshū*, 7. (pp. 239-252). Tokyo: Chikuma shobō.

Sakamoto, H. (Ed.). (1951). *Kōkoku gojūnenshi*. Tokyo: Nihon Denpōtsūshinsha.

Sato, B. (Hamil). (2003). *The New Japanese Women: Modernity, Media, and Women in Interwar Japan*. Durham and London: Duke University Press.

Satō, S. (1931). Fujin zasshi no henshū to kiji no torikata. In Tachibana, A. (Ed). *Sōgō jānarizumu kōza VII* (pp. 293-311). Tokyo: Naigai Shuppan.

Satō, T. (2002). *'Kingu' no jidai: Kokumin taishūzasshi no kōkyōsei*. Tokyo: Iwanami Shoten.

Shashi hensan iinkai. (1952). *Mainichi shinbun 70 nen*. Tokyo: Mainichi Shinbunsha.

Shashi hensan iinkai (Ed.). (1959a). *Kōdansha no ayunda 50 nen: Meiji Taishō hen*. Tokyo: Kōdansha.

Shashi hensan iinkai (Ed.). (1959b). *Kōdansha no ayunda 50 nen: Shōwa hen*. Tokyo: Kōdansha.

Shimizu, H. & Kobayashi, K. (1979). *Shuppan gyōkai*. Tokyo: Kyōikusha Shinsho.

Shufu no Tomosha, (Ed.). (1967). *Shufu no tomo no gojūnen*. Tokyo: Shufu no Tomosha.

Shufu no Tomosha, (Ed.). (1996). *Shufu no tomosha hachijjūnenshi*. Tokyo: Shufu no Tomosha.

Sparks, C. & Tulloch, J. (Eds.). *Tabloid Tales: Global Debates over Media Standards*. Lanham: Rowman & Littlefield, 2000. 131-146.

Sugiyama, H. (1935a). Jānarizumu sōmatō. *Gendai jānarizumuron* (pp. 3-90). Tokyo: Hakuyōsha.

Sugiyama, H. (1935b). Josei minoue sōdan jidai. *Gendai jānarizumuron* (pp. 453-465). Tokyo: Hakuyōsha.

Sukenari, Y. (2003, June). Seikatsu kaizen to seikatsugaku no tanjō. *Kon Wajirō kenkyū*, 1, 83-101.

Suzuki, S. (Ed.). (1996, March). Meijiki sōgōzasshi no buntai ni tsuite. *Shunposhion*, 1, 83-101.

Suzuki, S. (2001). *Zasshi 'Taiyō' to kokumin bunka no keisei*. Tokyo: Shibunkaku shuppann.

Takashima, B. (1922, March). Fujinzasshi no akukeikō. *Chūō Kōron*, 55-61.

Tōkyōdō, T. (1935). Saikin 8 nenkan zasshi uriage busū tōkei. In Tōkyōdō (Ed.). *Shuppan nenkan*. (frontispiece). Tokyo: Tōkyōdō.

Tosaka, J. (1937, May). Fujinzasshi ni okeru goraku to hiji. *Nihon hyōron (Japan Review)*, 342-349.

Tsugawa, R. (1930/1992). *Koete kita michi*. Tokyo: Fujokaisha, (reprinted by Tokyo: Ōzorasha).

Tulloch, J. (2000). The Eternal Recurrence of New Journalism. In C. Sparks & J. Tulloch (Eds.). *Tabloid Tales: Global Debates over Media Standards* (pp. 131-146). Lanham: Rowman & Littlefield.

Wakakuwa, M. (1995). *Sensō ga tsukuru joseizō: dainiji sekai taisenka no nihonjosei dōin no shikakuteki puropaganda.* Tokyo: Chikuma Shobō.

Watashitachi no Rekishi o Tsuzurukai. (1987). *Fujinzasshi kara mita 1930 nendai.* Tokyo: Dōjidaisha.

Yamamoto, M. (1981). *Genbunicchi no rekishi ronkō: ni zoku.* Tokyo: Ōbunsha.

Yomo, Y. (1995). Senjika ni okeru seiyakuwari kyanpēn no hensen: 'Shufu no tomo' no naiyō bunseki o chūshin ni. *Masu komyunikēshon kenkyū,* 47, 111-126, 238.

Zelizer, B. (Ed.). (2009). *The Changing Faces of Journalism: Tabloidization, Technology and Truthiness.* London and NY: Routledge.

CHAPTER TWO

REBALANCING JAPANESE NEWSPAPER COVERAGE

NATIONAL AND KANSAI NEWSPAPERS IN THE DIGITAL AGE

Sachiyo Kanzaki

INTRODUCTION

In July 2012, Tokyo media celebrated the birth of the first baby panda in Japan at Tokyo's Ueno Zoo. Problematic, however, is the fact that by this time Wakayama Adventure World in the Kansai region had already witnessed the birth of numerous baby pandas, and another baby panda had been born at the Kobe Oji Zoo in 2008. The reaction to the announcement by Tokyo media in Kansai was immediate, with Kansai television host Shinbō Jirō noting such arrogance by "Tokyo Media" as typical of the mass media concentration in Tokyo. Indeed, such Tokyo-centric reporting is routine: a three-minute train delay in Tokyo makes national news; noteworthy and nationally meaningful news from a local news service goes uncovered. And while criticism of this Tokyo-centric pattern of reporting abounds, among the voices raised, that of Kansai media is the loudest.

Tokyo Centralisation and the Media in Osaka

Media concentration in Tokyo is a fact of life in contemporary Japan, especially for television and magazines. While local satellite stations are located throughout Japan providing local service, the nation's major television broadcasting stations are located in Tokyo. As for magazines, concentrating in Tokyo saves time, particularly those that include content on the latest fashion and social trends. Major distributors Tohan and Nippan, both headquartered in Tokyo, control more than 75 percent of the national print publication and many of the other small distributors also have their offices in Tokyo (Nagahama, 2009). This Tokyo-centered distribution system means that most magazines pass through Tokyo, regardless of where they were produced and will be sold, and regardless of the fact that the third largest national distributor is named Osakaya and is headquartered in Osaka.

This media centralisation in Tokyo is, however, a result of recent trends rather than entrenched history. At the beginning of the 20th century, Osaka had the largest population of any city in Japan and was the economic powerhouse of the country. However, starting with the Meiji Restoration in 1868, when Imperial functions were transferred from Kyoto to Tokyo, Osaka gradually lost its position as Japan's economic center, particularly during the war period, with its intensive concentration on Tokyo. Still, as late as 1960, both Tokyo and Osaka played competing roles as epicenters of Japan commercial and political life. It was not only possible for a big company to exist while having its headquarters located somewhere other than Tokyo at this time, but it was also considered vitally important for major companies to have an administrative center in Osaka so as to be able to service western Japan. However, since 1980 Tokyo has become the dominant city of Japan, with the number of companies moving their headquarters to Tokyo continually increasing, many moving from Osaka. This concentration—political, administrative and financial—has affected all secondary fields of Japan's modern society. With the importance of Tokyo-centered politics and business as the sources of news information and advertising revenue, this has also been true for print media.

In this context, many media observers see Osaka media as important precisely because of its distance from Tokyo. This phenomenon is sometimes called *zure*, a term that reflects a function of space and distance. An example of this is a current popular talk show aired in Osaka titled *Takajin no sokomade itte iinkai (Getting to the facts with Takajin and his panel)*. A purely Kansai program which began airing in 2003, the show is not broadcast in the Kanto region. Indeed, the title of the show plays on the regional differences that emerge in the dialects of Japan. While the kanji characters used to write *iinkai* indicate the meaning as "panel" or "committee," when spoken in the Kansai dialect, it sounds similar to the expression *ii n kai*, which means "shall we?" rendering the show title something closer to *"let's get to the facts, shall we?"* The *zure* expectation is that this Kansai-based talk show will broach those topics not usually taken up on Tokyo-centered national broadcasts.

NEWSPAPER CLASSIFICATION: NATIONAL, REGIONAL AND LOCAL

This regional dynamic extends beyond broadcasting, to the realm of print media as well. In order to understand the tension between newspapers from Osaka and those from Tokyo, one must understand the overall structure of the Japanese newspaper industry. Newspapers in Japan are generally classified on the basis of three regional categories: national, regional (block) and local. The newspapers with national circulation have long been the *Asahi Shimbun,* the *Mainichi Shimbun* and the *Yomiuri Shimbun,* and more recently, the *Nikkei Shimbun* and the *Sankei Shimbun.* Regional (block) newspapers are also read broadly in their region, with their mastheads reflecting the regions they cover: the *Chūnichi Shimbun,* based in Nagoya and catering to readers in the central-Japan Chūbu region and the *Nishinippon Shimbun*, based in Fukuoka and catering to readers in the western-Japan Kyushu region. Finally, there are local newspapers with prefectural-level circulation, which, except for major national political and economic events, focus on local news.

Regionalism is powerful in Japan and in most Japanese prefectures, the local newspapers outsell the national brands. Indeed, as shown in Figure 1, regional and local newspapers are ranked first in popularity in all but ten of Japan's 47 (see Figure 1; Web Appendix). While the Kansai area lacks a block newspaper, the prefectures in the Kansai region surrounding Osaka each have either a prefectural or local newspaper. As for Osaka as a major city of western Japan, there is the *Osaka Nichinichi Shimbun*, with an Osaka-only distribution area and a circulation of only 7,700 copies. Until 2004, when it was taken over by the national *Sankei Shimbun*, the evening only *Osaka Shimbun* was published in the city as well. As for this dearth of newspapers in the Kansai region, as well as why the Kansai media is very sensitive to the concentration of media in Tokyo today, historical context is very important.

National Newspapers and Osaka

Osaka served as the cradle of many early Japanese newspapers. The *Asahi Shimbun* was founded in Osaka in 1879, after which it acquired the *Mezamashi Shinbun* of Tokyo, which then became the *Tokyo Asahi*; in 1940, these two regional papers merged into the *Asahi* we see today. Likewise, the *Mainichi Shimbun* was founded in Osaka in 1888 bearing the name *Osaka Mainichi Shimbun*. In 1906, it expanded its market to Tokyo and in 1911, incorporated the *Tokyo Nichinichi Shimbun*. These two papers then consolidated into the *Mainichi Shimbun* in 1943.

The *Sankei Shimbun* was originally the *Minami Osaka Shimbun*, founded in 1922, but changed its name to the *Yūkan Osaka Shimbun* the next year, and thereafter began publication as the *Nihon Kōgyō Shimbun* (The

Japan Industrial Newspaper). In 1942, due to the war-related restrictions affecting newspapers, the *Nihon Kōgyō Shimbun* became the *Sangyō Keizai Shimbun*, literally the Industry and Economy Newspaper, by consolidating specialized industry and economics newspaper companies operating in western Japan. However, in 1950, the newspaper started publishing in Tokyo, and changed the name to *Sankei Shimbun* after receiving financial support from Sumitomo Bank starting in 1958. The next year, the *Sangyō Keizai Shimbun*, still publishing in Osaka, also changed its name to *Sankei Shimbun* in order standardize the names. The *Nikkei Shimbun* (Japan Economic Times) started as a weekly market-quotation bulletin of Mitsui Company in 1876, becoming a daily in 1885. In 1942, it was merged with other industrial newspapers by consolidating industry and economy specialized newspapers operating in the East of Japan. However, the regional distinction remained, as the West was handled by the *Sankei Shimbun* and the East by the *Nikkei*. It was not until 1961 that the *Nikkei Shimbun* opened its office in Osaka, in other words, Western Japan.

On the other hand, the *Yomiuri Shimbun* was founded in 1874 in Tokyo and only established its Osaka branch, the *Osaka Yomiuri Shimbun*, after the Second World War, in 1952, after which the *Yomiuri* started to expand its business all over Japan. Indeed, the *Yomiuri* proudly recalls the newspaper's success in Osaka *after the war*, ignoring its absence earlier, during the Meiji period.

The Origin of "Osaka Journalism"

In Japanese journalism, the expression "Osaka journalism" qualifies the style of a newspaper article that is written from the point of view of the ordinary reader as opposed to the erudite elite. Some trace the origin to the literature of Ihara Saikaku and Chikamatsu Monzaemon during the Genroku period (1688-1704), when the culture of urban commoners of Osaka flourished. Takahashi (2008) offered that "Osaka journalism"—which is to say, the journalism of Osaka—has kept its characteristic plebeian *ko-shinbun* feel, vastly different from the prestigious *ō-shinbun* newspaper that targeted elites with high society ideals. At the beginning of Meiji era, when modern newspapers began to appear, Osaka saw the development of the woodblock print-based newspapers called *nishiki-e shinbun*. These newspapers illustrated news topics using *ukiyo-e* illustration techniques along with text accompanied by *furigana*, the small *kana* written over or alongside the kanji to indicate pronunciation. The accessibility of these *ko-shinbun* (small newspapers) provided for the rise of a reading public in Osaka, largely through the *Asahi Shimbun* as a leading *ko-shinbun*.

Later, the formats of these two newspaper types became more similar in nature, and this early distinction disappeared (Huffman, 1997). The first merging of these two types was the Tokyo *Nichinichi Shimbun Ōnishiki*. There were two views on this new mixed style of writing: some emphasized the accessibility provided through the pictorial portrayals of the news, while others emphasized its news-value and newspaper characteristics for what had been a non-news print media format. This is why the former is called *nishiki-e shinbun* and the latter *shinbun nishiki-e*. However, Ono Hideo (1972) attributed this terminological difference less to the characteristics of the newspapers and more to a fundamental difference between Tokyo and Osaka. While in Tokyo, such papers were viewed supplementary to the true newspapers, whereas in Osaka, these *ko-shinbun* were viewed as fully independent newspapers, which covered the affairs and accidents that are treated in social pages of today's newspaper. Tsuchiya (1995) pointed out that the people of Osaka received newspapers as a mass media of value from the beginning, and *nishiki-e shinbun* therefore enjoyed more popularity as well as status in Osaka than it did in Tokyo, with seventeen *nishiki-e shinbun* published in Osaka at one point.

Tsuchiya (2002) offered a lack of clear division between quality newspaper and more mass, popular newspapers in Japan as the reason why such *kokuminteki taishūshi* (popular national newspapers) emerged and prospered in Osaka. Specifically, there was no clear division between the *ō-shinbun* and *ko-shinbun* in Osaka, therefore there was no strong pushback against these equalizing trends. In addition, these newspapers were seen first and foremost as businesses in Osaka, allowing managers to influence the character of their paper and popular journalists to move freely between different newspapers. Osaka readers were interested in newspapers as a medium of information rather than as a status symbol or a source of literary copy. The managers, seeking profits and strong sales, and the journalists, free from factions and orthodoxy, produced *ko-shinbun* newspapers with factual reporting and series formats (*tsuzuki-mono*) that were responsive to market demands and yeilded stable sales. These combined *ō-shinbun* and *ko-shinbun* elements gave birth to what was called the *chū-shinbun* (middle newspaper) during the Taisho era (1912-1926). In the process of popularization of these early newspapers, the Osaka news industry had carved out a middle ground, a balance of content and a stable market product, a newspaper that would become the standard for *kokuminteki taishūshi*—today's national newspaper.

SOLIDIFICATION OF "OSAKA JOURNALISM"

The *Yūkan Osaka Shimbun*, launched in 1923 was this type of Osaka newspaper. Different from conventional newspapers of the time, which were usually founded and supported by a political party, a big company or a senior journalist, the *Yūkan Osaka Shimbun* was described in the *Japanese Newspaper Year Book*, published in 1924, as neutral, transparent and based on the "Osaka First Principle" *(Ōsaka daiichi shugi)* (Osaka Shimbunsha, 1997). The "Osaka First Principle" held that Osaka newspapers were businesses that served Osaka first and foremost. Takahashi (2008) contended that this view was important for Kansai media because newspapers needed to appeal to the public to generate sales. He refers to an anti-authority newspaper called the *Kokkei Shimbun* which started publishing in 1901. Lead by journalist Miyatake Gaikotsu (1867-1955), the newspaper as launched in Osaka with the support of Fukuda Tomokichi, who was at the time managing a printing publishing company *Fukudadō*. Miyatake was controversial: over his lifetime, he was fined by the government fifteen times and sent to jail four times. The *Kokkei Shimbun* was banned by the government in 1908, but continued to sell by changing its name to the *Osaka Kokkei Shimbun* until 1914. It sold 80,000 copies at its peak, was considered successful in its day and demonstrated that Osaka people supported both Miyatake's ideas and his passion.

Another example of Osaka journalism was *Asahi Shimbun's* 'White Rainbow Incident' (*Hakkō jiken*), which occurred in 1918, and is regarded as contributing to Japanese journalism's impartiality and its journalistic creed: *kyakkan hōdō*, objective reporting (Schäfer, 2012). At the time, the *Asahi Shimbun* criticized the administration of Prime Minister Terauchi Masatake for the Siberian Intervention and Rice Riots of 1918, with the *Osaka Asahi* making particularly stinging remarks. When the government forbade news coverage of the riots, the *Tokyo Asahi* simply led its front page with alternative content, whereas the *Osaka Asahi* responded with a blank space in lieu of an article that would have been about the riots. As the *Osaka Asahi* maintained its critical attitude in response to what it saw as infringement of its journalistic integrity, the government responded with a crackdown on the paper. This prompted an *Osaka Asahi* spokesperson to use the phrase "*A white rainbow piercing the sun* (*hakkō hi wo tsuranuku*)" at a Kinki (Osaka) newspaper rally, referring to the press censorship by the Terauchi cabinet by way of a reference to a peasant revolt in ancient China. The government, by saying this reference could be interpreted as threat against the emperor, initiated judicial proceedings to force *Asahi* out of business, but before judgment, *Asahi* officially apologized, and announced the resignation of its president and of all its chief editors. Although seen as a unifying event for Japanese press and journalism, major philosophical differences remained between the *Osaka Asahi* and the *Tokyo Asahi*. While Yanagita Kunio was penning editorials on Japanese folklore in the *Tokyo Asahi*, *Osaka Asahi* editorials were taking up issues of politics, philosophy and the fate of local people during tumultuous times. Takahashi (2008) asserted that the *Osaka*

Asahi reported on the 1928 Huanggutun Incident assassination plot in Manchuria factually, while *Tokyo Asahi's* reports followed the scenario offered by the Japanese military. The lesson many took from these instances spoke to the importance of *zure*, the offset distance from central authority; the anti-authoritarian strength of Osaka journalism was seen as a function of its distance from Tokyo.

"Osaka Journalism" After the War

Although the end of the Second World War saw various maneuvering with regard to governmental restrictions on newspapers, this period also gave birth to a different kind of independent evening newspaper in Kansai. Seeking a measure of journalistic freedom from the structural pressures of the big newspaper companies, many journalists of the existing newspapers joined these emerging and progressively managed evening papers. Unfortunately, this golden period of evening newspapers for Kansai journalism was short-lived. Ex-journalist Adachi Ken'ichi (1913-1985) cited the end of the Kansai evening paper as coming in 1949, when the larger national newspapers were also allowed to publish evening versions, the circumstances of which he described in his 1981 work *Yūkan Ryūseigō: Aru Shimbun no Shogai*, based on his experiences at *Shin-Osaka Shimbun*. However, in Osaka, notably at the kiosk of the Umeda subway station, independent evening newspapers such as the *Osaka Nichinichi Shimbun* and the *Kansai Shimbun* continued to be popular and sold until the 1980s. The *Osaka Nichinichi* in particular, which originated in the *Minami Osaka Shimbun* and gave birth to the *Sakei Shimbun*, brought such remarkable figures as historical novelist and social critic Shiba Ryōtarō (born Fukuda Teiichi, 1923-1996) to the forefront of Japanese journalism. These evening newspapers provided continuing evidence of "Osaka journalism" in the form of distinctly local newspapers of Osaka.

When talking about Osaka journalism today, people often refer to former Osaka *Yomiuri Shimbun* journalist Kuroda Kiyoshi (1931-2000), born in Osaka and a graduate of Kyoto University. He was particularly well known for his original reporting style, an example of which is when he made reports during the Mitsubishi Bank kidnapping incident in 1979. The Tokyo version of the same paper, the *Tokyo Yomiuri*, refused to use Kuroda's articles in its editions and produced their own articles based predominantly, if not exclusively, on TV reports and *Jiji Press*. Kuroda also wrote a popular regular feature titled *Mado* (window) in the *Osaka Yomiuri*, in which he commented on various aspects of daily life based on letters he had received from readers. The themes were sometimes heartbreaking; one letter described a mother who had lost her 6-year-old son in an accident and another a 28-year-old girl who had attempted suicide after a wedding refusal because of her *buraku* origin. His comments were often critical of the status quo. This was not the usual stuff of newspapers at the time, certainly not the stuff of the *Tokyo Yomiuri*, but Kuroda did not hesitate to quote these letters directly; he considered these voices as those most deserving faithful treatment by the press, more so than politicians and celebrities. Kuroda eventually left the *Yomiuri* after 35 years of service and wrote a book in 1987 titled *Shimbun ga suitai suru toki (When the Newspapers Perish)*. Newspaper history is not without controversy; it is also said that Kuroda was pressured to leave by the chief executive of the *Osaka Yomiuri*, who was said to be following the directions of *Tokyo Yomiuri's* top management (Uozumi, 2000; Nagai, 2009). That said, Kuroda's influence is certainly part of the powerful and enduring narrative surrounding "Osaka journalism" and how it took on its anti-authority character. But, much like before the war, even such a powerful contribution as that of Kuroda's could not counter the rise of the concentration of media in Tokyo. As newspapers were uprooted from Osaka after becoming national, Osaka journalism began to fade.

In 2004, the *Sankei Shimbun Osaka* released a series of articles written by Minagawa Takeshi titled *Osaka era–when it lost its shine,* which highlighted the trend of national newspapers publishing *kakuitsuteki,* essentially identical news items, which as a consequence, brought over-representation of a Tokyo view with less space for local news (Minagawa,

2005). Minagawa was awarded the Sakata Memorial Journalism Award, an award dedicated to Kansai journalism, for this series in 2005. Nagai (2009), a retired journalist of the *Yomiuri Osaka*, believes that the success of the *Yomiuri* in Osaka was largely attributable to the fact that, in Osaka, the newspaper hired local journalists rooted in their community, who then provided news that was of interest to the readers. He also predicted that papers would lose their readers if this *kakuitsuteki* news tendency continued.

Although contextualized here as an Osaka-Tokyo phenomenon, the *kakuitsuteki* news problem is related to the overall state of Japanese journalism, particularly with regard to the institution called *kisha kurabu* (Press Club). Described as information cartels that encourage, if not demand, self-censorship (Freeman, 2000), the *kisha kurabu* operates on the principle that journalists of media outlets who are members of the Club are obliged to follow the content conformity that the Club demands. Press Club journalists from different newspapers often exchange their notes after press conferences or interviews to ensure this conformity (Gamble and Watanabe, 2005), a practice freelance journalist Uesugi Takashi (2011) asserted has become more organized recently thanks to recorders and the exchange of e-mails between journalists. This tendency is also reinforced by cross-media ownership in Japan, where each TV network is related to a national newspaper. For example, Nippon Television Network, key station of NNN network, is held by the Yomiuri Shimbun Holdings. The FNS network, whose key station is Fuji television, is in a similar manner linked with the *Sankei Shimbun*, while ANN network, whose key station is *Asahi Hōsō*, is affiliated with the *Asahi Shimbun*. As a result of Press Club practices and media consolidation, news on domestic Japanese politics has become virtually identical regardless of newspaper.

Today, all the national newspaper companies have their headquarters in Tokyo, with only the *Asahi Shimbun* maintaining their main office in Osaka. The once-strong media in Osaka has been suffering from this centralization and the continued corporate concentration in Tokyo.

However, Kansai does still have a media story to tell, based on its three distinctive geographical centers: Osaka, of course, but also Kobe and Kyoto. It is this distinct media localism that holds the key to the present vitality and future viability of Kansai media.

The Kobe Shimbun and the Kyoto Shimbun

The *Kobe Shimbun* is based in Kobe, Hyogo prefecture. The morning edition sells around 550,000 copies (*Kobe Shimbun*, 2013) and is the top newspaper in Hyogo prefecture. The newspaper was founded in 1898, but has experienced near fatal disasters on three occasions. Early in its history, the company building was burned down during the Rice Riots of 1918. The company however could manage to continue to publish thanks to the printing facilities of an affiliated company in Hyogo. The next crisis the newspaper faced was in the bombing of Kobe in World War II in 1945, which again destroyed the newspaper's building. This time, the *Asahi Shimbun* of Osaka helped with printing such that the Kobe newspaper could continue publishing activities. In the last of these three calamities, the company building was destroyed yet again in the Great Awaji Earthquake of 1995. As in the past, the newspapers publication capabilities were lost, this time because the computers were destroyed. However, thanks to a cooperation agreement that had been signed with *Kyoto Shimbun* just a year earlier, they could continue to edit, print and deliver their paper to readers in Kobe.

The newspaper's mission statement holds that: "As newspaper people, we will try to improve the welfare and development of the community" (translations by author). As a characteristic Japanese local newspaper (Rausch, 2012), the *Kobe Shimbun* puts emphasis on regional development and its contribution to their area of circulation. Kamata (2002) cites *Kobe Shimbun* ex-Chief Editor Satō Kimihiko as pointing out that the greater the distance from a local community, the more the mass media seeks sensationalized information. This is what Satō had observed in the media coverage of the murder of a 14-year-old boy in

1997 in the Hyogo prefecture. In this case, local residents sought concrete information as opposed to the sensationalized coverage provided by national media, coverage that ultimately brought only apprehension and heartache. For the *Kobe Shimbun*, understanding the point of view of their Hyogo prefecture reader and the information they are looking for are the most important characteristics of their newspaper identity.

Kyoto also has a local newspaper, the *Kyoto Shimbun.* Unlike the *Kobe Shimbun*, the *Kyoto Shimbun's* philosophy does not specifically refer to "community," focusing instead on universal values: "Through comprehensive information based on the speech coverage, the *Kyoto Shimbun* will contribute to the enrichment of humanity". Founded in 1879, the paper now sells approximately 490,000 copies of its morning edition (*Kyoto Shimbun,* n.d.). Considering circulation figures for newspapers in the prefectures surrounding Tokyo (about 168,000 copies for the *Chiba Nippō* (*Chiba Nippō*, n.d.) and about 210,000 for the *Kanagawa Shimbun* (*Kanagawa Shimbun,* n.d)), the relatively local *Kyoto Shimbun* seems to be rewarded for its efforts.

According to the newspaper's chief editor, any newspaper company that is close to a big city needs a balance of urban refinement and homespun charm, adding that local newspapers need this refinement more than any national newspaper in order for their business to survive (Kamata, 2002). This combination, for the *Kyoto Shimbun*, is found in the high level of local cultural-related content the paper carries. As proof of this committent and reflecting the historical reality of Kyoto and the local consciousness of its local readers, the newspaper has more staff in the cultural section of its operation than for other similar sized papers and even has a reporter specializing in temples. According to one staff reporter, the *Kyoto Shimbun* does not focus on scoops, which are valuable only when the news is "hot" (personal interview, 30 March 2010). This does not mean they ignore breaking stories, but they consider most scoops, the stuff of scandal and intrigue, as less important for their survival, allowing the Tokyo media outlets in the Kyoto area to focus their coverage on such matters. In addition to the local and highly cultural orientation identified in these two newspapers, journalists at both the *Kobe Shimbun* and the *Kyoto Shimbun* say they also recognize the importance of supporting their local communities in terms of business and reputation. These local journalists stressed their focus on collaboration with local companies and the respective university research communities in the development of the cities (personal interview, 4 March 2010).

The Japanese Print Media Industry in the Digital Era

As with print media around the world, the expanse of Japanese print is shrinking year by year; sales figures for Japanese publishing companies have been declining, from 50 billion to 100 billion yen every year since 1996, when 2.66 trillion yen in sales were recorded (NHK, 2012). This is not only due to the fact that the Japanese economy is itself shrinking, but can also be viewed in terms of the arrival of the digital era. Indeed, when Japan hosted the *Internet 1996 World Exposition*, it was clear people across Japan had already begun a transition to the Internet and were including it as a media and information source. Overall market statistics bear this out: compared with 2011, books sales in 2012 decreased by about 20 billion yen and magazine sales fell by about 40 billion yen (Zenkoku shuppan kyōkai, 2013). However, at the same time the traditional print market was absorbing this 60 billion yen loss, digital books sales in Japan increased by approximately 10 billion yen, from 62.9 billion yen in sales in 2011 to 72.9 billion yen sales in 2012 (Intanetto Media Sōgō Kenkyūjo, 2013). In this context, it is worth noting that the bulk of sales of electronic publications in Japan has been in manga on smartphones (Intanetto Media Sōgō Kenkyūjo, 2012). Indeed, of the 62.9 billion yen in Japanese e-book sales in 2011, sales of digital manga through electronic phones accounted for roughly three-quarters of the market (Japan Fair Trade Commission, 2013). Impress Business Media (2013) welcomed this trend as a sign of the development of e-publishing in Japan. More and more popular manga magazines are entering into e-publishing: a biweekly manga magazine *Morning* launched its electronic version *D-Morning* in May 2013, and the popular weekly manga magazine *Shōnen Jump* launched its special electronic version in August 2013.

However, this does not mean that they have transitioned completely from paper to digital publication. Shimada Eijirō, editor of the *Morning* manga magazine, explained that their profit margin is based on readers who buy their manga. For them, the weekly magazines they publish, on paper or electronically, are still meant to target the same readers. The number of manga magazines sold is decreasing, but manga sales remain stable; any problem with a decrease of manga sales is rather a problem with the potential decrease of readers who buy manga rather than the format (*Mainichi Shimbun*, 2013). This implies something about e-publishing in Japan: people spend money to buy electronic publications as long as they are affordably priced and mobile, which is to say, something they can consume and discard. A good example may be the new market of e-business books, which can be easily downloaded and just as easily deleted. Indeed, this points to a meaningful conclusion regarding newspapers: readers should as well be interested in electronic versions of newspapers more than their paper versions. Their advantage would lie in their portability, space and use efficiency and ease of discarding.

Moreover, Yamada (2012), chief editor of Kobunsha Publishing and contemporary media critic, believes that paper publication persists in Japan largely because neither paper nor electronic publication has achieved dominant commercial success over the other. If any particular publication consists only of text, it is relatively easy to produce in an electronic version, even though it still needs modification for different formats, devices and versions. However, if a publication requires layout or processes that necessitate printing plates, publication requires manual verification by the publisher. For the moment, this digitalization process takes more time and raises costs over that of the paper versions. It has only been possible for large publishing companies with sufficient means to invest the necessary resources for digitalization, meaning that only

The Arrival of the "Digital Newspaper"

Along with the economic decline in the fortunes of Japanese print media in general, Japanese newspaper sales have also decreased. Beyond the ups and downs that followed the industry's peak in 2000, sales have continually declined by around 100 billion each year since 2006, from 2.522 trillion in 2000 to 2.332 trillion in 2006 and to 1.953 trillion by 2011 (Japan Newspaper Publishers & Editors Association, n.d.). While the decline in population alone led publishers not to expect any increase in circulation, print-advertising revenues are now also being upstaged by online-advertising revenues. Several alarming books were published in the early 2000s about the bleak future of the Japanese newspaper industry, including one that warned of *The End of Newspapers* (Utagawa, 2005). While this may be true based on the premise of *paper* in a newspaper, newspapers have now become new online content-providers based on the convergence of mass media and the Internet. As outlined by Aoki and Yukawa (2003), when diversifying their media outlets, newspaper companies have tried to differentiate the content of paper media and digital media. For their paper versions, they present content requiring careful reading and contemplation, while the news flashes and short stories have become the preferred content for their digital versions; now most newspapers in Japan update their websites multiple times a day.

In Western countries, particularly the United States, many newspapers have launched online versions, most with pay-walls. This system allows for anyone to access the website, but requires some form of payment to access further content. Cost considerations aside, global potential is an asset: it is now possible for Japanese to read newspapers such as the *Washington Post* or the *New York Times* without having to find a specialized magazine shop and pay for a single paper copy. In the case of the *Wall Street Journal,* which has opted for a "pay model" since the launch of their website in 1996, readers could access all the content of an

further concentration of the publishing industry that Tokyo presents will make it possible to fully cross this digital threshold.

online *Wall Street Journal* for a very reasonable weekly fee. Still, updating of the pay model has been necessary and, in 2009, the paper changed its policy from a weekly payment system to a by-article basis.

In Japan as well, the national newspapers have begun charging for digital editions, with varying types of charge models. However, many are seeking innovative approaches; since the arrival of the Internet and the possibility of e-publishing, the conventional publishing industry in Japan has been preparing to establish a system where paper and electronic versions are published at the same time, with the newspaper industry gearing up for the same compatibility. The first to start such a system was the *Nikkei*, which launched its website *NIKKEI NET* in 1996 and offered free viewing of its articles. However, the system was closed upon launch of a for-pay web version of the *Nihon Keizai Shinbun Denshiban* (Web-kan) newspaper in March 2010. *Asahi Shinbun Digital* started its digital version in August 2011 after providing content free of charge with their website asahi.com since 1995. At present, subscribers of the paper version of *Asahi* or *Nikkei* can have access to the online version by adding a supplement. In the case of the *Yomiuri Shimbun*, access to the digital version costs an additional fee on top of the actual paper subscription but as of October 2013, the *Yomiuri Shimbun* does not offer a digital-only subscription. The *Mainichi Shimbun* launched its digital version in June 2010 as *Mainichi RT (Real Time)*, but announced in August 2013 that they will be launching a digital version nationally before 2014 by following the *Yomiuri* model. A unique feature of the Mainichi approach is use of social networks to allow the public to rank their articles. *Sankei* offers different prices depending on multiple options: a computer view of the newspaper as an image; news for Japanese phones such as imode, Yahoo! Japan, and ezweb in forms adapted specifically for these devices; and, as of April 2013, a service for iOS and Android OS that provide horizontally-written texts. While many of the national newspapers in Japan are working to adapt to a new media environment with a range of services and payment schemes, the conclusion, for the moment, is that Japanese papers are still to be struggling to find the best way to survive in the digital era.

Online Platforms: The End of Newspapers? Local Newspapers?

The final question of this chapter is thus: how does the Internet and e-publishing affect the Japanese newspaper industry as a whole, and do the notions of regional, national or local still have a meaning in a world open to cyberspace? To be sure, in the past, all national papers had Kansai versions of their webpages focusing on Kansai news. However, the *Asahi Shimbun* and the *Nikkei Shimbun* have now closed these Kansai-centered pages and have replaced them by the prefectural division versions as they have upgraded to digital publishing. Further, local newspapers have also started publishing digital versions. The *Tōōnippō* newspaper of Aomori Prefecture was the first among local Japanese newspapers to go digital, beginning with an Internet presence in October 2008. Other local newspapers have begun to offer similar services, where the reader can view the newspaper as an image. While rudimentary given the rapid advances in digital technology, such an approach enables people living in remote regions to read these newspapers, where delivery costs have made access to paper version prohibitive.

Meanwhile, with the development of the digital technologies (HTML5, for example), different types of devices are being enabled to display a variety of web content (video, music and texts), so consumers need fewer different devices, such as DVD players, MP3 players, or e-book readers, in order to access media texts. Indeed, younger generations can now meet their media consumption needs with just a smartphone. As such, national newspapers are changing their approaches and policies to adapt to the complex combination of evolving consumer preferences, expanding technical capabilities and effective monetization models. It is in this context that the *Kobe Shimbun* recently launched their "integrated" digital version, a mixture of the type of content that had been provided earlier by the national newspapers, but localized.

While the price structure for this electronic version is less than for a delivered paper version, the newspaper also included an e-mail notification service, a newspaper viewer, access to a database of old articles dating back up to one year, and access to a range of content. Readers can access from any device and even log in from different devices at the same time. This pricing scheme shows that, as it is highly unlikely for those who do not pay for newspapers outright to subscribe for an electronic version no matter what the price, the aim by *Kobe Shimbun* is to maintain their current reader base by offering better online services. However, if they sell electronic newspaper access for much less than the paper version, there is the risk of losing some of their existing paper customers and thus reducing their revenues. Further, those subscribing only to the digital version pay the fee by credit card, whereas the paper reader pays through the local delivery agent as they used to, thus guaranteeing revenues for the distribution system as well.

Such technical issues aside, Ōmachi Satoshi (2013), Assistant General Manager of the digital business division of *Kobe Shimbun*, says that they are also trying to differentiate their digital media service from that of the national newspapers by adopting a regional standpoint. The electronic versions of newspapers offered by the national newspapers provide various functions that in fact require large financial and labor investments that local newspapers could not afford. Therefore, as outlined by Ōmachi, local newspapers have to determine and choose the most valuable functions for local newspapers. Since the costs of implementating a transactional subscription management system are prohibitively high, *Kyodo News* has offered to share its system with affiliated companies. As for the content of their electronic version, they view online platforms such as social media and individual blogs as their competitors, rather than the national newspapers. Therefore, these newspapers consider it more important to prioritize local news of their region as content. In the case of the *Kobe Shimbun,* like their paper version, they devote a different page to each of the twelve regions of Hyogo prefecture, which the local branches update with the latest news. They send their readers e-mail notifications through smartphones with weather news, news flashes, and disaster and traffic information relevant to Hyogo Prefecture. In this process, according to Ōmachi, journalists, who at first wondered if the technological shift would increase their workload, began to see new possibilities. They came to understand the importance of news flash reports for the online version; they began using video footage taken between photo shots to augment news content on blogs provided exclusively to subscribed readers.

The journalists of the *Kobe Shinbun* and the *Kyoto Shinbun* that I interviewed both admitted that they do not have any concrete problems due to the emergence of the Internet. Rather, they welcome the diversification that is made possible through the advances of information technology as a counter-balance to the media concentration that has long been the trend in the Japanese newspaper industry. In the 1980s, the Kansai media railed against the problem of media centralisation in Tokyo, charges that reflected their lack of information sharing with other media outlets (Komatsu, 1994). Reflecting this sentiment, the local media should be seen as working dual roles, both as a receiver of information and an information provider on levels both local and regional or national. With the combined front of a paper newspaper and a website made possible through information technology, local newspapers can reach readers both within and outside of their circulation area. In this context, the unique strength of local newspapers can be fostered.

The point of this journey through the tensions of Tokyo-centric and national newspapers versus the local newspapers of Kansai has been to illustrate the value of local journalism. News consumers anywhere can indeed get the latest news—particularly Tokyo-based or national news—easily and at low cost through information technology. Moreover, an increasing number of local newspaper publishers have adopted technology, and are trying to reach their traditional audience, that within their immediate area, as well as an expanded audience dispersed across Japan, directly via the Internet. While local news consumers tend to prefer local newspapers, where locally important, immediate and useful information can be obtained, as time passes, the transition from print-based media to information technology platforms benefits the local newspaper companies, those traditionally at a disadvantage when gathering national and governmental news. This transition shows that, while prioritizing the local connection with their local readers, *zure*, the offset of distance between central Tokyo and outlying areas, also offers the Kansai media an opportunity to explore new forms of news dissemination. It is in the continuation of "Osaka journalism," a resistance to the Tokyo-centric model of news publishing, that allows outlying newspapers to maintain, if not further pursue their interpretation of journalistic integrity.

References

Adachi, K. (1981). Yūkan ryūseigō : aru shimbun no shogai. Shinchōsha.

Aoki, N., & Yukawa, T. (2003). Netto wa shinbun o korosunoka: Henbōsuru masumedia. NTT Shuppan.

Chiba Nippō. (n.d.) Retrieved 20 October, 2013, from http://www.chibanippo.co.jp/pdf/baitaishiryou.pdf

Fujiwara, O. (2007). Netto jidai 10-nengo shinbun to terebi wa kō naru. Tokyo: Asahi Shinbunsha.

Gamble, A. & Watanabe, T. (2004). A public betrayed: an inside look at Japanese media atrocities and their warnings to the West. Regnery Publishing.

Huffington Post Japan. (2013, Augsut 8). Ushinawareta shōhizei nihyau gojū okuen, gaikoku kigyō ni kazei dekiruka. Retrieved October 20, 2013, from http://www.huffingtonpost.jp/2013/08/08/consumption_tax_n_37 22851.html

Huffman, J. L. (1997). Creating a public: people and press in Meiji Japan. Honolulu, Hawaii: University of Hawai'i Press.

Japan Fair Trade Commission (Kōsei torihiki iinkai). (2013, July 26). Denshi shoseki shijō no dōkō ni tsuite. Retrieved from http://www.jftc.go.jp/cprc/reports/index.files/cr-0113.pdf#page=1&zoom=auto,0,621.

Japan Newspaper Publishers & Editors Assciation (Nihon Shinbun Kyōkai). (n.d.). Shinbunsha no sō uriage daka no suii. Retrieved October 20, 2013, from http://www.pressnet.or.jp/data/finance/finance01.php

Kamata, S. (2002). Chihōshi no kenkyū. Tokyo: Ushio Shuppansha.

Kanagawa Shimbun. (n.d.). Baitai dēta. Retrieved October 20, 2013, from
http://www.kanagawa-shimbun.jp/ad/date.html

Katsuya, M. (2007, March 14). Yūkoku no koramunisuto Katsuya Masahiko san: "Osaka koku" ga mirai no nihon, Sankei Web. Retrieved from http://www.sankei.co.jp/culture/enterme/070314/ent070314006.htm

Kobe Shimbun. (2013). Retrieved October 20, 2013, from
http://www.kobe-np.co.jp/ad-data/contents/pdf/2013ad-data_Part01.pdf

Komatsu, S. (1994). Kochira kansai. Bungei shunjū.

Kyoto Shimbun. (n.d.). Hakkōbusū. Retrieved October 20, 2013, from http://www.kyoto-np.co.jp/ad/profile/busuu_01.htm

Mainichi Shimbun. (2013, August 26). Shūkan mangashi: denshika, hyōgen hirogeru kanōsei—D mōningu·janpu LIVE, Mainichi Shinbun. Retrieved from http://mainichi.jp/feature/news/20130826ddm004040028000c.html

Matsumoto, H. (2012, July 4). Denshishoseki wa shoten renkei wo jūshi— rakuten mikitani shachō to kōdansha noma shachō, PC Online. Retrieved from http://pc.nikkeibp.co.jp/article/news/20120704/1054943/

Mediarisāchisentā (Media Research Center). (2013). Zasshi shinbun sōkatarogu: 2013. Tokyo: Mediarisāchisentā.

Minagawa, T. (2005). Ano Osaka wa shindanoka. Tokyo: Fusōsha.

Nagahama, J. (2009, August 26). Nippan to Tōhan, nidai toritsugi ga kasen suru nihon no shuppan ryūtsū jijō, Business Media Makoto. Retrieved from http://bizmakoto.jp/makoto/articles/0908/26/news015.html

Nagai, Y. (2008). Tōkyō kara ōsaka e: Yomiuri shinbun no baai. In M. Senda (Ed.), Kansai o sozosuru (pp. 190-205). Osaka: Izumi Shoin.

Nagai, Y. (2009). Osaka janarizumu no keifu: Saikaku chikamatsu kara netto jidai e. Osaka: Forum·A.

NHK. (2012, December 30). Shuppan uriage icchō hassen oku en shitamawaru mitōshi. NHK Online. Retrieved from http://www3.nhk.or.jp/news/html/20121230/k10014530671000.html

Intanetto Media Sōgō Kenkyūjo. (2012). Denshi shoseki bijinesu chōsa hōkokusho: 2012. Tokyo: Impress R&D.

Intanetto Media Sōgō Kenkyūjo. (2013). Denshi shoseki bijinesu chōsa hōkokusho. Tokyo: Inpuresubijinesumedia (Impress Business Media).

Okumura, H. (2009). Tettei kenshō Nihon no godai shinbun. Tokyo: Nanatsumori Shokan.

Ōmachi, S. (2013). "Kōbe Shinbun NEXT" wa denshiban no chihōhi no moderu ni naruka. Janarizumu (Journalism), 272, January (1 gatsu gō), Asahi Shinbunsha.

Ono, H. (1972). Shinbun nishikie. Tokyo: Mainichi Sinbun.

Osaka Shinbunsha. (1997). Osaka Shinbun 75-shunen kinenshi. Osaka-shi: Osaka Shinbunsha.

Pharr, S. J., & Krauss, E. S. (1996). Media and politics in Japan. Honolulu: University of Hawai'i Press.

Rausch, A. S. (2012). Japan's local newspapers: Chihoshi and revitalization journalism. London ; New York: Routledge.

Schäfer, F. (2012). Public opinion, propaganda, ideology : theories on the press and its social function in interwar Japan, 1918-1937. Leiden; Boston: Brill.

Shinbō, J. (2012, July 10). Tōkyō hatsu wa nihon hatsu? Panda sōdō de kanjita chihō e no mukanshin, Sports Hochi Osaka-ban. Retrieved from http://hochi.yomiuri.co.jp/osaka/column/shinbou/news/20120710-OHO1T00150.htm

Takahashi, T. (2008). Kansai no media jijō. In M. Senda (Ed.), Kansai o sozosuru (pp. 171-189). Osaka: Izumi Shoin.

Tsuchiya, R. (1995). Osaka no nishikie shinbun. Tokyo: Sangensha.

Tsuchiya, R. (1999). Nishikie shinbun towa nanika, Nyūsu no tanjō: kawara ban to shinbun nishikie no jōhō sekai, Tokyo University digital Museum. Retrieved from http://www.um.u-tokyo.ac.jp/publish_db/1999news/03/301/0301.html

Tsuchiya, R. (2002). Taishūshi no genryū: Meijiki koshinbun no kenkyū. Kyoto: Sekai Shisōsha.

Uesugi, T., & Ugaya, H. (2011). Hōdō saigai genpatsuhen: jijitsu o tsutaenai media no taizai. Tokyo: Gentosha.

Uozumi, A. (2000). Watanabe Tsuneo: Media to kenryoku. Tokyo: Kōdansha.

Utagawa, R. (2005). Shinbun ga naku naru hi. Tokyo: Sōshisha.

Yamada, J. (2012). Shuppan shinbun zetsubō mirai: Tōyō Keizai Shinpōsha.

Yomiuri Shinbun 100-nenshi Henshū Iinkai. (1976). Yomiuri shinbun hyakunenshi. Tokyo: Yomiuri Shinbunsha.

Yoshino, T. (1980). Miyatake Gaikotsu. Tokyo: Kawade Shobō Shinsha.

Zenkoku shuppan kyōkai. (2013). Nihon no Shuppan Tōkei. Retrieved October 20, 2013, from http://www.ajpea.or.jp/statistics/index.html

Chapter Three

New Journalism in Japan

Using Independent Digital Sources for Social Research

Akihiro Ogawa

Introduction: My New Research Routine

We all have research routines; a recent addition to my routine includes checking digital media news sites. By "digital," however, I am not referring to digital forms of traditional newspapers. News content is currently and commonly sold on the Internet instead of via the *paper* newspaper, but this represents, in fact, the same content as in the actual newspaper. Rather, my new routine involves searching and viewing video clips broadcast via "independent journalism" formats. My favorite is popularly called *IWJ* (for *Independent Web Journal*), a digital news medium available only on the Internet (at http://iwj.co.jp/). Using Ustream, a video streaming service, *IWJ* maintains channels to broadcast press conferences and grassroots protests by citizens, briefings by government officials, and a range of interviews, primarily from Tokyo, but also from across Japan.

These new forms of "independent journalism" provide the viewer "news" raw data in a straightforward manner, for example, by broadcasting a press conference, uninterrupted and unedited and from beginning to end. In the past, such news would only have been accessible to registered reporters who are members of a particular press club. Now, however, because I can watch the broadcast, I can follow every minute of the conference; I can note how each person presents his or her materials and how reporters interact with that person. I can confirm exactly what words were actually used in what way, and I am a witness to facial expression and body language. Whereas researchers have conventionally used newspapers as a primary source, newspaper articles are in fact, secondary sources. Newspaper content is "manufactured," made up of words and phrases, by reporters to condense the volume and make the news content clearer and easier to understand. However, in the course of this "manufacture," the original words and phrases might be altered, with some inevitably cut. This process reflects value judgments regarding the news, prioritizations made by the reporters themselves, as well as by the political stance of the media outlets. Hence, researchers need access to the original news data, that which has not been manufactured or colored in some manner by the process of reporting or editing.

This chapter explores new possibilities for researchers when they use such independent digital media sources in their social research. By using independent digital sources, I argue that researchers can take direct initiative in pursuing news and that they are afforded an independent opportunity to judge the news for value in a critical manner. In this chapter, I first introduce my own research experience as an example, bringing a comparative perspective on how traditional newspapers and independent media actually covered the widespread anti-nuclear demonstrations that occurred across the country following the Fukushima disaster in March 2011 (see Ogawa, 2013a; Ogawa, 2013b, forthcoming). In particular, I present how I dealt with specific pieces of news in order to comment on contemporary Japan. Second, I will provide a brief overview of the emergence of digital media in Japan, focusing on the practical perspective of using them as research tools in social research. Finally, I will conclude this chapter with some personal reflections on the practice of traditional journalism from my five years of experience as a staff reporter at a major Japanese wire service.

Covering Anti-nuclear Rallies Post-Fukushima

In the course of extensive fieldwork in Japan, one of my current research interests is to document ethnographically the development of anti-nuclear sentiments in Japanese society following the March 2011 Fukushima disaster. This topic has become part of my broader interest in researching the development of Japanese civil society (Ogawa, 2009). My original research approach on anti-nuclear social movements used a combination of sources conventional to social anthropology: combining participant observation in anti-nuclear demonstration sites, an extensive series of interviews with anti-nuclear rally participants, and media analysis, including newspapers and magazines. Recently, however, I have begun to focus more on independent digital media sources as I have come to realize that limitations to my research emerge if I follow conventional mass media sources alone.

The Fukushima disaster triggered several anti-establishment demonstrations across Japan, with one of the first, which was directed against Japan's nuclear energy policy, happening on March 12, just one day after the great earthquake. A small group of citizens, about 10 people, demonstrated at the Ministry of Economy, Trade, and Industry (METI), the government agency in charge of energy policymaking in Japan. The group appealed for Japan's energy policy, which has depended heavily on nuclear power, to be changed, and called for halting the operation of current nuclear power plants. One of the group members said, "It is time for people who are still in Fukushima to evacuate as soon as possible. The situation is becoming worse and worse." As they were protesting, they learned by a news report from a mobile phone service that one of the nuclear plant workers at Fukushima Daiichi had died.

This was probably the first modern anti-nuclear demonstration in Japan, and it came from grassroots voices against nuclear energy sources shortly after the Fukushima disaster. I learned about this demonstration when I watched a live broadcast by *IWJ*, which continued for nearly two hours. For several days after the demonstrations, I found no newspaper articles reporting on it—even though this anti-nuclear protest was carried out right in front of the METI building, which meant that there should be several reporters from major media within the METI press club housed in the METI building. It seemed that the reporters were not interested in covering this demonstration or that publication of articles that had been written was stopped by desk editors, most likely due to pressure from power companies, major sponsors of Japanese newspaper companies. In fact, in the year before the Fukushima disaster, the Tokyo Electric Power Company (TEPCO), operator of the collapsed Fukushima nuclear reactors, spent 11.6 billion yen on advertising, according to the earning reports distributed at the shareholders' meeting on June 28, 2011. This advertising money went to the major Japanese media conglomerates, including those who publish the *Yomiuri*, *Asahi*, *Sankei*, and *Nikkei* newspapers. Later, I had a chance to talk about this matter with an ex-colleague working with a major newspaper (we were press club members together when I was a reporter in the mid-1990s). He did not say very much about the matter, but he did allow that anti-nuclear rallies were deemed "too partisan to cover."

My subsequent research indeed revealed that newspaper articles on anti-nuclear rallies did not often appear in major newspapers, as I had now come to expect. Because I work outside Japan, I subscribe to the international edition of the *Asahi* newspaper; in addition, almost every day I check the websites of the five major newspapers read by residents throughout Japan: the *Asahi*, *Mainichi*, *Yomiuri*, *Sankei*, and *Nikkei Shimbun*. I also checked the websites of the *Tokyo Shimbun* and the Tokyo edition of the *Chūnichi Shimbun*, a Nagoya-based local newspaper, and peruse the *47News* (www.47news.jp/), a website made by *Kyodo News* and its 52 affiliated local newspapers.

While sifting through these various sources for information on the grassroots mobilization against nuclear energy, I always came back to *IWJ* as my primary source. This digital medium, which was started in 2010, increased its broadcasting quantity—in terms of both coverage hours and range of events covered—with its coverage of issues related to the Fukushima disaster. In particular, from shortly after the disaster until the following summer, I began to use video streaming services like *Ustream* because during the initial post-disaster stages, the state-run television NHK was broadcast all day on *Ustream* free of charge, primarily for the convenience of the disaster victims. From overseas, I could keep an eye on *Ustream,* and I was made aware of *IWJ* because it was also broadcasting via *Ustream.*

Since early 2011, beginning with the first anti-nuclear demonstration after Fukushima on March 12, 2011, anti-nuclear power rallies have come to be held with increasing frequency across Japan (see documentation in Ogawa, 2013a). In this regard, I confirmed several crucial developments via *IWJ*: March 20, 2011, was the date of one of the first demonstrations against TEPCO. One month after the earthquake, on April 10, 2011, perhaps 15,000 people, mostly young people, marched in protest against nuclear energy in Koenji, Suginami, a hub of youth culture in Tokyo. On May 7, this demonstration was extended to Shibuya, Tokyo. Seven days later on May 14, another anti-nuclear protest was organized at the TEPCO headquarters, as well as at the Tokyo branch of the Chubu Electric Power Company. The next day, another demonstration was held in Yoyogi Park in central Tokyo, highlighting the importance of exploring alternative energy sources. Viewing the event through the broadcasting by *IWJ,* it was apparent that thousands of people were there, shouting "*mirai no tameni ene shifuto*" (shift energy sources for our future).

In the following week, another demonstration was organized in front of the Ministry of Education, Culture, Sports, Science, and Technology (MEXT), this one in response to its determination that a level of 20 millisieverts per year (mSv/y) would be used as the radiation safety standard for schools in Fukushima Prefecture. On April 19, 2011, the MEXT notified the Board of Education and related institutions in Fukushima Prefecture that this figure would be the standard used for school grounds and buildings. According to the information aired by *IWJ* broadcasting as part of the demonstration participants' appeals, 20 mSv/y is equivalent to 3.8 microSv per hour (as measured outdoors), which is roughly six times the level specified for "Radiation Controlled Areas" (0.6 microSv/h or more). The Japanese Labor Standards Act prohibits those under the age of 18 from working under these conditions, and forcing children to be exposed to such radiation doses was deemed by protestors to be an exceedingly inhumane decision, hence the demonstration targeting MEXT. This protest against MEXT has continued every week from this period until July of 2013. The parents of 14 children who attended schools in Koriyama, Fukushima Prefecture filed a provisional injunction against the City of Koriyama on June 24, 2011, at the Koriyama Branch of the Fukushima District Court, to demand the collective evacuation (*shūdan sokai*) of children amid strong fears of health damage from radiation emitted by the Fukushima Daiichi nuclear power plant. The Sendai High Court rejected the demand in April 2013, even as it acknowledged the radiation risks for health. Further, the Citizens' Committee for 10 Million People's Petition to Say Goodbye to Nuclear Power Plants (*Sayonara genpatsu 1 senman nin akushon*) has regularly organized demonstrations against nuclear energy since the Fukushima disaster. One of the major events was a rally of 60,000 people in Meiji Park in September 2011, with vast crowds chanting *"Genpatsu Iranai"* (No More Nuclear Power).

It must be emphasized that details of these initial developments concerning anti-nuclear actions in the first six months, mobilized by grassroots citizens in Japanese society, were only minimally available in conventional media outlets; the major newspapers hardly covered them. In fact, the abovementioned demonstration in September ended its march in Yoyogi Park, next to the NHK headquarters. However, the state-run TV did not broadcast a single word on this anti-nuclear movement on the 7 p.m. national news program that day. I would not have been aware of this new grassroots dynamism if I had followed only the conventional mass media, including major newspapers like the *Asahi* and the *Yomiuri*. Further, Independent digital media like *IWJ* have built up extensive and high quality digital archives following the Fukushima disaster. Most (though not all) of the major anti-nuclear developments were recorded as well as being broadcast, and anyone can access these archives freely. Hence, independent digital journalism has the potential to be a great source for social research on Japanese society.

SUMMER 2012 IN TOKYO

In summer 2012, I was in Tokyo where I witnessed a series of anti-nuclear demonstrations every Friday evening in front of the prime minister's office. The demonstrations originally started on March 29, 2012, and I was there on July 13, 2012. The number of participants reached a peak of 150,000 (although the police reported only 10,000), with member of the crowd shouting *"Saikadō hantai, Oi wo tomero"* (Say no to nuclear power plant restarts; stop the Oi operation). This development followed Prime Minister Yoshiiko Noda's authorization to reactivate two nuclear reactors in Oi, Fukui Prefecture, during the previous month. By the end of August 2012, the total number of Friday rally participants actually had risen to nearly one million, according to figures released by the organizers (Manabe, 2013). This series of protests was orchestrated by a group of networks named the Metropolitan Coalition Against Nukes (*Hangenren*)—a platform organized by thirteen Tokyo-based informal citizens' groups, all of which are active in energy and environmental issues—together with independent individuals. These demonstrations were becoming major events in Japan solely at the instigation of ordinary people who were only now fully exploring nuclear energy policy and developing an anti-nuclear energy stance.

I learned of this Friday evening rally in front of the prime minister's office only via *IWJ*. Again, the rally site was just on the opposite side of the press club building from reporters covering the National Diet (*kokkai kisha kaikan*). Thus, it seems that the reporters would have been the first witnesses of these highly visible and highly charged and continually increasing anti-nuclear demonstrations. Nonetheless, coverage from the major newspapers, including the *Asahi Shimbun* and the *Yomiuri Shimbun*, was very limited in terms of the Friday evening rallies from late March through early June. Meanwhile, the *Tokyo Shimbun*, a liberal paper, covered the development well, as did the *Akahata*, a Japanese communist paper. I shared this impression with an older woman at one of the rallies. One of the anti-nuclear rally participants, she said that she had been reading the *Asahi* over the past five decades but that it had not had been covering the series of anti-nuclear rallies happening in this country. Thus, she had stopped subscribing to the *Asahi* and had begun to read the *Tokyo Shimbun*, which she thought would be more informative and useful for her.

Notable in the coverage were the differences in the numbers of participants reported among newspapers when they covered the Friday demonstrations. On June 29, for example, the organizers announced 150,000 participants, whereas the police announced an estimate of 17,000—a scale difference that is clearly intentional. In its coverage, the *Asahi* estimated 150,000 to 180,000, whereas the *Mainichi* reported the numbers announced by both the organizers and the police. The *Sankei* mirrored the police estimates, putting the number at less than 20,000. Interestingly, the *Yomiuri* did not write a single line about it, totally ignoring the fact that thousands of people were actually getting together in front of the Japanese prime minister's office to protest the nation's energy policy. Finally, the state-run television NHK covered the anti-nuclear rallies on the 7 p.m. news on July 20 for the first time since they had started in March, when former Prime Minister Yukio Hatoyama appeared on the rally site. In this, it was clear that any news value was judged to be based on the appearance of the former prime minister and his comments, instead of on the basis of a rally by thousands of, if not over a hundred thousand, ordinary people. Such a conclusion seems inescapable for the simple reason that had the rally itself had been of interest, a national news station of that caliber had had plenty of chances to cover the demonstrations previously but had neglected to do so. Hatoyama supported the anti-nuclear rally, shouting to the crowd, "I regret that politics has strayed far from the people's wishes...." A former prime minister apologizing to hundreds of thousands of citizens, yet the whole affair was given just 15 seconds airtime.

During this time, on the other hand, new digital media like *IWJ* continuously broadcast these ongoing political demonstrations live from the very beginning. While attending the Friday mass rally during part of my summer research in Tokyo, I also used the *IWJ* archives to check the overall developments of the demonstration. During the demonstrations themselves, I could not often move up to the front of the demonstration or just in front of the prime minister's office where participants were making powerful appeals. However, all the appeals were recorded by *IWJ*, and I could document the specifics of the appeals in my field notes later at home. Further, by watching the *IWJ* archives, I could identify who was actually leading the demonstrations, which helped me to plan further research, including scheduling interviews, for example. In addition, the live broadcasts were accompanied by comments from Twitter users who were watching the broadcast. These contained a mixture of anti- as well as pro-nuclear messages, providing me with a full grasp of the real sentiments of the grassroots population in Japan.

During this summer research, I also took advantage of the full coverage of Prime Minister Noda's meeting with anti-nuclear activists of *Hangenren* on August 22, 2012, inside the prime minister's office. Prime Minister Yoshihiko Noda met with the anti-nuclear activists, but the meeting was apparently only to show that he was attempting to take anti-nuclear sentiment among both the public and his own Democratic Party of Japan into account before the party's leadership election, which was scheduled for September. Permission to get into the meeting for the purpose of research observation was difficult to obtain in a timely manner (the meeting was canceled once and then rescheduled suddenly; I wanted to be physically present at the meeting, but I could not manage it). Thus, I believe watching *IWJ* was the only way for me to find out what was actually happening on the site.

Via *IWJ*, the impression that I took was that Prime Minister Noda looked cautious, even nervous, in front of the activists. On the other hand, a female leader and other members from *Hangenren* sat in front of Prime Minister Noda, and I was struck by how brave they appeared —images provided clearly via *IWJ*. More than the impressions of the participants provided by *IWJ*, this was indeed a historic moment for Japan. This event represented the first time in Japanese post-World War II history that a prime minister had met directly with members of a citizen's group. Further, one *Hangenren* member was bold enough to say to Prime Minister Noda, "Don't use us to get votes. ... We didn't come here to play politics. We came here to stop nuclear power."

While all of the major newspapers and televisions more or less covered the meeting, their reports, in terms of both quantity and quality, were relatively short and not well detailed. The articles simply devoted a couple of paragraphs to the incident, saying that Prime Minister Noda met with members of citizens' groups at his office. Given the significance of the event, both in terms of a sitting prime minister meeting with a citizen's group and the implications of this meeting in reflecting citizen anti-nuclear sentiments, such minimal coverage by traditional media was troubling. Indeed, one of my key interests was to document how the activists would present their anti-nuclear agenda to the top person in Japanese politics and to observe the actual interactions between Prime Minister and the activists. During the 30-minute meeting, however, I did not see any interaction between them—a research conclusion made possible only through using *IWJ* as a source. The time was used mainly for the activists' presentations, and Prime Minister Noda was listening to what they had prepared, which was mostly about the anti-nuclear creed, voices from Fukushima victims, etc., and he spoke to them for only three minutes.

Noda asserted, "Our basic stance is to explore post nuclear society. We are now building up a new energy policy in the middle/long term, not depending on nuclear energy. ... Regarding the restart of the nuclear plant, the safety standard is the most important thing. I decided the restart of Oi nuclear plants, based on our expert knowledge and experiences. I also wanted to tell you that the restart has nothing to do with any particular economic or industry organizations. ... We will continue to make serious efforts to enhance safety issues. There are no upper limits for guaranteeing safety. The safety will be confirmed by an independent regulation committee, which is likely to be started in September. ..."

Promptly responding to Prime Minister Noda's comment, the above-mentioned *Hangenren* leader asserted,

> "We are not at all satisfied with your answer" (*shōfuku itashi kaneru*). The current situation, including the collapsed Fukushima plant, is not safe enough. In what way can the current government, which cannot even confirm the safety of the Fukushima plant, guarantee safety in the future? How can we trust our government?"

The conventional mass media, including the *Nikkei*, simply reported the activist's comment that the group was not satisfied with Noda's answer without providing the important context of her additional comments. However, I thought her response presented an important point for understanding their rationale. A safer tomorrow would be the supreme agenda for the activists. Thus, what Prime Minister Noda and his government were doing was the opposite of what they were seeking. I did not see that the conventional media outlets reported this point.

Another activist also maintained that their calculations showed that the quantity of electricity available would be enough for surviving the summer. The rationale for why the restart was necessary was simply related to bookkeeping by electric power companies. Their financial situation would be in the red unless the nuclear power plants were operated. I believe this last issue provides a key for understanding contemporary Japanese society and energy politics after Fukushima, but the conventional mass media did not, indeed could not, deliver this opinion, likely because the sponsors of those media outlets are electric power companies. I saw great value in this point, even though the mass media ignored it.

During the whole meeting I observed via *IWJ*, however, Prime Minister Noda's style of speech impressed me as very monotonous. He was like a robot, repeating something already programmed into his brain, and his facial expression did not change at all. Furthermore, former Prime Minister Naoto Kan, who was sitting next to Noda and who had also helped arrange the meeting, did not have any chance to talk to the activists. Thinking about Kan's background as a civic activist and as a former prime minister, I believe he should have played a more active, direct role in responding to the points raised by the anti-nuclear activists. During his tenure as prime minister, he himself clearly showed an anti-nuclear stance following the Fukushima disaster, saying that nuclear power was a risk Japan could not afford.

Based on this extended and detailed research activity, I published a journal article titled "Demanding a Safer Tomorrow" in *Anthropology Today* (Ogawa, 2013b). I combined my ethnographic findings directly stemming from participant observation on anti-nuclear rallies with my reflective, critical accounts of Japanese energy politics as generated by viewing *IWJ* broadcasts.

Digital Media as a New Research Source

As outlined above, Japanese society is seeing the emergence of independent digital media. This is important not just in that it provides an alternative source to the traditional and conventional mass media in the dissemination of information to citizens, but also in the fact that it provides an alternative source for researchers to use in social research. Understanding the background of such emerging independent media as *Independent Web Journal (IWJ)*, together with other notable outlets such as *Our Planet TV* and *Nico Nico Dōga*, is an important part of being able to use these sources in research.

IWJ was established in December 2010 by Mr. Iwakami Yasumi, a freelance journalist, and who retains full responsibility for the distributed content. *IWJ* has more than 130 stream channels on the website and an archive with more than 1500 items available. The first page of the website (http://iwj.co.jp/) states clearly that *IWJ* is an Internet medium that is attempting to explore a new style of journalism in Japan, a style catering to grassroots citizens. In addition to its staff reporters, *IWJ* is also supported by citizen or lay journalists who can broadcast by carrying small video cameras for reporting; *IWJ* gives such amateur journalists the opportunity to publish these video-tapped materials. In fact, the Friday mass rally, which I referred to in the previous section, was in fact held at sites across the country, not being limited to the site in front of the prime minister's office. Similar demonstrations were organized in many other locations through Japan, including Hokkaido, Aomori, Iwate, Fukushima, Ibaraki, Aichi, Ishikawa, Osaka, and Ehime. The broadcasts of these demonstrations by lay journalists were also made possible through *IWJ* channels and are included as part of its archive system.

In order to watch *IWJ*, one can simply access the site link. There is no charge for simple access, but to watch the material in the archives, one must purchase a membership, which is quite reasonably priced. Further, if one wishes to watch the material in the expanded archive, which includes some original interviews covered exclusively by *IWJ*, one must purchase a support membership, again quite reasonably priced. Iwakami (2013) stated on Twitter in July 2013 that *IWJ* has 4,949 memberships (including both regular and support memberships), and that he aims to increase the membership to 5,000 in order to promote stable long-term management of the site.

Another contemporary alternative to traditional media is *Our Planet TV* (http://www.ourplanet-tv.org), which was established in 2001 by video journalist Ms. Shiraishi Hajime as an independent alternative video medium. Via the Internet, *Our Planet TV* produces documentary stories and interviews on gender issues, children and family life, environmental problems, and human rights, under the mission slogan of "Standing Together, Creating the Future." Reflecting on the Fukushima disaster, they have a comment on the situation of the Japanese media on their home page:

> Even after the tragic accident on March 11th at the Fukushima nuclear power plant, the government and TEPCO continued to underestimate and underreport the severity of the accident and the potential effects on the surrounding population. The mainstream media followed this lead by not questioning the information they were getting from the government and TEPCO and simply passed along what they were being told.... (Our Planet TV, 2013; translation by author)

It would thus seem that *Our Planet TV* is trying to be consistent in offering transparent information about the Fukushima incident. They have paid particular attention to children's health issues and safety problems in daily life during the post-Fukushima period because they believe that it is crucial for parents living close to the nuclear incidents' epicenter to have access to objective information regarding the disastrous situation.

Organizationally, *Our Planet TV* is a nonprofit organization (NPO) established under the 1998 NPO Law. For its revenue, this medium depends primarily on donations, which vary from 500 to 100,000 yen, and the donated money is used specifically for program production. Meanwhile, the regular yearly membership for individuals starts at 10,000 yen and for corporations at 50,000 yen. In order to maintain independence, the organization accepts money neither from businesses nor from any level of government.

Lastly, I should mention *Nico Nico Dōga* (http://www.nicovideo.jp/), which might be one of the most popular digital media outlets in contemporary Japanese society. It is simply a video hosting service where anyone can post video clips. Thus, one does not see any particular journalistic message on this service, as is often the case with *IWJ* and *Our Planet TV*; rather, it functions like a politicized form of YouTube. Materials broadcast live can be viewed without any fee, and users can access the archive if they purchase a premium status by paying 525 yen per month (as of July 2013). *Nico Nico Dōga* emerged out of a change in Japanese election law. In July 2013, the ban on the use of the Internet for election campaigns was lifted for the Upper House election campaign. Political parties and candidates campaigned over the Internet, taking advantage of the live streaming provided on a special webpage of *Nico Nico Dōga* (http://ex.nicovideo.jp/saninsen2013). Online campaigns indeed enabled candidates to engage in more detailed debates with their prospective constituents, examine the campaign platforms of their opponents, and refute any slanderous accusations without the need for mountains of cash. Lifting the ban on Internet usage also gave everyone, including researchers, a solid chance to access and interact with raw materials or to hear and see direct messages from political parties and candidates through video streaming. These new channels of direct information are a welcome addition to conventional public debate meetings and reports from such mass media as newspapers and television. Instead of depending on possibly biased comments by conventional mass media outlets, the public and researchers alike can now generate our own opinions independently.

SOME PERSONAL REFLECTIONS

I believe the independent digital media developments described herein can eventually make a significant change in the Japanese news industry, which I must say is closed, offers little challenge to the authorities, and is deadlocked in some ways. Using independent digital sources offers researchers the possibility of taking direct initiative in accessing news and judging it for value in a critical manner, instead of merely depending on mainstream and conventional journalism. This appraisal of the conventional media and the potential offered by digital media is based on my own deadening experience when I worked in the traditional mass media in Japan.

After graduating from college and before starting graduate school in the mid-1990s, I spent five years as a staff reporter at *Kyodo News*, a Japanese major wire service, which is equivalent to British Reuters and the American Associated Press. For the first two and half years, I was based in Maebashi, the capital of Gunma Prefecture in northern Kanto. I covered a variety of issues relating to such venues as police, civil court, municipal and prefectural government administration, local economy and businesses, citizen involvement in environmental issues, and protection of migrants' human rights. These last two became my favorite topics to cover, and I expanded my own network on these issues.

Upon college graduation, I had been originally hired as an English-language reporter instead of a regular reporter. Thus, after experiencing just one local bureau, I was moved to the Tokyo headquarters where I belonged to the English language news section. My transfer to Tokyo was early, compared to those of my cohort reporters. My reporter career extended further in Tokyo where I covered economic and financial news at the Tokyo Stock Exchange and the Bank of Japan, both centers of Tokyo financial markets.

Reflecting on my experience as a reporter in Japan, I remember mostly that I was extremely busy—in particular, over the last two years of my journalism career when I was covering the Tokyo financial markets. Every day at the press club was packed. I was a relatively young reporter, in my 20s. Most of my colleagues there were in their late 30s and 40s; they had moved up to Tokyo after spending 10 years in lesser Japan cities. Under the dominant seniority system at Japanese companies (even though the atmosphere at *Kyodo* itself was very liberal), I must admit that I felt isolated. Further, I was the only English language reporter among all of the *Kyodo* reporters in the press club.

When I covered the stock market, I arrived at the press club by around 8 a.m. at the latest. The market opened at 9 a.m., so I checked all of the newspapers, picking up relevant articles that could influence the market of the day. During trading, I attended daily market lectures (twice a day—morning and afternoon) that were given by officials of Nikko and Yamaichi—two of the major Japanese brokerages in the mid-1990s. I also called my informants, actual traders as well as economists in securities firms based in Tokyo. I wrote short articles at 9 a.m. and 10 a.m. The morning trading ended at 11 a.m., and until 11:15, I sent out my articles about the morning market. Sometimes I scheduled lunch with my informants; otherwise, I had a quick lunch with my colleagues. The afternoon trading started at 12:30 p.m. and continued until 3 p.m. I needed to submit a daily market report, about 2,000 words, by 3:20 pm at the latest; we were in competition, in terms of time and quality, with Japanese competitors, *Jiji Press*, as well as with foreign wire agencies like Reuters and Bloomberg, which were trying to expand their services in Tokyo at that time. I always wrote my stories under the strong time pressure exerted by desk editors. After articles were submitted, press conferences were usually scheduled until 6 p.m. I would write a couple of articles following the press conferences, and by around 7 p.m., I would be totally exhausted. Honestly speaking, at this point in the day, my brain could no longer think seriously about anything. However, as with most of my colleagues, this was not end of my day. I often had to go out drinking with my informants as well as with my colleagues, mainly to enhance communication. Sometimes, I would join with a senior colleague to do *yomawari*—a Japanese practice in journalism that consists of visiting some important official's private house in the evening to get or confirm information gained during the daytime.

This was a typical day. I could not leave the press club during market hours. Every reporter experiences a similar daily routine—I do not believe that mine was a special case. Simply, I was doing what *Kyodo* expected me to do: produce daily market reports to be distributed earlier than those of *Jiji*, another press service in Japan, and foreign press counterparts, and to cover press conferences held at the Tokyo Stock Exchange press club. In addition to the daily market reports, I also produced weekly market reports and *Kyodo* also regularly expected me to write feature articles. I think I did all these expected things well, though I spent my day doing only what I was expected to do. Under the circumstances, however, I must admit that I began to realize that I was losing my sharp edge in terms of my ability to examine issues. Just sitting at the press club is the safest (and easiest) way for staff reporters protected by lifetime employment at media companies to operate because then it would be rare that they would miss an important announcement. I gradually lost my motivation in being a staff reporter, mainly because I had no time to pursue my own interests and because I wanted to work outside of the press club—a practice that is hard wired in Japanese journalism.

While I was a reporter, though, I was gradually defining my own research interest—the development and state of Japanese civil society. A particular journalistic experience relevant to my scholarly interests was seeing the initial steps Japan was taking to become less regulated, this in order to stimulate the economy and energize society. I gained a first-hand understanding of the Japanese policymaking process and made contacts with the newsmakers of the time. Furthermore, my journalistic experiences, combined with my experience in local Maebashi, enhanced my original research interests concerning collaborative grassroots civic activism in a policymaking framework, which led me back to graduate school. I left journalism in the summer of 1998 to pursue an academic career.

For more than a decade, digital technology has developed with amazing speed. Conventional mass media, the newspapers and television that were the staple of information, are nowadays not the only resources for us as we seek to observe and discover what is actually happening in society. Thanks to the current expansion of the Internet, independent digital sources like *IWJ* have now gained momentum and legitimacy. Researchers can easily access independent digital media sites in order to seek the truth, including most specifically, what the mass media does not report. In Japan, journalism as it is currently practiced operates on the basis of a closed press club system to protect a web of vested interests (electric power companies, for example). This circumstance will likely not change and, rather, may only worsen. In fact, Japan fell from 11th to 22nd out of 179 countries in the 2011–12 World Press Freedom Index, in part because of poor coverage of the Fukushima disaster. Thus, I have high hopes for the further development of a new style of journalism—independent digital media—in challenging and activating the current listlessness of Japanese journalism. And with that independent journalism as a vital part of the media landscape, I have high hopes that we researchers will view this new media more seriously and take advantage of such sources in our social research.

References

Iwakami, Y. (2013, July 28). https://twitter.com/iwakamiyasumi.

Manabe, N. (2013). Music in Japanese antinuclear demonstrations: The evolution of a contentious performance model. The Asia Pacific Journal, 11(42:3).

Ogawa, A. (2009). The failure of civil society? The third sector and the state in contemporary Japan. Albany, NY: State University of New York Press.

Ogawa, A. (2013a). Precariat at the forefront: Anti-nuclear rallies in post-Fukushima Japan. Inter-Asia Cultural Studies, 14(2), 317–326.

Ogawa, A. (2013b). Demanding a safer tomorrow: Japan's anti-nuclear rallies in the summer of 2012. Anthropology Today, 29(1), 21–24.

Ogawa, A. Forthcoming (2013, November). Civil society: Past, present, and future. In J. Kingston (Ed.). Critical issues in contemporary Japan. London, England: Routledge.

Our Planet TV. (2013). http://www.ourplanet-tv.org/?q=node/287, accessed on July 22, 2013.

SECTION TWO

JAPANESE JOURNALISM AND SOCIAL DISCOURSE

Chapter Four

The Ambiguity of Memory in East Asian Newspapers

Journalistic Representations of War Memories

Choonghee Han

Introduction

This chapter explores the politics of memory as it has unfolded in recent years in East Asia. The politics of memory in the region has been a struggle to define one's identity against others', to direct and divert blame, and to take a superior position in moral judgment. The investigation presented in this chapter concerns journalistic representations and discursive constructions of war memories from the Asia-Pacific Theater of World War II. News stories drawn from three newspapers in East Asia were analyzed through a lens of a critical discourse analysis. The three newspapers, the *China Daily* of China, *The Daily Yomiuri* of Japan, and *The Chosun Ilbo* of South Korea, are major in their respective countries. The *China Daily* is the only state-run English newspaper in China and the *Yomiuri* and the *Chosun* are the English language editions of the *Yomiuri Shimbun* and the *Chosun Ilbo* respectively. The thematic discourse of this chapter is "the ambiguity of memory," which indicates a paradoxical arbitrariness in the process of articulating memory in the present time.

East Asia endured a tumultuous period from the late nineteenth century to the end of the first half of the twentieth century. Japan's militaristic empire building and the warfare it waged resulted in the loss of more than three million Japanese lives, nearly twenty million Asians, and more than sixty thousand Western Allied personnel (Bix, 2000; Kosaka, 1992). Japan, China, and South Korea have long been at odds over the appropriate interpretations of memories from this period. In this chapter, those disputes will be called "the war of memories," as memories that have taken center stage in political debates and social discourses in East Asia.

This chapter posits that nationalism in the three countries has grown over time, particularly in recent years, as a function of this "war of memories." It also suggests that journalistic institutions have contributed to the political uses of memory by invoking national memories. A number of scholars have found that media outlets are agents of social, national, and cultural memory (Edy, 1999; Zelizer, 2004), with Zelizer (2008b) outlining the relationship between journalism and social memory as:

> Memory and journalism resemble two distant cousins. They know of each other's existence, acknowledge their shared environment from time to time and proceed apace as autonomous phenomena without seeming to depend on the other. And yet neither reaches optimum functioning without the other occupying a backdrop. Just as journalism needs memory work to position its recounting of public events in context, so too does memory need journalism to provide one of the most public drafts of the past. (p. 79)

Moreover, media representations of the past become media spectacles that work to make media stories more resonant (Edelman, 1988). As a result, memories in news stories end up serving political aims rather than a reflexive remembrance of past occurrences. As Elsaesser (1985) notes, "the act of representation makes history the phantom signifier of endlessly interchangeable referents" (p. 40). As such, any ambiguity of memory signifies the fluidity of the interpretation of memory.

THE THREE SITES OF MEMORY

While there is ample historical material, this research took up three enduring controversies: the Yasukuni Shrine visits, the "Comfort Women" issue, and the Japanese textbooks revisionism controversy, concentrating in the analysis herein primarily on the Yasukuni Shrine controversy. These three controversies are guided entries (Nord, 1989; Smith, 1989; Stempel & Westley, 1989) to the discourse practices of presenting war memories in the newspapers.

The Yasukuni Shrine controversy is rekindled every time Japanese politicians visit the shrine. The most revealing case in this controversy has been the annual visits made by former Prime Minister Junichiro Koizumi (2001-2006). Although a shrine for the Japanese native religion Shintō, the point of contention is that among the Japanese war dead commemorated in the shrine are wartime Prime Minister Hideki Tōjō and thirteen others who were sentenced to death by the International Military Tribunal for the Far East in 1948 for their roles in human rights violations during the war. Contrary to Japanese politicians assertions that they visited the shrine to pay their respects to the war dead in general, these have been seen as symbolic of Japanese militarism, historical revisionism, and political populism (Bass, 2006; Kristof, 1998; Shibuichi, 2005).

The second lingering controversy concerns the "Comfort Women," a euphemism for the sex slavery, in which an estimated 200,000 to 300,000 Asian women, from mostly Korea and China, were forced to provide sex for Japanese soldiers during the Asia-Pacific War (Coomaraswamy, 2001; Eckert, 2007). Unresolved and still volatile, the "Comfort Women" issue became international in 2007 when legislative bodies of several countries, including the US, Canada, and the Netherlands, sought to pass resolutions aiming to urge the Japanese government to deliver an official apology and compensation to former "Comfort Women" (Soh, 1996; Tanaka, 2001). The third controversy concerns Japanese history textbook revision, the "screening" (i.e., censoring) of textbooks by the Ministry of Education to ensure that the subject matter is "suitable" to be taught in elementary, junior high, and high schools (Kishimoto, 2004, p. 34). This issue revolves around alleged "distortion and beautification" (Rose, 2005) of the terminology used in Japanese government-approved textbooks to describe Japanese invasion of Asian countries along with domestic protests by conservative groups regarding inclusion of controversial content in approved Japanese textbooks (Gluck & Graubard, 1992; Jeans, 2005; Rose, 1998).

Theoretical Framework

The research rests on two theoretical groundings. The first is the politics of memory and the second the culturological approach to journalistic representation. The politics of memory implies the arbitrary appropriation of collective memory in the service of the present political climate. It starts with the theories of collective and cultural memory, and expounds a variety of ways memories are utilized to serve politics. The premise of the culturological approach to journalistic presentation is that journalism has a symbiotic relationship with its host society, and, therefore, it is necessary to examine the historical, traditional and religious superstructure of the society.

The Politics of Memory

Researchers in memory studies have developed a wealth of concepts to describe memory beyond the personal level or individual faculty (Connerton, 1989). Media scholar Schwartz (1991) defines "collective memory" as "a metaphor that formulates society's retention and loss of information about its past in the familiar terms of individual remembering and forgetting" (p. 302). French sociologist Halbwachs (1980; 1992) postulates that collective memory is a dynamic discursive process of construction and representation of the past developed through social interaction among members of a society. The theory of "cultural memory" focuses on the amorphous and unconscious memory that directs behavior and experience in the interactive framework of a society and is that which is passed down to next generations through repeated social rituals and initiation processes (Assmann, 2006). Cultural memory enables imagination and dynamism of thoughts, and, unlike collective memory, includes "non-instrumentalizable, heretical, subversive, and disowned" memories (p. 27). These constructs identify a common feature, that of the social and constructive dimension of memory. Herein, the term "collective memory" will be used to refer to the social, cultural, and constructive nature of memory (Connerton, 1989; Kattago, 2001; Zelizer, 2008a).

In a political sense, the substance of memory neither remains the same over time and space, as memory is volatile and subject to change, nor exists by itself or holds any significance if left alone. If a particular memory is accepted among a group in power, the memory can emerge as an authentic interpretation of the past. However, it has to be connected with social and political circumstance or present ideological orientation in order to (re)create its value. In this sense, memory is seen as a "usable past," which "implies the active engagement of users, through whose agency collective and personal histories are continued" (Zamora, 1997, p. ix). This brings the possibility that one particular constructed memory is more prevalent than other constructions in a circumstance, and that certain groups try to participate in the construction of a memory to stay valid in terms of political power and socially dominant norms.

One example of the role of memory in politics was the Bitburg controversy in 1985. At issue was the planned visit by US President Ronald Reagan, in the company of West German Chancellor Helmut Kohl, to the Bitburg Military Cemetery, to celebrate the normalization of relations between the two countries on the fortieth anniversary of the end of World War II. The visit was considered as Kohl's attempt to rewrite recent

German history and gain support from conservative constituents for his political agenda; on the US side, conservatives also endorsed Reagan's (Elsaesser, 1985; Jensen, 2007; Levkov, 1987). Problematic was the fact that Bitburg Cemetery contains the graves of 49 members of the Waffen-SS, the armed wing of the SS (*Schutzstaffel*) of war time Nazi Germany.

After the White House announced that Reagan and Kohl would lay a wreath at the cemetery "in a spirit of reconciliation, in a spirit of forty years of peace, in a spirit of economic and military compatibility" (Miller, 1990, p. 47), Reagan referred to the soldiers buried there as victims (Jensen, 2007), which drew angry responses from the Jewish community and political liberals. The Reagan administration attempted to allay the anger by including a Nazi concentration camp site at Bergen-Belsen in his itinerary, but this further offended the Jewish community, who viewed this as equating the German soldiers with victims of the Holocaust. Ignoring the mounting criticism, Reagan and Kohl visited both sites on May 5, 1985. Biro (2003) asserted that the revisionism in the Bitburg controversy was a form of memory interpretation that identified with the German participants and represented them as victims. The visit also "relativized" the Holocaust by not only comparing it to other acts of genocide, but also by partially excusing it (p. 127). What happened in Bitburg in 1985 was indicative of the two different approaches to the past: reflexive remembering with critical thinking and the construction of a national conventional identity (Habermas, 1979), and exemplifies the construction of collective memory, identity, and national unity.

The Ambiguity of Memory

That memory is ambiguous is an indication that memories are presented neither in a clear manner nor as truthful facts. The ambiguity of memory is the absence of a clear contour of the past; it signals that there is "contestation and debate about whose memory and whose past are remembered or forgotten" (Kattago, 2001, p. 29). Memories are highly malleable; as Halbwachs (1992) notes, "depending on its circumstances and points in time, society represents the past to itself in different ways: it modifies its conventions" (pp. 172-173). Historical events and memories are recalled only if they fit in the contemporary interests and circumstances. Once so called up, memories get modified to serve the needs of the present time. Collective memory adjusts to and shapes a system of present-day beliefs (Ben-Amos & Weissberg, 1999). Since memories are constructed and deployed by those in power in order to create an "appropriate" history, the process of remembering is intrinsically political. The manufacturing of memory in any society is unpredictable, being greatly influenced by ever-changing sociopolitical circumstances. This unpredictability reflects the fact that a memory is open to a number of arbitrary interpretations, some in agreement and some in opposition, which result in disputes over the validity of different interpretations. There is no such thing as an original "official memory;" official memories are made up in processes of reinterpretation, recreation, and approval. Since political communities seek cohesion and unity, power forces a limited number of "official memories." As such, the representation of memory and its conversion to history always depend on the political power. These "official memories" constitute the dominant and hegemonic narratives that underpin and organize remembrance and commemorations at the level of the nation-state (Ashplant, Dawson, & Roper, 2000). The imbalance between competing memories reaffirms the fact that memories are lived history being negotiated at any present time, with strong bias toward that present (Kansteiner, 2002). Therefore, it is not surprising that the controversies introduced in this chapter have been provoked by the ambiguity of memory as manipulated by political leaders and groups.

JOURNALISM AS SITES OF MEMORY

To be internalized by members of a society, collective memory needs to be represented in certain forms that are institutional, symbolic or physical, in manners that are material, symbolic or functional. Nora (1989) writes:

> [Site of memory] originate with the sense that there is no spontaneous memory, that we must deliberately create archives, maintain anniversaries, organize celebrations, pronounce eulogies, and notarize bills because such activities no longer occur naturally. (p. 12)

In this theorization, the ways of representing memory are called *lieux de mémoire* (sites of memory). Sites of memory are "meaningful entity of a real or imagined kind, which has become a symbolic element of a given community as a result of human will or the effect of time" (Kattago, 2001, pp. 16-17). Sites are where memory gets displayed, interpreted, and politicized; sites of crystallization and articulation. We encounter innumerable sites of memory everyday, as places, ideas, practices, and objects (Nora, 1989).

The historical controversies of this chapter are also sites of memory. While the Asia-Pacific war took place decades ago, people in East Asia still live with its consequences. Whether memories of heroism, achievement, humiliation, tragedy, or victimization, those memories are scattered and unorganized, the very reason the role of the media becomes critical. The media organize, criticize, validate, and explain, giving back to people their own versions of memory. In that sense, the media are also sites of memory. Sites of memory, therefore, are not a dormant stockpile of past occurrences. Rather they are active playgrounds of social discourses where different political and societal players flex their muscles, proclaim their presences, and seek the support from the public.

Scholars have theorized various modes of communication considering process, efficiency, and veracity. Advertising, for example, is a form of communication intended to persuade audiences to purchase products, ideas, or services. Journalism, distinctive yet similar to other forms of communication, focuses on precision, specificity from the author to the reader, and its role in supporting democracy (Glasser, 1999). Journalism witnesses and conveys its observations to the public. Witnessing is both a distinct mode of perception and "the discursive act of stating one's experience for the benefit of an audience" (Peters, 2001, p. 709). However, witnessing cannot be neutral; each individual and society uses its own psychological and societal constructs to experience events and later bear witness to them (Kelly & Maher, 1979). Peters (2001) notes that in witnessing, there must be judgment; conveying a message of witnessing includes not just offering a factual text but also supplying an interpretive framework. Frosh (2006) uses the concept of "conjecture" to explain this feature of public communication. Upon receiving a text, audiences create "not just an imaginative experience regarding the subject of its discourse but also conjecture that this text is a witnessing text, that the event described really happened and that the text was designed to report it" (p. 276). In other words, witnessing is not just a testimonial of what was seen, it is the construction of meaning.

Berkowitz (2011) notes that there are three vantage points of journalism: journalistic, socio-organizational, and cultural. The cultural approach, according to Berkowitz, views texts as artifacts of the culture that represent key values and meanings. People live in a social environment that is formed by personal, social, and cultural memory, and each memory is subject to active interpretation and crystallization. Ironically, the notion of collective and cultural memory directly contradicts the primacy of objectivity, the core tenet of the professional journalistic paradigm. Since journalists live in the same society and breathe the same social cultural memory, they area also subject to sociopolitical memory. In fact, "journalism is full of pasts" (Edy, 1999, p. 132), and journalists and their organizations enable particular memories to resonate with their audiences better than others. In that sense, the mass media are battlefields in which reconstruction of memory are performed and perpetuated.

Research Question

While history is never a purely neutral account of past events, this dynamic becomes more complicated in the case of collective memory. Collective memory is a product influenced by political, social, historical, geographical, and psychological contexts. Different groups with varying discursive constructions reflecting different sociocultural contexts produce highly contested interpretations of the past. When such interpretations emerge as political remarks and actual policy statements, they are neither neutral nor transparent, but are often made to mark a line identifying a permissible range of interpretations on certain topics. In situations where national collective memory is involved, comment and policy often reflect ideological orientations and political goals. Such arbitrary reconstructions of memory and the politics of memory this yields are common to contemporary politics and journalistic outlets play a role in this process as the authoritative interpreter of social discourse (Zelizer, 1990).

Building on the theories of discursive memory construction memory and the role of journalism as the authoritative interpreter of government policy and national collective memory, the research question this chapter proposes concerns the three newspapers' treatments of the three sites of memory. The research asks what these constructions of ambiguous memories tell us about the politics of memory and the role of journalism therein?

Conceptual Framework of Analysis

The analytical method used in this chapter is critical discourse analysis (CDA) grounded in the theories of collective memory and informed by the examination of the three sites of memory in recent East Asian history. This analysis is supplemented by an interpretive policy analysis of the official stances of the three countries with respect to war memories.

The critical discourse analysis of this chapter is an interpretive approach that investigates news texts to find thematic discourses presented by the three newspapers through their construction of war memories. The production of texts can be traced by examining normative use of discourse types (Fairclough, 1995) and by the processes in which text and statements are made and fed into other debates (Jacobs, 2006). It is important to note that qualitative studies focus on social practices and meanings of communicative events in specific historical and cultural contexts (Lindlof & Taylor, 2002), and they examine how various levels of meanings are expressed, where meanings include intentional meanings as well as hidden and often unintended meanings (Bettig & Hall, 2003). Such cultural and historical contexts combined with the theoretical framework ensure the reliability of interpretative analysis this chapter makes.

Construction of social and cultural meaning is connected to the process by which power is created and maintained on the basis of ideology and hegemony (Cormack, 1992). In order to investigate meanings created through social and cultural constructs, Lindlof & Taylor (2002) suggest that an interpretive paradigm revealing human behavior is necessary. This principle penetrates observable behavior to access inherent bias found in human acts. The construction of war memories in the news media is an ideal topic to which this interpretive paradigm can be applied. When memory is represented through the media, the representation is a practice of sociopolitical and cultural discourse, where CDA fits a subject matter that is historical, cultural, and international.

Texts and Analysis

News texts for this chapter were analyzed from two online academic news databases (*LexisNexis Academic* and *Access World News*) and the Internet websites of the three newspapers, with relevant search words identified for each historical controversy. Also analyzed were policy statements issued by the foreign ministry of each country, which were cross-examined with the news texts that relayed the statements. The time frame of the news texts covers the period between 2000 to 2007.

Society represents the past to itself in different ways depending on its circumstances and points in time (Halbwachs, 1992). Historical events are recalled only if they fit in the framework of contemporary interests and society subsequently modifies recollections to make them consistent with its present needs. During the analysis, it became clear that the three sites of memory were closely intertwined, and it was difficult to separate them from one another. When one of the three controversies was in the spotlight, perhaps a function of timeliness, e.g. Japanese Prime Minister Koizumi's visit to the Yasukuni Shrine on Aug. 15 each year, the anniversary of Japan's surrender, the other two became linked to the story as well. Ultimately, the three separate controversies come to be treated as one larger historical issue.

Politicians skillfully played to domestic public sentiment regarding these issues. Conservative political leaders were at times extremely hawkish about historical controversies, provoking a sense of national sovereignty and unity, while also being cautious not to irritate either constituents with other opinons or the citizens of neighboring countries on such controversial matters. This attitude was particularly true with Japanese political leaders, due mainly to the fact that Japanese actions could be seen as at the center of much of the controversy. Japanese political leaders were highly ambiguous when questioned about their thoughts and intentions on these issues; the ambiguity of memory surrounding the sites of memory led to an ambiguity of attitude on the part of political leaders, and vice versa.

"Appropriate" Memory

The appropriateness of interpretations and actions was one of the most troubling discourses appearing in the news coverage of the issues. Very little effort was evident in clarifying the appropriateness of memory and what made a particular interpretation of the past inappropriate. In a sense, defining an appropriate memory was impossible because everyone had their own construct to measure appropriateness. In spite of this, the word "appropriate" was routinely used in public debates in reference to a particular action or response.

Japanese Prime Minister Junichiro Koizumi frequently used the terminology of "appropriateness" in reference to the Yasukuni Shrine issue. While he was hawkish in his determination to visit the Yasukuni Shrine, he was cautious not to speak specifically about either his thoughts or specific historical facts, deliberately creating a gray area regarding the controversy. When asked whether he would visit the shrine, he routinely answered, "I will decide it appropriately" (Hidaka & Imai, 2005). When urged not to visit the shrine by Chinese President Hu Jintao in 2004 Koizumi responded that, "he would deal with the issue appropriately" ("Koizumi Won't," 2005). On another occasion, he asserted that his visits had been turned into "a diplomatic and political issue" and he "should not elaborate on it," again promising to "address the matter appropriately" ("Invasions Caused," 2006).

As Koizumi neglected to define "appropriate" from "in appropriate," others fed on this ambiguity. No doubt calculating the political gains he could gain by visiting Yasukuni Shrine, his ambivalence was communicatively convenient and politically useful. As long as he said he was trying to "address the matter appropriately," he was granted latitude to explore public sentiment both in Japan and neighboring countries. Other Japanese politicians took advantage of this rhetoric of appropriateness. In 2006, a group of lawmakers from the ruling Liberal Democratic Party presented a proposal for creation of a state-run memorial facility for war dead. Due to the ambiguity of the ensuing discussions, the proposal did not see a meaningful outcome. While the *Yomiuri* asserted in its coverage of the proposal that "Japan, as an influential member of the international community, needs to pay appropriate attention to neighboring countries when the government holds memorial services for war dead and prays for peace at state-organized events" ("Lawmakers Question," 2006), the newspaper relied on reiterating convenient rhetoric while not clarifying what constituted "appropriate."

Chinese leaders also spoke about "appropriate" understanding of the past. In 2004 when Koizumi met Chinese Premier Wen Jiabao at international summit talks in Laos, Koizumi was told to "act appropriately" regarding historical matters ("Japan, China," 2004). Prior to their meeting, the foreign ministries of the two nations had agreed that Koizumi would pledge to "take appropriate actions" on the Yasukuni Shrine dispute. However, Japanese Foreign Minister Nobutaka Machimura refused to comment further on the issue in public after the talks, meaning it was impossible to predict what actions the Japanese and the Chinese governments would take. This ambiguity again seemed intentional, designed to allow the political leaders to evade explaining where exactly they stood in the dispute. When they knew they could not reach an amicable conclusion, the political leaders from both sides turned back to the ambiguous rhetoric of "appropriateness."

The importance of such "appropriateness" in political negotiations lies in its ambiguity. The word "appropriate" opens up numerous possible ways of interpretation. What's appropriate to one can be inappropriate to someone else. Something that was appropriate a decade ago may not be appropriate now. An appropriate historical understanding in one country would not be appropriate in a different country, especially if the two share a history of confrontation and war. The vexing question in East Asia was whether politicians triggered such ambiguity of memory intentionally for their political gain. A number of studies have concluded that there were political calculations behind the ambiguous stance over historical controversies (Min, 2003; Saaler & Schwentker, 2008; Seraphim, 2006; Ueno, 2004) and that Koizumi's ambiguous stances were propelled by political populism that sought to win over Japan's social and political conservatives. He tried to take advantage of the nostalgia of the public for the glorious past, while disrupting neither domestic political opponents nor encouraging nationalistic sentiments in China and South Korea. The "appropriate" rhetoric was the result of such a complex negotiation of domestic and international politics.

"Respecting" the Past

Another ambiguous expression identified in the research was "respect." The word "respect" generally means to consider someone or something worthy of high regard (Merriam-Webster Online Dictionary, 2010). This meaning, however, depends on the circumstance in which the word is used. Thompson (2006) held that respect is recognition reflecting a particular institutional location and therefore respect is essentially political, dependent upon the different political orientations of the people expressing respect. Topics are controversial, thus, making a statement of personal reverence can be regarded as a political action. Respect vis-à-vis the past is an act of collective memory, and therefore is often viewed as disputable and inconsistent (Dwyer & Alderman, 2008), as well as reactionary, resonant, or reflexive, depending on whether the respected action was political, and by whom for whom and on whom. Thus, the dynamic of collective memory becomes more complicated when it encounters the discourse of "respecting the past."

There were many articles concerning the three sites of memory in which the term "respect" appeared. A *Yomiuri* article published on June 9, 2005 read:

> In an interview with reporters, the sources said, the prime minister will explain the purpose of his visit by saying he had visited Yasukuni Shrine "to pay respect and express gratitude to the war dead." ("Yasukuni Key," 2005)

To Koizumi, paying "respect" meant going to Yasukuni to "mourn for victims who lost their lives" ("Koizumi To," 2005). It was not clear, however, whom among so many victims of different nationalities he was specifically referring to. In fact, he never clarified the nationality of the victims when he mentioned about "war dead" in his speeches.

The word "respect" was used differently in the Chinese political context. On April 12, 2005, when asked to comment on anti-Japan demonstrations in his country, Chinese Premier Wen Jiabao stated, "Only the country respecting history, with the courage to take responsibility for history and obtaining the trust of the people in Asia and the world could play greater role in international affairs" (MFA of China, 2005). In so doing, Wen made it clear that China would oppose Japan's bid to become a permanent member of the UN Security Council. Wen's "respect" was interpreted by the *China Daily* as his indicating Japan's "accepting responsibility of war crimes and offering apology to victims inside and outside Japan" ("Building Mutual," 2005). Wen thus "respect" connected with historical issues as leverage to foil Japan's desire to become an important member in the UN.

The *China Daily* also quoted a Chinese historian who demanded that Japan step out of the historical shadows, show their "respect for history," and try to resolve post war issues ("Invasion Anniversary," 2004). South Korean politicians used the word "respect" in the same context when President Rho Moo-hyun was quoted in a *Chosun* article as saying that the Japanese government should have "respect for historical truth." He asserted that the lingering "Comfort women" issue and "visits to the militarist Yasukuni Shrine" were signs of Japan's "disrespect for history" ("Roh Calls," 2007). Such use of the words "appropriate" and "respect" thus created a unique discourse whose diverging meanings were sometimes difficult to decipher. The true memories of the war were forgotten in the midst of such diplomatic, but political rhetoric.

OFFICIAL VISITS VERSUS PRIVATE VISITS

When asked in 2001 whether he would visit Yasukuni Shrine officially as Prime Minister, Koizumi rebuffed the question saying, "The question over whether (the visit) is private or public is nonsensical" ("Koizumi To," 2001). Koizumi went on to say, "I never oppose whatever kinds of ceremonies other countries may take to commemorate their wartime victims." However, the "nonsensical" question about the distinction between an official visit and a private visit has been one of the most ambiguous yet contentious issues in the politics of memory in East Asia.

As the three newspapers extensively covered Koizumi and other Japanese politicians' visits to the shrine, the focus has always been the format of their visits; whether the visits were made in an official capacity or as a private person was of the most importance. Japanese politicians have always tried to avoid criticism inside and outside the country by stating that their visits were based upon national tradition, having nothing to do with imperialism or militarism. They have also argued that paying respect to "victims" of wars should not be interpreted as a political action. The Koizumi administration, and Koizumi himself, was extremely cautious to define the nature of his visits as such, drawing criticism both from within and outside the country.

In an editorial published a week before his first visit to the shrine, the *Yomiuri* concluded that Koizumi had no other choice but to go ahead with his visit as planned. The newspaper suggested if he decided not to go, it would mean backing down in the face of foreign pressure from a "belief" he had professed. When the format of visit became fodder for a heated controversy in Japanese domestic politics, the focus became the constitutionality of those visits. Articles 20 and 89 of Japan's postwar Constitution mandate the clear separation of religion and state. The *Yomiuri*'s view on the constitutionality question mirrored that of Japanese conservatives holding that the Constitution did not make a clear distinction between an official visit and a private visit. Indeed, a *Yomiuri*'s editorial called on its government to change its interpretation of the distinction:

> Some argue that private visits are constitutional, but that visits in a public capacity are not. But a 1985 government statement said that an official visit to Yasukuni Shrine by cabinet ministers is constitutional if it does not involve Shintō-style rituals. Thus, this (anti-visit) argument is in effect demanding that the government change its official stance regarding prime ministerial visits to the shrine. ("Japan Sends," 2006)

In a different editorial *Yomiuri* argued that there was only a "thin line" between an official and a private visit because "it is extremely difficult to tell where the public persona ends and the private persona begins." The newspaper criticized the lukewarm attitude of the government, pointing out that the lack of clarification had "caused the government to swing back and forth on its official stance on the private-or-official question" ("Editorial: Let's," 2001).

The Japanese government was not alone in showing such ambiguity toward the constitutionality question. Japanese courts have made conflicting determinations on the issue as well, with the media quick to point out such contradictions. The *China Daily* reported that while the Fukuoka District Court in southwestern Japan stated that the prime minister's visit to Yasukuni on August 13, 2001 violated the constitutional separation of religion and state ("Koizumi Vows," 2004), the Chiba District Court rejected a damages suit disputing the constitutionality of the visit to the shrine ("Koizumi Should," 2005). In contrast, the *Yomiuri* portrayed the different rulings, with a tinge of chagrin, as the "swinging" of Japanese society. It is possible to assume that *Yomiuri*'s characterization of the rulings, the "swinging," emboldened Koizumi to speak bluntly later on about the constitutionality question, saying "It's strange, I don't know why it violated the constitution" ("Koizumi Vows," 2004). In truth, the *Yomiuri* did not cover the different rulings as extensively as the *China Daily* did, and when it did, it did so through editorials and op-ed columns. Instead of relaying factual information about the court rulings, the *Yomiuri* dedicated its space to dissecting political stances and opinionating on the issue.

Nonetheless, while the *China Daily* and *Chosun* did report on the constitutionality question, reporting factual information regarding the constitutionality debate in Japan, they ultimately allowed that questions of constitutionality were ultimately a Japanese domestic political issue. Their focus instead was on the visits; for the *Chosun*, most important was the fact that Japanese prime ministers had bowed to Class-A war criminals, not the constitutionality question. The newspaper always coalesced the shrine visit issue with other ongoing historical controversies, attempting to raise awareness of what it called Japan's irresponsible attitude toward the past. A *Chosun* editorial carried when Koizumi visited the shrine on August 13, 2001, two days before the anniversary of the Japanese surrender, said that:

> Japanese imperialism and Japan's actions in events such as the Manchurian Incident, the invasion of China, and the War in the Pacific took the lives of 20 million people in Asia. The mortuary tablets of Hideki Tōjō and thirteen other war criminals, men who orchestrated the war that took so many lives, are enshrined at Yasukuni... Combine this with the issue of Japanese middle school textbooks that distort Japan's plundering of Asia, and the distrust and concerns are magnified. ("Editorial: Koizumi," 2001)

Similar to *Chosun*'s caustic criticism, the *China Daily* reported on August 16, 2006, a day after Koizumi's visit, that China "condemned" Koizumi's visit to the Yasukuni Shrine, bemoaning that the visit challenged international justice and trampled upon the conscience of mankind ("Koizumi's Provocation," 2006). It conveyed Foreign Minister Li Zhaozing's statement that Koizumi's visit had severely "hurt the feelings of the people of the victim countries, and undermined the political foundation of China-Japan relations." The fact that Koizumi's visits took place in the midst of other historical controversies can explain why the constitutionality question did not garner much attention from *China Daily* and *Chosun*. The two newspapers did not have to mull excessively over the constitutionality question in order to criticize the revisionist moves in Japan. They already had other historical issues and discourses to turn to, one of these being the discourse of victimhood. They emphasized that their countries were victims in the war and were ravaged by the Japanese invaders. The constitutionality question was not as resonant a topic to their respective readers and constituents as was the victim narrative.

Conclusion: Strategic Ambiguity, a Political Strategy

The ambiguous stance of political leadership shown in this chapter has recently become the subject of criticism as each of the three Asian newspapers has accused politicians of capitalizing on historical ambiguity for political gain. The *Chosun* argued in an editorial that China was engaging in strategic ambiguity in its foreign relations, writing:

> Take the diplomatic principle of a "peaceful rise." The phrase itself contains an ambiguity. If China's diplomacy is criticized abroad for being aggressive, China stresses "peaceful"; if domestic criticism arises that its diplomacy is weak-kneed, China emphasizes "rise." The mother of ambiguity is the diplomatic principle of "bide our time, build our capacities," where appearance hides an altogether different reality. Thus, when China opposes Japanese leaders' visits to Yasukuni Shrine, we had better think twice before breaking into applause. China, as a master of ambiguity, always deals with Japan with its own national interests and the possibility of reconciliation for their sake firmly in mind. ("Editorial: China," 2007)

What *Chosun* wanted to stress to its readers was that China could not be a reliable ally in South Korea's dealing with Japan over historical issues. The newspaper's assessment showed the political reality in East Asia, where domestic politics and myopic national interest routinely capitalize on historical ambiguity.

In Japan, the *Yomiuri* asserted that Prime Minister Shinzō Abe, who succeeded Koizumi, had adopted a policy of "strategic ambiguity" on the issue of visiting Yasukuni. Although he vowed to adhere to Koizumi's policies, he could not afford to disregard the pressure from China and South Korea. Japanese internal politics and the necessity of working with other political parties in a ruling coalition and acknowledging different voices in the public sphere, was another reason for Abe to take an ambiguous stance. The *Yomiuri* noted that Abe refused to say "whether he would or would not go, or whether or not he visited the

The Ambiguity of Memory in East Asian Newspapers 97

shrine, in an attempt to blur the issue as a focus of political and diplomatic discord" ("Editorial: Mark," 2007).

Coverage of these three sites of memory in the three newspapers adopted varied rhetoric and different narratives while employing remembering that included ambiguity, elaboration, omission, and appropriation of memory. These different ways of dealing with memory were seamlessly connected to national identity formation and the internal politics in each country. The *Yomiuri* once characterized the textbook controversy as being provoked by "self-tormenting liberals," and stated that a revisionist history "can make the Japanese people proud of the nation's history" ("Editorial: ROK," 2005). The ambiguity of memory surrounding Japan's history was the easiest and most strategically sound means for political leaders to use. Such phrases as "appropriate memory," "respect of the past," and "official or unofficial visit" became socially sticky, as leaders failed to be clear on the events for which these terms were employed.

There was little consistency in ways the newspapers dealt with the ambiguous stance of politicians; each represented and constructed the same historical events in different ways, mirroring the sociopolitical circumstance of their own countries. Sometimes they were cautious not to go too far beyond what was said by political leaders. At other times, they admonished leaders for their lack of clarity. Such differences notwithstanding, one commonality across the newspapers was that they constantly reminded their readership of the importance of national unity and "appropriate" understanding of the nation's past. In that sense, the newspapers were also sites of memory where social, political, and cultural forces are mixed together to create a national discourse of collective memory.

This analysis has shown that the three newspapers were not providing the proverbial "first draft of history" regarding the historical controversies remarked upon. The historical incidents took place decades earlier, and the three countries have since undergone remarkable political and economic changes. Many of the journalists and columnists who wrote the news stories and op-ed columns had no direct experience with the events. Nevertheless, their coverage of these sites of memory showed that these historical issues remain remarkably volatile topics in each country as well as internationally, and that the newspapers are active producers of memory discourses. They constructed multiple discourses: of victimhood, aggression, national unity, and many more.

The three newspapers' active involvement in the historical controversies exceeded what scholars commonly describe as "commemorative journalism." In general, journalistic representations of the past are expected to comprise such conventional journalistic practices as reviewing, revisiting, commemorating, or objectively investigating historical events (Edy, 1999; Zelizer, 2008b). The role that the three newspapers took in their coverage of these memory sites was that of arbitrators; the newspapers not only represented the memories but also actively engaged in the reconstruction, solidification and homogenization of certain interpretations that converged into discourses of national unity and identity. Such a nationalistic approach to collective memory may not be unique to East Asia, but is still emblematic in terms of understanding East Asian journalistic culture and the news coverage on the difficult past in the region.

References

Ashplant, T. G., Dawson, G., & Roper, M. (2000). *The politics of war memory and commemoration.* London; New York: Routledge.

Assmann, J. (2006). *Religion and cultural memory.* Stanford, Calif.: Stanford University Press.

Bass, G. J. (2006, August 5). A shrine to Japan's tainted past. *New York Times,* pp. 13.

Ben-Amos, D., & Weissberg, L. (1999). *Cultural memory and the construction of identity.* Detroit: Wayne State University Press.

Berkowitz, D. A. (Ed.). (2011). *Cultural meanings of news: A text-reader.* Thousands Oaks, California: Sage.

Bettig, R. V., & Hall, J. L. (2003). *Big media, big money: Cultural texts and political economics.* Lanham: Rowman & Littlefield.

Biro, M. (2003). Representation and event: Anselm Kiefer, Joseph Beuys, and the memory of the holocaust. *Yale Journal of Criticism, 16*(1), 113.

Bix, H. P. (2000). *Hirohito and the making of modern Japan.* New York: HarperCollins.

Building mutual trust needs time and wisdom. (2005, April 20). *China Daily.*

Connerton, P. (1989). *How societies remember.* Cambridge England; New York: Cambridge University Press.

Coomaraswamy, R. (2001). *Violence against women: Report of the special rapporteur.* (No. E/CN.4/2001/73). U.N. Office of the High Commissioner for Human Rights.

Cormack, M. J. (1992). *Ideology.* Ann Arbor: University of Michigan Press.

Dwyer, O. J., & Alderman, D. H. (2008). *Civil rights memorials and the geography of memory.* Center for American Places at Columbia College Chicago: University of Georgia Press.

Eckert, P. (2007, Feburary 15). At U.S. hearing, WW2 sex slaves spurn Japan apologies. *Reuters.*

Edelman, M. J. (1988). *Constructing the political spectacle.* Chicago: University of Chicago Press.

Editorial: China, master of ambiguity. (2007, January 24). *The Chosun Ilbo.*

Editorial: Let's end Yasukuni controversy. (2001, July 27). *The Daily Yomiuri.*

Editorial: Mark end-of-war anniversary calmly. (2007, August 15). *The Daily Yomiuri.* pp. 4.

Editorial: ROK interfering in Japan's affairs. (2005, March 19). *The Daily Yomiuri.*

Edy, J. A. (1999). Journalistic uses of collective memory. *Journal of Communication, 49,* 71-85.

Elsaesser, T. (1985). Between Bitburg and Bergen Belsen. *On Film, 14.*

Fairclough, N. (1993). Critical discourse analysis and the marketization of public discourse: The universities. *Discourse & Society, 4*(2), 133-168.

Fairclough, N. (1995). *Critical discourse analysis: The critical study of language.* London; New York: Longman.

Frosh, P. (2006). Telling presences: Witnessing, mass media and the imagined lives of strangers. *Critical Journal in Media Communication, 23*(4), 265-284.

Glasser, T. L. (1999). The idea of public journalism. In T. L. Glasser (Ed.), *The idea of public journalism* (pp. 3-20). New York; London: Guilford Press.

Gluck, C., & Graubard, S. R. (Eds.). (1992). *Showa: The Japan of hirohito.* New York: Norton.

Habermas, J. (1979). *Communication and the evolution of society* (T. McCarthy, Trans.). Boston: Beacon Press.

Halbwachs, M. (1980). *The collective memory* (F. J. Ditter Jr. & V. Y. Ditter, Trans.). New York: Harper & Row.

Halbwachs, M. (1992). *On collective memory* (pp. 37-193). Chicago: University of Chicago Press.

Hidaka, T., & Imai, T. (2005, December 10). Iraq pullout timing difficult: SDF's eventual withdrawal faces diplomatic, logistical hurdles. *The Daily Yomiuri.*

Invasion anniversary commemorated. (2004, September 20). *China Daily.*

Invasions caused great damage. (2006, October 9). *China Daily.*

Jacobs, K. (2006). Discourse analysis and its utility for urban policy research. *Urban Policy and Research, 24*(1), 39-52.

Japan sends envoy; S. Korea not to back down on islands row. (2006, April 22). *China Daily.*

Japan, China put own spin on talks. (2004, December 6). *The Daily Yomiuri.*

Jeans, R. B. (2005). Victims or victimizers? useums, textbooks, and the war debate in contemporary Japan. *The Journal of Military History, 69*(1), 149-195.

Jensen, R. J. (2007). *Reagan at Bergen-Belsen and Bitburg.* College Station: Texas A&M University Press.

Kansteiner, W. (2002). Finding meaning in memory: A methodological critique of collective memory studies. *History & Theory, 41*(2), 179.

Kattago, S. (2001). *Ambiguous memory: The Nazi past and German national identity.* Westport, Conn.; London: Praeger.

Kelly, G. A., & Maher, B. A. (1979). *Clinical psychology and personality: The selected papers of George Kelly.* Huntington, N.Y.: R. E. Krieger Pub. Co.

Kishimoto, K. (2004). Apologies for atrocities: Commemorating the 50th anniversary of World War II's end in the United States and Japan. *American Studies International, 42*(2), 17-50.

Koizumi should honor his words. (2005, May 25). *China Daily.*

Koizumi to honor pledge to visit Yasukuni Shrine. (2001, July 27). *The Daily Yomiuri.*

Koizumi to make WWII remarks. (2005, August 15). *The Daily Yomiuri.*

Koizumi vows to continue shrine visits. (2004, April 8). *China Daily.*

Koizumi won't visit Yasukuni over New Year holiday season. (2005, January 3). *The Daily Yomiuri.*

Koizumi's provocation condemned. (2006, August 16). *China Daily.*

Kosaka, M. (1992). The Showa era. In C. Gluck, & S. R. Graubard (Eds.), *Showa: The Japan of Hirohito* (pp. 27-48). New York: Norton.

Kristof, N. D. (1998). The problem of memory. *Foreign Affairs, 77*(6), 37-49.

Lawmakers question Yasukuni visits' legality. (2006, June 16). *The Daily Yomiuri.* pp. 2.

Levkov, I. I. (1987). *Bitburg and beyond: Encounters in American, German and Jewish history.* New York: Shapolsky Publishers.

Lindlof, T. R., & Taylor, B. C. (2002). *Qualitative communication research methods.* Thousand Oaks, Calif.: Sage Publications.

Merriam-Webster Online Dictionary. *Respect.* Retrieved May 14, 2010, from http://www.merriam-webster.com/dictionary/respect

MFA of China. (2005). *Premier Wen Jiabao meets with journalists, talking about 3 achievements of his visit to India.* Ministry of Foreign Affairs of the People's Republic of China.

Miller, J. (1990). *One, by one, by one: Facing the Holocaust.* New York: Simon and Schuster.

Min, P. G. (2003). Korean "comfort women": The intersection of colonial power, gender, and class. *Gender and Society, 17*(6), 938-957.

Nora, P. (1989). Between memory and history: Les lieux de memoire. *Representations,* (26, Special Issue: Memory and Counter-Memory), 7-24.

Nora, P. (1996). *Realms of memory: Rethinking the French past* (A. Goldhammer, Trans.). New York: Columbia University Press.

Nord, D. P. (1989). The nature of historical research. In G. H. Stempel, & B. H. Westley (Eds.), *Research methods in mass communication* (pp. 290-315). Englewood Cliffs, N.J.: Prentice Hall.

Peters, J. D. (2001). Witnessing. *Media, Culture & Society, 23*(6, November), 707-724.

Roh calls on Japan to respect historical truth. (2007, March 2). *The Chosun Ilbo.*

Rose, C. (1998). *Interpreting history in Sino-Japanese relations: A case study in political decision-making.* London; New York: Routledge.

Rose, C. (2005). *Sino-Japanese relations: Facing the past, looking to the future?* New York: RoutledgeCurzon.

Saaler, S., & Schwentker, W. (2008). *The power of memory in modern Japan.* Folkestone, UK: Global Oriental.

Schwartz, B. (1991). Iconography and collective memory: Lincoln's image in the american mind. *The Sociological Quarterly, 32*(3), 301-319.

Seraphim, F. (2006). *War memory and social politics in Japan, 1945-2005.* Cambridge, Mass.: Harvard University Asia Center.

Shibuichi, D. (2005). The Yasukuni shrine dispute and the politics of identity in Japan. *Asian Survey, 45*(2).

Smith, M. Y. (1989). The method of history. In G. H. Stempel, & B. H. Westley (Eds.), *Research methods in mass communication* (pp. 316-330). Englewood Cliffs, N.J.: Prentice Hall.

Soh, C. S. (1996). The Korean "Comfort Women": Movement for redress. *Asian Survey, 36*(12), 1226-1240.

Stempel, G. H., & Westley, B. H. (1989). *Research methods in mass communication*. Englewood Cliffs, N.J.: Prentice Hall.

Tanaka, Y. (2001). Comfort women in Dutch East Indies. In M. D. Stetz, & B. B. C. Oh (Eds.), *Legacies of the comfort women of world war II* (pp. 42-68). Armonk, N.Y.: M.E. Sharpe.

Thompson, S. (2006). *The political theory of recognition: A critical introduction*. Cambridge: Polity.

Ueno, C. (2004). *Nationalism and gender* (B. Yamamoto, Trans.). Melbourne, Vic.: Trans Pacific.

Yasukuni key to LDP presidency. (2005, June 9). *The Daily Yomiuri.*

Zamora, L. P. (1997). *The usable past: The imagination of history in recent fiction of the Americas*. Cambridge, U.K.; New York: Cambridge University Press.

Zelizer, B. (1990). Achieving journalistic authority through narrative. *Critical Studies in Mass Communication, 7*, 366.

Zelizer, B. (2004). *Taking journalism seriously: News and the academy*. Thousand Oaks, CA: Sage.

Zelizer, B. (2008a). *Explorations in communication and history*. Milton Park, Abingdon, Oxon; New York: Routledge.

Zelizer, B. (2008b). Why memory's work on journalism does not reflect journalism's work on memory. *Memory Studies, 1*(1), 79-87.

CHAPTER FIVE

JAPANESE NEWPAPER'S INFLUENCE ON SOCIETAL DISCOURSE AND GOVERNMENTAL POLICY TOWARD NORTH KOREA, 1998-2006

Seung Hyok Lee

INTRODUCTION

On August 31, 1998, the Democratic People's Republic of Korea (DPRK: North Korea) test-launched a multi-stage ballistic missile, the Taepodong, eastward in the direction of Japan. The missile flew over the northern Japanese main island, through its airspace, and a portion of it then fell into the Pacific Ocean (*Asahi Shimbun,* 1998). Although it was later confirmed as a failed satellite launch (*Asahi Shimbun Editorial*, 1998), the incident and its subsequent impact on Japanese society and politics was later described as "the Taepodong shock."

Initially, the Japanese government reacted to the North Korean provocation with verbal condemnations. Japan pushed for an official statement of protest by the United Nations (UN) Secretariat, but it had to eventually settle for a less assertive press statement. Apart from verbal condemnations, the Japanese Ministry of Foreign Affairs held up food aid to the North that had been scheduled before the launch, and froze its financial contribution to the Korean Peninsula Energy Development Organization (KEDO), an international organization which had reached agreement with North Korea in 1995 for supplying a light water reactor in return for North to giving up the nuclear program it had initiated in 1994 (Gaimushō, 1999).

Considering that it's airspace had been jeopardized by a potentially catastrophic missile belonging to a not-so-friendly neighbor, Japan's reaction as a sovereign state was in fact quite restrained. If we were to compare its response to how other states would most likely have dealt with a similar provocation, it is clear that Japan's actions were modest.

Eight years later, North Korea once again launched a multi-stage ballistic missile Taepodong-2. On July 5, 2006, it conducted a series of short and medium-range missile exercises, during which the modified version of Taepodong was launched from North Korea's eastern seaboard. The debris fell into the international waters a few hundred kilometers between the western part of the Northern Japanese main island of Hokkaido and the Maritime Province of Russia (*Asahi Shimbun*, 2006a; *Yomiuri Shimbun*, 2006a).

The 2006 missile neither penetrated the Japanese airspace nor flew over Japan as in 1998. Although the maritime security of other regional neighbors—Russia and China—were similarly affected, and the actual threat posed by the missile was comparatively not as direct as in 1998, this time the Japanese government immediately implemented unilateral sanctions against North Korea (*Asahi Shimbun*, 2006a, 2006b, 2006c; Gaimushō, 2007; *Yomiuri Shimbun*, 2006a). In the following months, Japan would implement additional unilateral sanctions in order to punish North Korea (*Asahi Shimbun*, 2006c, 2006d; *Yomiuri Shimbun*, 2006c; *Yomiuri Shimbun Editorial*, 2006a, 2006b, 2006c).

Interestingly, the Japanese government in 2006 also took the leading role in drafting the UN Security Council resolution condemning North Korea and actively persuaded other member states to join the Japanese unilateral sanctions; this stands in drastic contrast to settling for a UN Secretariat press statement eight years before *(Asahi Shimbun*, 2006c; *Yomiuri Shimbun*, 2006c). The policy reaction by Japan in 2006 was, therefore, strikingly different from its stance in 1998. For the first time in post-World War II history, Japan unilaterally imposed sanctions against a regional state and took the most active part in drafting and submitting a UN resolution specifically aimed at condemning a neighbor.

For any scholar interested in Japanese security foreign policy, the question of why the Japanese reactions to the two North Korean provocations of a similar kind but eight years apart substantially differed constitutes a fascinating empirical puzzle. It could be simply argued that it is common sense for a state—just like an individual—to be more angry when provoked a second time. But the question still remains as to why Japanese government shifted its policy specifically in favor of a particular form of unilateral sanctions. This chapter asks whether other domestic factors were at work behind this policy shift.

The Role of Societal Discourse and Newspapers in Publicized Foreign Policy

This chapter engages this puzzle by tracing the cause and the nature of the North Korean case leading up to 2006, focusing on domestic processes within Japan that influenced subsequent foreign policy change toward North Korea. The paper argues that analyzing the process of mutual interactions among Japanese domestic factors– *especially the influential role played by newspapers in representing and leading mainstream public/societal discourse concerning North Korea that eventually influenced Japanese government's foreign policy*—is the best means to provide a contextually valid explanation for the type of sanctions implemented in 2006.

In the contemporary East Asian regional security interactions, the North Korea factor has always been a highly complex issue and thus this chapter is aware of the high-politics level dealings in the Six Party Talks (SPT) involving the United States, China, the two Koreas, Japan, and Russia concerning the North Korean nuclear and missile programs that unfolded at the same period in question. Understandably, the North Korean issue has been mainly analyzed in the realm of international relations and policy studies, and thus the chapter does not claim that regional governmental interactions and high-politics are insignificant. What this chapter argues, conversely, is that domestic discursive influence on Japanese policy change vis-à-vis the North and the role of Japanese media have been seriously overlooked, as mainstream works have been overly and solely focused on the unfolding of the government and elite-level dealings while domestic currents are often mentioned only in passing.

In any consideration of a media role in social events, the use of particular terminology is important. In the present research, the term "public/ societal" encompasses the notion of domestic, non-governmental interest groups in Japan linked to North Korean issues or national security. The term is used to broadly embrace ordinary Japanese citizens at the mass level of all occupational, educational, and regional backgrounds. Of course, as in any democratic state, Japanese citizens embrace diverse opinions and show varied degrees of interest in foreign policy issues. There are, however, certain foreign policy issues which draw a high degree of public interest, and these well-publicized policy areas tend to produce a mainstream/ majority opinion. The present research is thus geared toward analyzing the shifts of such mass-level, mainstream emotions and ideational trends that are observable.

Likewise, the term "discourse" here is a contextual and narrated-in-detail form of public opinion, formed by debates and discussions (often through the medium of domestic newspapers) concerning a foreign policy issue. Japanese society and politic broadly understand public opinion as a "viewpoint of society that is perceived and recognized by its members to be strong and influential in a particular issue area" (Kabashima, Takeshita & Serikawa, 2007, pp. 116-117). Two additional terms widely interchangeable with public opinion in the Japanese context are "*iken no kazamuki*" and "*kūki*." The former can be translated literally as "the wind-direction of opinion," and the latter more figuratively as "atmosphere" (Kabashima, Takeshita & Serikawa, 2007, pp.134-135; see also Yamamoto, 1983). These terms have connotations of societal inclination toward a particular viewpoint and a strong pressure on individuals to voluntarily conform to mainstream ideational current.

In the Japanese context specifically, however, there is no clear demarcation between public opinion and public discourse, as there is no equivalent vocabulary for the latter in Japanese; should a distinction between the two be necessary, the *katakana* term "*disukōsu*" is used. Public opinion is usually expressed in opinion polls in any democratic country, and it refers to citizens' responses to pre-determined and framed questionnaires. But societal discourse, on the other hand, points to the background ideational current or narratives that led those citizens to answer in such a way to the opinion polls in the first place. Discourse is, therefore, a source from which we can contextually understand the nuanced background of how and why citizens have come to react in a certain fashion to a particular issue.

In Japan, closely following the contextual "tone" of mass media sources, especially in the editorials of the major newspapers and the articles in major weekly/monthly magazines, is one of the most valid and accessible approaches for tracing representative, mainstream voices and discursive societal trends concerning publicized foreign policy issues. This is because Japanese mass media are accepted as the country's most prominent reflective medium by both the public and the government. Major newspapers in particular are well-established societal organizations that enjoy an especially high level of respect as credible sources of such information in Japan (Tadokoro, 2000). The media have been the chief "institutional transmission belts" of public opinion as well as being even regarded as a supplement of civil society (Katzenstein, 1998, p. 39). It is little wonder that government officials and foreign policy makers consider mass media as the primary source for gaining access to public opinion and they consistently monitor the expressions and interpretations of the people's mandate written in newspapers. "Voices from all strata of the public, comments and editorials of journalists, letters from the ordinary readers and the viewers, columns with coverage on how ordinary citizens are reacting to a certain issue, and opinion polls" all introduced and transmitted through newspapers, magazines, and television, are always closely watched and viewed by policy-makers (Kabashima, Takeshita & Serikawa, 2007, p. 119). In this chapter, editorials of the two most widely-read newspapers–the *Yomiuri Shimbun* and the *Asahi Shimbun*– are used as the representation of moderate-right conservative and liberal discourses respectively.

This chapter brings strong emphasis to "publicized" foreign policy versus that which is non-publicized, and North Korea related issues have been one of the most vivid illustrations of the former type in the late 1990s and to the mid-2000s in Japan before the so-called "China factor" took over that role in more recent years. When a given political or foreign policy issue is "publicized," it means that it is sufficiently known to the public to the extent that a vast majority of members are aware of the issue's existence and are emotionally involved in its unfolding. Any analysis of publicized policy that does not incorporate the role of public opinion and societal discourse would be incomplete. This is especially true when a publicized foreign policy issue is shocking enough to affect citizens' nationalism and to stir their emotional involvement, and Japanese mass media and particularly the newspapers play the role of the mirror of public sentiment whenever such occasions arise.

Japanese newspapers are fully capable of fulfilling such a role, as they strive to be accessible in their tone so as to ensure that they are not out of touch with the overall attitudes of the public. Their receptiveness to the current mainstream voices (or their flexibility to accommodate them whether voluntarily or reluctantly) has been the core assets of the major Japanese media agencies in sustaining their respective positions within society. Indeed, Ōtake argued that the Japanese media tend to "fawn over" readers and viewers and that they are especially prone to be swayed by direct criticism from the public (Ōtake, 2003, p. 237).

Of course, when a political phenomenon is not highly publicized—as in the everyday politics of issues not significant to state or public interest— the direct, influential role of the media in accommodating and representing mainstream discursive current and influencing governmental decisions is comparatively vague. As is well known, major Japanese newspapers are widely positioned in domestic political spectrum, but despite each newspaper's political inclinations, they are in most cases quite flexible in their tones in order to accommodate their diverse pool of readers. However, when the nature of the topic is such that there is strong societal emotional participation from the beginning and the formation of a clear mainstream, public discursive undercurrent, the media often end up merely reflecting ongoing public sentiment as one. Media in such a scenario are generally compelled—by correctly "reading" the societal atmosphere—to report on the majority opinions of the public, and thus further provide a more concrete, discursive focal point for the citizens by their own act of news coverage.

In short, the society-media-government relationship varies depending on the foreign policy issue at hand and whether it is highly publicized or not. The influence-structure between the public and the media, and the linkage between governmental policies and public opinion mirrored by the media, are thus directly issue-dependent. Focusing on these various aspects of Japanese newspapers, public discourse, and their relations to the government decision-making, is the key for understanding why the Japanese government was compelled to shift its policy toward North Korea—one of the most publicized issues in the postwar Japan—between 1998 and 2006.

Tracing the Empirical Case

From here, this chapter traces empirically trends in Japan between 1998 to 2006 after the first North Korean Taepodong missile launch from the viewpoint of three separate levels. The first concerns bilateral incidents involving North Korean breaches of Japan's sovereignty. This is followed by societal reaction and the Japanese public's interpretation of these incidents, together with the unfolding of public discourse on the North Korean threats facilitated by Japanese newspapers' band-wagoning with the public's rapidly-worsening attitude toward North Korea. Lastly, the chapter notes the nature and the behavior of the political decision-makers, particularly in terms of their increasing susceptibility to the public discourse, which led them to adopt the policy shift toward the unilateral sanctions in 2006 when an opportunity presented itself.

Bilateral Level Incidents involving Japan and North Korea

Between the two ballistic missile launches in 1998 and 2006, there had been a number of other highly provocative and publicized North Korea-linked incidents which stirred Japanese security consciousness and their negative image toward the North in the late 1990s and early 2000s. On two occasions (March 25, 1999, and December 21-23, 2001), unidentified vessels, so-called mystery/spy ships (*fushinsen*), suddenly appeared within the maritime sovereignty of Japan. While they disguised themselves as Japanese fishing boats, they were presumed—and later confirmed—to be from North Korea. In both cases, Japanese Maritime Self Defense Forces

(MSDF) and the Japanese Coast Guards (JCG) ships were dispatched to the area. These instances marked the first post-World War II instance of Japanese naval vessels firing warning shots (1999) (*Asahi Shimbun Editorial,* 1999), and the first postwar use of deadly force in a naval engagement (2001), as in the second encounter, the JCG vessels fired on the mystery ship and sank it (Samuels, 2007a, 2007b). On top of the ballistic missile incident of 1998, these additional breaches of sovereignty in 1999 and 2001 highlighted the bizarre nature of the regime in North Korea to the Japanese public.

Considering that Japan maintained a careful and non-aggressive stance toward North Korea throughout the Cold War period, the shift in Japanese public view toward the North from the late 1990s as a result of these publicized incidents is highly indicative. During the Cold War, Japan's basic stance toward the Korean Peninsula in general and toward North Korea in particular was largely confined to the careful support of regional stability and the status quo (Kamiya, 2000). The Japanese were reluctant to openly express their concern over security issues of the peninsula, since any Japanese initiative beyond supporting inter-Korean dialogue could be perceived by Koreans as a sign of interference (Hwang, 2006, Murata, 2004). Such caution was not confined to government foreign policy. The public was equally passive concerning Japan's role in any potential contingency on the peninsula, even if it would have a direct consequence on Japanese security. For example, as late as 1997, a year prior to the first Taepodong missile launch, 39% of the Americans who were asked about contingencies in Korea responded that they expect a military response from Japan as an ally should the United States got involved, while only 2% of the Japanese favored their country's participation (Murata, 2004).

In addition, Japan's non-political contacts with North Korea were maintained throughout the Cold War. After signing private sector agreements on trade in 1972 and fishing in 1977, other moderate steps were also taken in economic and cultural spheres (Togo, 2005b), and bilateral trade was stable around US$500 million per year, even into the 1990s

(Green, 2001, p. 117). Reflecting the general societal trend of the period, Japanese media throughout the 1960s to 1980s emphasized the need for maintaining "peace and friendship (*heiwa to yūkō*)" between Japan and the North, despite a number of North Korean terrorist activities against South Korea which occasionally destabilized regional security (Yamakoshi & Hirai, 2008, p. 48).

But incidents originating from North Korea from 1998 onward had significant impact on changing Japanese public views about the nature of its neighbor and gradually formulated its threat perception and security discourse vis-à-vis the North. More than any other previous incidents, events in 2002 would arguably become the most shocking of North Korea-linked incidents in postwar Japanese history, and it would frame North Korea policy and public stance of Japan ever since up to the present day. On September 17, 2002, Prime Minister Koizumi Junichiro visited Pyongyang and met the then-head of state of the North Korea Kim Jong-il, the first by an acting Prime Minister of Japan in postwar history. Despite the previous incidents that had already marred the relations between the two countries, they managed to conclude a historical bilateral agreement in the form of the "Pyongyang Declaration."

Koizumi's initiative to visit the North when public perception toward the country was deteriorating was perceived by many experts to be an important stepping stone for Japan, as he was determined to resolve one of the last remaining agendum of the World War II legacy—diplomatic normalization with the North—and thereby achieve greater diplomatic leverage for Japan in the region (Togo, 2005b). The "Pyongyang Declaration" dealt with all previous historical and security related issues that had hindered the normalization process in the past: Japan would initiate economic aid to North Korea; both parties would mutually cede their right of claim for properties and other assets from the pre-World War II period; North Korea would take appropriate measures to prevent further occurrence of incidents that endanger Japanese citizens' lives and security; and North Korea would cooperate with Japan on regional security (*Yomiuri Shimbun*, 2002b).

The most significant breakthrough of the declaration, however, was Kim Jong-il's official admission and apology of North Korea's abductions (*rachi*) of Japanese citizens in the past. Although the possibility of North Korea abducting Japanese had been raised by some media (notably *Sankei Shimbun*), politicians, family members of the disappeared in the 1980s, and most mainstream journalism had never investigated in depth and the accusation was seen as a sort of "conspiracy theory" even among Japanese policy circles during the Cold War period. But in September 2002, it was revealed that North Korean agents had abducted Japanese citizens during the 1970s and 1980s to be trainers for North Korean spies infiltrating South Korea disguised as Japanese. Another purpose of the abductions was providing Japanese who were semi-permanently residing in North Korea (for example, the Japanese Red-Army faction members who hijacked the airliner JAL 351 "Yodo-gō" in March, 1970 and flew to North Korea to seek asylum) with Japanese spouses (Steinhoff, 2004; Wada, Yamamuro, Yamaguchi, Mizuno, Takasaki, Tanaka, Shimizu, Komori, Kimiya, Kang, Kawasaki & Ishizaka, 2008; *Yomiuri Shimbun Political Section*, 2006). Kim informed the Japanese that among thirteen Japanese victims that the North Korean government confirmed, eight had already died and five were still living in North Korea (*Yomiuri Shimbun*, 2002b).

Although the then-North Korean dictator Kim Jong-il offered his personal and official apology and explained that the kidnappings were "voluntarily" conducted by special units without Kim's "prior knowledge," (*Yomiuri Shimbun*, 2002b) the shocking revelation that a neighboring state had intentionally abducted Japanese citizens from their homeland and had deliberately hidden the fact for decades understandably caused an unprecedented outcry and anger in Japanese society. From this point on, the charged emotional atmosphere that had emerged has never fully subsided, and the abduction issue, more than any other North Korea-linked incidents, would bar any possibility of bilateral rapprochement, reconciliation, or negotiation. Koizumi, as a politician wanting to reach his final goal of normalizing diplomatic relations with the North, thereby enabling Japan to take the leading role in security affairs in the East Asian region, tried to save the 2002 framework by visiting Pyongyang again in May 2004. It was a political gamble, as he faced public uproar against the North and ever-increasing societal and media resistance against their government still prioritizing "dry politics" when an unprecedented violation of the human rights of Japanese citizens has been uncovered. The second visit was thus aimed at bringing the abductees' remaining family members from North Korea and to convince the public that there was some movement toward some closure to abduction issue, so as to provide Koizumi with justification to proceed with the long-delayed diplomatic normalization. However, despite Koizumi's gamble, the effect of his trip would not be sufficient to mollify the already-prevalent Japanese societal anger toward North Korea.

As we shall see below, this single incident, more than any other previous North Korean provocations combined, has fundamentally influenced the trajectory of Japanese policy toward the North leading to the 2006 sanctions, all through the engagement of Japanese public and the bandwagoning of major newspapers.

The Unfolding of the Japanese Discourse on Security and Threats

For most Japanese, these North Korean provocations and shocks—and especially the abduction issue—were unlike other international-level incidents in the post-Cold War period. To be sure, other rather distant incidents—such as the first Gulf War and the 9/11 attacks, for example—had already given Japanese policy-makers a wake-up call to re-evaluate Japan's traditional postwar "pacifist" security principles of self-limiting the use of force or diplomatic/economic coercion (as governed by the "Peace Clause" of the Constitution). But those events had largely failed to provoke the public's committed and consistent participation in debates about national security once the memories of the incidents subsided in public minds.

North Korean threats, on the other hand, pushed the public to increasingly problematize Japan's traditionally restrained security policies, especially toward its neighbors. This attention is understandable, as North Korea's constant and highly visible provocations in a short time span directly affected Japanese maritime and territorial sovereignty, unlike any distant war or terrorism. The *fushinsen* incidents of 1999 and 2001 became a source of anxiety in the minds of many Japanese citizens, and forced recognition that their country was lacking even basic means of enforcing its maritime sovereignty. The incidents encouraged public belief that East Asia was a dangerous place and that Japan must be more sensitive to external military threats from North Korea (Murata, 2004; Samuels, 2007b). For example, while 20% of respondents to a *Yomiuri* newspaper survey in August 1998—just before the Taepodong incident—felt threatened by North Korea, the figure jumped to 50% in October, 2001. From this period on, more frequent criticisms from major newspaper editorials toward an "almost theological adherence" to the so-called "peace naivety" (*heiwa-boke*) of the postwar period, which had prevented realistic and effective countermeasures against a clear and present violation of Japanese sovereignty appeared (*Yomiuri Shimbun Editorial*, 1999a, 1999b). During this eight-year period from 1998 to 2006, North Korea had demonstrated to the Japanese public that the traditional, postwar self-limitations on the use of the "sovereign right of the nation" against its neighbors—a direct extension of Japan's Peace Constitution and "pacifist" and "antimilitaristic" tendency to resolve international disputes diplomatically without relying on any forceful, punitive measures—were problematic in their original, dogmatic form (Ishihara & Abe, 2003; *Yomiuri Shimbun Editorial*, 2002).

Although some politicians belonging to the nationalist and other "rightist" camps had advocated for a change of the traditional stance from time to time without winning any substantial public support in the past, the highly illustrative and proximate nature of the "North Korea factor" gave this line of thought a noticeable domestic legitimacy from 1998 on. As the public was increasingly convinced that Japan's timid diplomatic stance during the Cold War was at the core of an inability to prevent such a North Korean "abuse" of Japanese postwar security institutions, actual and accumulating examples of North Korean breaches of Japanese sovereignty and the abductions of Japanese citizens gave strength to a public discourse concerning the use of "national power" to prevent and punish such actions, evidenced in a discursive trend seen in such representative examples as mainstream newspaper editorials (*Asahi Shimbun Editorial*, 2002a, 2002b; *Asahi Shimbun*, 2003; *Yomiuri Shimbun Editorial*, 2002b, 2002c).

Throughout this period, the role of Japanese mass media at the societal level was crucial. The tendency in Japan's media in publicized foreign policy issues reinforced the ongoing societal discourse concerning North Korea from 1998 onwards, providing a public stage on which people's anger toward the North could gain focus and momentum. Japanese journalism realized how the mainstream public viewed North Korea, and they promptly bandwagoned in an unprecedented degree in the post-World War II Japan. More "objectively-minded" experts could observe this trajectory, in which the claim that society's over-fixation on the abduction issue could limit Japan's broader opportunity to play a leading role for regional peace, was increasingly becoming a statement too "audacious against near-uniformity in emotional criticism of the North" (Togo, 2005a, pp. 31-32). Particularly after the 2002 summit, experts monitoring Japanese media observed that journalists were self-censoring minority interpretations to go along with the main trends in viewing the North, with few willing to challenge the prevailing tone of the "hawks dominating the public discourse" on North Korea (Yamaguchi, 2005, p.54). Liberal editorializing—in the *Asahi Shimbun*, for example—"always fold(ed) back on itself two or three times." (Yamaguchi, 2005, p.54)

The main "storyline"—the content of the mainstream public discourse—concerning North Korea and the abductions that took shape through the interaction between an emotionally-engaged public and the newspapers after 2002 disclosure of the abduction issue, was of a peaceful and democratic state's human rights—an integral part of national sovereignty (*kokka-shuken*)—being utterly violated by an individual-worshipping and criminal dictatorship located dangerously close to Japan. For many Japanese, the disclosure of abductions was closely linked to their understanding of the importance of national sovereignty and the role of the government in that. One major daily editorial—in a tone that largely represents the societal atmosphere of the time—suggested that it was now time to discuss the proper role of the state in protecting the lives and properties of its citizens, as the abduction now provided Japan with a clear example of a violation of its state sovereignty (*Yomiuri Shimbun Editorial*, 2003b). Between 1998 and 2006, the Japanese media thus performed primarily in the role of confirming the already-prevalent societal discourse by further advocating a negative image of North Korea. This is the domestic environment in which the idea of putting pressure on North Korea under some form of sanctions first emerged, as public anger gradually turned to more policy-relevant ideas with the help of newspaper editorials and "ideational entrepreneurs" outside the government even before the second missile launch actually materialized in 2006 (Maruyama, 2003, p.128; Morris-Suzuki, 2003a, 2003b).

THE GOVERNMENT'S SUSCEPTIBILITY TO THE PUBLIC DISCOURSE AND THE FORMATION OF SANCTION OPTIONS PRIOR TO 2006

Before moving on to how public discourse as led and represented by mass media framed subsequent foreign policy toward North Korea, a note on Japanese government's increasing susceptibility to public opinion that coincided with the North Korean issues in the early 2000s must be included. Starting in 1998, the Japanese government, led by the Liberal

Democratic Party (LDP), experienced the first large-scale generation shift, as an influx of a post-World War II generation of Diet members started to replace traditionally-minded politicians who had preferred more factional and elitist means of policy-making. In addition, the LDP regained the Prime Ministership after the political turmoil in the immediate aftermath of the post-Cold War period when political leadership had briefly shifted to the hands of other parties. With this new political balance taking hold, the election of Koizumi Junichiro as the Prime Minister in 2001 further facilitated an environment in which the LDP Cabinet could formulate foreign policies relatively free from the pressures of other coalition allies and traditional LDP factional considerations. Koizumi won his position through his "populist" tendency of reaching out directly to ordinary citizens, and his image as a new type of politician, bold enough to make political decisions on his own initiatives, was initially widely supported by the constituency and the new generation of Diet members (Kabashima, Takeshita & Serikawa, 2007; Ōtake, 2006; Shinoda, 2007).

Koizumi's rise and the nature of his political power during the crucial years of the early 2000s, as a result, led to a style of decision-making that put more powerful policy initiatives in the hands of the Prime Minister, at the cost of undermined bureaucratic and LDP factional considerations (Pempel, 2007; Shinoda, 2007). As Koizumi's power base strongly depended upon public support, the nature of his Prime Ministership gave popular preferences and societal atmosphere a significant influence on the government's decision-making process in both domestic and foreign policy areas (Tanaka, 2009).

This structural change in the political landscape had crucial implications on how North Korea policies would unfold. Already soon after the 2002 summit, negative public opinion against North Korea was starting to become a "wall of deterrence" hindering Japanese government from simply following the agreed steps of the Pyongyang Declaration. The government (The Cabinet and the bureaucracy)—as well as the LDP—were therefore forced to turn cautious in their North Korea-related statements in order to avoid potential societal criticism, in case they were viewed as too conciliatory (*Asahi Shimbun*, 2002; *Yomiuri Shimbun*, 2002c).

In the midst of such a domestic environment, demand for "foreign policy cards" to put pressure on North Korea to sincerely re-investigate the whole story behind the abduction issue and "return" the eight victims who were presumed dead—but still widely thought by a large number of Japanese public to be alive and hidden by North Koreans—began to take hold among informed citizens and mainstream newspapers and politicians receptive to such voice. This hostile consciousness toward the North allowed the idea of pressuring North Korea to permeate into public discourse and develop further into a more concrete agenda. Gradually, the term "economic sanction" replaced "foreign policy cards," as both media and politics widely adopted the terminology.

In this regard, it is important to note that the first demand for sanctions against North Korea that took hold during 2003 and 2004 was first proposed and supported by political parties and members of the wider public, not by the bureaucracy or the Koizumi Cabinet (with an exception of Abe Shinzō). Once the possibility of sanctioning North Korea was on the table, more detailed public discussions involving newspaper editorials, public opinion, and political pundits began to appear with increasing frequency, and the specific options of banning North Korean ships from entering Japan, and revising foreign exchange laws that would prohibit money to be sent to the North from within Japan, became the two pillars of the sanction options widely popularized in the Japanese media.

The banning of North Korean vessels from entering Japanese harbors —especially the passenger liner Mangyonbong-92—was the first pillar of the sanctions proposal that appeared in newspaper editorials as a realistic possibility at Japan's disposal. Once the Metropolitan Police Department announced in January 2003 that the liner could have functioned in the past as a command center for North Korean spies in Japan, media support for the ban became even more widespread (*Yomiuri Shimbun Editorial*, 2003a). In May and June of 2003, societal support for another pillar of the "pressure option"—the revision of foreign exchange laws—also gained momentum. The public was more convinced than ever that blocking Japanese goods and money from flowing into North Korea could not be complete unless the capital transfer to Pyongyang by pro-North, ethnic Korean residents in Japan (*Chōsen-Sōren*) was strictly controlled. Throughout 2003, societal discourse of supporting the two options became mainstream, with wider public understanding. By the end of 2003, mainstream Japanese newspapers realized that there was already a "national consensus in principle" (*kokuron*) among politics and public concerning the validity of pressuring North Korea (*Yomiuri Shimbun Editorial*, 2003c).

As a logical consequence, on January 29, 2004, "The Amendment of Foreign Exchange and Trade Laws" (*Gaikoku Kawase/Gaikoku Bōeki-hō Kaisei-an*–abbreviated as "*Kawase-hō*") enabling Japan to unilaterally stop the transfer of capital and goods to North Korea passed the plenary session voting in the Lower House *(Asahi Shimbun Editorial,* 2004a). On June 14, 2004, another pillar of the proposed sanction bills that would, once imposed, prohibit North Korean vessels from entering Japan also passed the Diet as the "Special Legal Measures Prohibiting Particular Vessels from Entering Japanese Harbors" (*Tokutei Senpaku Nyūkō Kinshi Tokubetsu Sochi-hō*) (*Asahi Shimbun*, 2004; *Yomiuri Shimbun*, 2004).

The passing of the two sanction legislations was possible, only because majority public and media were in support, and in fact strongly demanded them from the start. For example, an opinion poll conducted in February, 2004 by Yomiuri Shimbun showed that 78 percent of the public welcomed the revised foreign exchange laws, and also supported passing the "Law Prohibiting Particular Vessels from Entering Japanese Harbors" (80%). In fact, the poll found that the majority of Japanese felt even stronger sanction measures were desirable (*Yomiuri Shimbun Editorial*, 2004b). Media of both left and right political inclinations also accepted this public voice as a legitimate reaction by the people whose national sovereignty and human rights had been violated (*Asahi Shimbun Editorial*, 2004b; *Yomiuri Shimbun Editorial*, 2004c).

Although there were expert voices in and out of Japan questioning the real effect the bills would have on the North, Diet discussions did not stop but snowballed to expand the scope beyond the two options, once they became official foreign policy weapons with clear public backing. The Diet, more than targeting North Korean vessels, started to consider the possibility of rejecting the issuance of re-entry permits to particular "foreigners with permanent-resident status" (*eijyū gaikokujin*) —the majority of them being ethnic Koreans—by revising the immigration control laws (*Shutsunyūkoku Kanri-hō Kaisei-an*) (*Yomiuri Shimbun Editorial*, 2004a).

2006 NORTH KOREAN MISSILE LAUNCH AND THE IMPOSITION OF UNILATERAL SANCTIONS

When Taepodong-2 was launched in July 2006, the Japanese government swiftly announced the same day that it would impose unilateral sanctions against the North Korea. The announcement was divided into twelve parts, the first nine stating how Japan would conduct the sanctions by domestic means, with the latter three urging other states and international organizations—the United States, the United Nations (UN) Security Council, the member states of the SPT and the G8—to cooperate with Japan and participate in pressuring the North (*Asahi Shimbun*, 2006b; *Yomiuri Shimbun*, 2006b).

The first nine clauses included the following five notable points: (1) the immediately-effective banning of the North Korean passenger liner Mangyongbong-92 from entering any Japanese harbor for six months; (2) a ban on North Korean government officials entering Japan, along with heightened security and immigration checks for anyone who had traveled to the North; (3) the cessation of issuance of re-entry permits to ethnic Korean residents in Japan with affiliations with the North (mostly the officials of *Chōsen-Sōren*), once they had left Japan; (4) the cancellation of Japanese government visits to the North and also a call for citizens to refrain from traveling to the destination for personal and business reasons; and (5) a ban on North Korean air flights from making a stop at any Japanese airport. In addition, one clause expressly made public that the above measures were only the beginning, and that the government was already considering imposition of stronger measures – the ban of foreign exchange, capital transfer, and trade – depending on North Korean reactions (*Asahi Shimbun*, 2006b; *Yomiuri Shimbun*, 2006b).

What is significant is that the sanctions imposed on July 5 closely reflected the legislation and other legal proposals prepared during 2003-2004, when the abduction issue was the focus of Japanese public discussion concerning North Korea. On September 19, 2006, the government announced that Japan was additionally imposing the second part of the sanctions, and the additional measure was legally based on "The Amendment of Foreign Exchange and Trade Laws" (*Gaikoku Kawase/ Gaikoku Bōeki-hō Kaisei-an*) passed in 2004, as it included bans on sending cash to the North as well as freezing all North Korean assets in Japan.

The sanctions in 2006 were, therefore, not a spontaneous Japanese reaction to the missile launch itself. The contents of the unilateral sanctions reveal that they were rather an application of already-prepared punitive measures originally thought out for a different issue, the abductions. All plausible scenarios for Japan's own sanctions had already been considered—with strong public and journalism backing—much earlier by a Diet task-force when the primary national concern—as far as the public was concerned—was the abduction. In short, the Taepodong launch in 2006 provided a timely and suitable opportunity for the implementation of the scenarios for unilaterally punishing North Korea, even if the means applied had been prepared before the event and for a different purpose. (Abe, 2006; Abe & Sakurai, 2008).

Conclusion

This chapter has argued that one of the most significant security-related policy changes of Japan introduced in recent years—the unilateral sanctions in 2006 against North Korea—was directly motivated by public backing through societal stages provided by a bandwagoning mass media, the mainstream newspapers in particular. By identifying and analyzing the evidence at three separate levels—international, societal, and governmental—and tracing the unfolding of processes at these levels, this chapter has provided a contextual understanding of the often-overlooked collective influence of media and society on the formation of the sanction policy.

When domestic developments taking place between 1998 and 2006 are empirically traced, they demonstrate that during this juncture these three levels mutually reinforced interactions among them in the following way: accumulating North Korean provocations and shocks visibly convinced the public of the image of North Korea as the most direct threat to Japanese security (international/bilateral); the resulting public shock and re-evaluation of Japan's traditional foreign policy posture led to a hardened domestic discourse toward North Korea, facilitated by the media's unprecedented level of bandwagoning to this public emotion (societal); a concurrent, structural power-shift within the political realm, in turn, made public preferences more influential in foreign policy decision-making than in the pre-1998 period, and politicians were pressured to incorporate the changing security discourse into their subsequent North Korea policies (political). Viewed in this context, one can conclude that it is unlikely that the unilateral Japanese economic sanctions of 2006, engaged immediately following the second *Taepodong* launch, would have been realized in the form in which they were in the absence of the particular interactions that had taken place beforehand in and between these three society levels.

Tracing this process has thus provided us with a persuasive conclusion that the sanctions of 2006 were more of an unintended consequence of larger domestic factors than simply government action. The discursive change in Japan toward North Korea as a result of various provocations by the North, especially by the official disclosure of the abduction issue in 2002, compelled the trajectory of Koizumi's government's punitive approach to North Korea toward a particular direction. It could be thus argued that the extent of public-media-government interaction in this particular case is one of the most vivid examples of Japanese foreign policy influenced by non-governmental societal discourse led by media in post-World War II Japanese history.

References

Abe, S. (2006). *Utsukushii Kuni e*. Tokyo: Bungeishunjū.

Abe, S. & Sakurai, Y. (2008). Futatabi Tatsu! Dare ga Kono Kuni wo Mamorunoka. *Seiron*, 48–61.

Asahi Shimbun. (1998, September 1). pp. 1.

Asahi Shimbun. (2002, September 28). pp. 3.

Asahi Shimbun. (2003, September 17). pp. 2.

Asahi Shimbun. (2004, December 25). pp. 2.

Asahi Shimbun. (2006a, July 5). pp. 1–2.

Asahi Shimbun. (2006b, July 6). pp. 1.

Asahi Shimbun. (2006c, July 17). pp. 1.

Asahi Shimbun. (2006d, September 19). pp. 1.

Asahi Shimbun Editorial. (1998, September 18). *Asahi Shimbun*, pp. 5.

Asahi Shimbun Editorial. (1999, March 25). *Asahi Shimbun*, pp. 5.

Asahi Shimbun Editorial. (2002a, November 13). *Asahi Shimbun*, pp. 2.

Asahi Shimbun Editorial. (2002b, December 9). *Asahi Shimbun*, pp. 2.

Asahi Shimbun Editorial. (2004a, January 30). *Asahi Shimbun*, pp. 2.

Asahi Shimbun Editorial. (2004b, March 12). *Asahi Shimbun*, pp. 2.

Gaimushō (The Ministry of Foreign Affairs of Japan). (1999). *Bluebook 1999* (p. Part 1, Chapter 1, Section 2(2)). Gaimushō (The Ministry of Foreign Affairs of Japan). Retrieved from http://www.mofa.go.jp/mofaj/gaiko/bluebook/99/1st/index.html

Gaimushō (The Ministry of Foreign Affairs of Japan). (2007). *Bluebook 2007 online edition* (p.Chapter 2 (1)). Gaimushō (The Ministry of Foreign Affairs of Japan). Retrieved fromhttp://www.mofa.go.jp/mofaj/gaiko/bluebook/2007/pdf/pdfs/2_1.pdf

Green, M. J. (2001). *Japan's Reluctant Realism: Foreign Policy Challenges in an Era of Uncertain Power*. New York: Palgrave.

Wada, H., Yamamuro, J., Yamaguchi, N., Mizuno, S., Takasaki, H., Tanaka, S., Shimizu, Y., Komori, T., Kimiya, S. K., Kawasaki, A. & Ishizaka, K. (2008). *Kyodo Teigen: Tai Kitachosen Seisaku no Tenkan wo. Sekai.*

Hwang, B. (2006). Seoul's Policy towards Pyongyang: Strategic Culture and the Negligibility of Japan. In L. Hagström & M. Söderberg (Eds.), *North Korea Policy: Japan and the Great Powers* (pp. 53–72). Oxford: Routledge & The European Institute of Japanese Studies, Stockholm School of Economics.

Ishihara, S. & Abe, S. (2003). Kangan-Kokka tono Ketsubetsu no Toki. *Bungeishunju,* 112–120.

Kabashima, I., Takeshita. T. & Serikawa, Y. (2007). *Media to Seiji.* Tokyo: Yūhikaku ARMA.

Kamiya, M. (2000). Japanese Foreign Policy toward Northeast Asia. In T. Inoguchi & J. Purnendra (Eds.), *Japanese Foreign Policy Today: A Reader* (pp. 226–251). New York: Palgrave.

Katzenstein, P. J. (1998). *Cultural Norms and National Security: Police and Military in Postwar Japan.* Ithaca: Cornell University Press.

Maruyama, N. (2003). Kenshō Rachi Hōdō–Jiyū de Shinjitsu no Hōdō wa Dekiteiruka. *Sekai,* pp. 127–135.

Morris-Suzuki, T. (2003a). Hisuterī no Seijigaku – Amerika no Iraku, Nihon no Kitachōsen. *Sekai,* 230–240.

Morris-Suzuki, T. (2003b). The Politics of Hysteria: America's Iraq, Japan's North Korea. *Japan in the World (Sekai),* Number 710.

Murata, K. (2004). Japanese Domestic Politics and the U.S.-Japan-ROK Security Relationship. In T. Kim & B. Glosserman (Eds.), *The Future of U.S.-Korea-Japan Relations: Balancing values and interests* (pp. 140–149). Washington D.C.: Center for Strategic and International Studies.

Ōtake, H. (2003). *Nihon-gata Popyurizumu–Seiji e no Kitai to Genmetsu.* Tokyo: Chūōkōron Shinsha.

Ōtake, H. (2006). *Koizumi Junichirō Popyurizumu Kenkyū – Sono Senryaku to Shuhō.* Tokyo: Toyo Keizai Shimposha.

Pempel, T.J. (2007). Japanese Strategy under Koizumi. In G. Rozman, K. Togo, & J. P. Ferguson (Eds.), *Japanese Strategic Thought toward Asia* (pp. 109–133). New York: Palgrave Macmillan.

Samuels, R. J. (2007a). New Fighting Power! Japan's Growing Maritime Capabilities and East Asian Security. *International Security, 32*, 84–112.

Samuels, R. J. (2007b). *Securing Japan: Tokyo's Grand Strategy and the Future of East Asia.* Ithaca: Cornell University Press.

Shinoda, T. (2007). *Koizumi Diplomacy: Japan's Kantei Approach to Foreign and Defense Affairs.* Seattle: University of Washington Press.

Steinhoff, P. (2004). Kidnapped Japanese in North Korea: The New Left Connection. *The Journal of Japanese Studies, 30*(1), 123–142.

Tadokoro, M. (2000). The Media in US-Japan Relations: National Media in Transnational Relations. In G. Curtis (Ed.), *New Perspectives on US-Japan Relations* (pp.175–212). Tokyo: Japan Center for International Exchange.

Tanaka, H. (2009). *Gaikō no Chikara (The Power of Diplomacy).* Tokyo: Nihon Keizai Shimbun Shuppansha.

Togo, K. (2005a). Greater Self-Assertion and Nationalism in Japan. *The Copenhagen Journal of Asian Studies, 21*, 8–44.

Togo, K. (2005b). *Japan's Foreign Policy 1945-2003: The Quest for Proactive Policy.* Leiden: Brill Academic Publishers.

Yamaguchi, A. (an interview by Katsuyuki Yakushiji). (2005). Liberal Journalism in Japan: An Endangered Species, *Japan Echo*, 49–55.

Yamakoshi, S. & Hirai, T. (2008). Media Hōdō to Seron Chōsa ni miru Nihon no Jiko Imēji. In Y. Ōishi & N. Yamamoto (Eds.), *Imēji no Naka no Nihon – Sofuto Pawā Saikō* (pp. 39–57). Tokyo: Keio University Press.

Yamamoto, S. (1983). *Kūki no Kenkyu.* Tokyo: Bungeishunjū. *Yomiuri Shimbun.* (2002a). *Nihon no Yoron (Japanese Public Opinion).* Tokyo: Kobundo.

Yomiuri Shimbun. (2002b, September 18). pp. 1.

Yomiuri Shimbun. (2002c, September 20). pp. 2.

Yomiuri Shimbun. (2004, September 17). pp. 3.

Yomiuri Shimbun. (2006a, July 6). pp. 1–2.

Yomiuri Shimbun. (2006b, July 6). pp. 1.

Yomiuri Shimbun. (2006c, July 7). pp. 3.

Yomiuri Shimbun Editorial. (1999a, January 1). *Yomiuri Shimbun*, pp. 3.

Yomiuri Shimbun Editorial. (1999b, May 3). *Yomiuri Shimbun*, pp. 3.

Yomiuri Shimbun Editorial. (2002a, May 3). *Yomiuri Shimbun,* pp. 3.
Yomiuri Shimbun Editorial. (2002b, October 16). *Yomiuri Shimbun,* pp. 3.
Yomiuri Shimbun Editorial. (2002c, December 5). *Yomiuri Shimbun,* pp. 3.
Yomiuri Shimbun Editorial. (2003a, January 30). *Yomiuri Shimbun,* pp. 3.
Yomiuri Shimbun Editorial. (2003b, April 27). *Yomiuri Shimbun,* pp. 3.
Yomiuri Shimbun Editorial. (2003c, December 14). *Yomiuri Shimbun,* pp. 3.
Yomiuri Shimbun Editorial. (2004a, February 1). *Yomiuri Shimbun,* pp. 3.
Yomiuri Shimbun Editorial. (2004b, February 26). *Yomiuri Shimbun,* pp. 3.
Yomiuri Shimbun Editorial. (2004c, April 23). *Yomiuri Shimbun,* pp. 3.
Yomiuri Shimbun Editorial. (2006a, July 24). *Yomiuri Shimbun,* pp. 3.
Yomiuri Shimbun Editorial. (2006b, September 20). *Yomiuri Shimbun,* pp.3.
Yomiuri Shimbun Editorial. (2006c, October 13). *Yomiuri Shimbun,* pp. 3.
Yomiuri Shimbun Political Section. (2006). *Gaiko wo Kenka ni shita Otoko– Koizumi Gaiko 2000 nichi no Shinjitsu.* Tokyo: Shinchosha.

Chapter Six

Reporting of the World's Biggest Single Plane Crash

Christopher Hood

Introduction

Journalism needs a steady diet of news. A good newspaper, however, will have a healthy balance of different news stories covering what its readership likes to read. Different newspapers have different readerships with different demands, and so the content between newspapers inevitably varies. Furthermore the way in which newspapers cover the same story may also vary due to the demands of its readership, the focus of the newspaper, and its access to information. But there are some types of news stories that lead to the usual diet being put to one side. Amongst these are disasters. These are stories on which journalists and readers alike will gorge themselves.

There are many types of disasters. What unites most of them is the human factor. Even so-called "natural disasters" are often disastrous due to their impact on humans rather than nature. There are many reasons why people take an interest in the news about a disaster: compassion and concern for others, an almost pornographic desire to see in reality an event which they can usually only see portrayed in a movie, the unusual and scale nature of such events, and a desire to be informed. For most, there is also a feeling of "at least it did not happen to me." And so it was with my initial interest in the crash of a Japan Airlines flight in the mid-1980s.

Background

On August 12, 1985 I was on holiday in the South of France. The headlines of the evening newspapers were about a plane crash in Japan. It was, as far as I remember, the first time I saw Japan in the news. Even upon returning to the UK a few days later, the crash of JAL flight 123 was still the leading news story. Indeed, this was no ordinary crash. This was the first time that a Boeing 747, the original "jumbo jet" and the symbol of the modern jet-set age, had crashed seemingly due to anything other than pilot error or terrorism. The death toll was also unprecedented; 520 had lost their lives. Remarkably there were also 4 survivors. The passenger manifest included one Japanese victim known internationally: Kyū Sakamoto (real name Hisashi Ōshima), who remains the only Japanese to have topped the US Billboard charts (in 1963 with *Ue-o Muite Arukō*, more commonly known as *Sukiyaki*). In the days following the crash, notes (*isho*) written by passengers during the 32 minutes between the plane developing a problem and its eventual crash were also found. The news even highlighted the timing of the disaster: August 12 marks the start of *Obon* (Festival of the Dead), when many Japanese return to their ancestral home towns to see family and relations and to pay respects to their ancestors.

In 1985 I had no idea that I would ever go on to conduct research about this crash. Indeed, at the time I had no particular connections to Japan and the idea of studying the language and country came to me only years later, with the decision to become an academic in 1993. After completing my PhD and a book about education reforms in Japan (Hood, 2001), I completed a book about Japan's *shinkansen* high-speed train and how it combinatively reflects and influences many aspects of Japanese society (Hood, 2006). And so I was ready to embark on a new study. Around this time I learned that a friend working at JAL, Keith Haines, had been the person who looked after the family of the sole British victim of the crash. I inquired if he would be willing to speak to my students about the events and his experiences. In the end, Keith was joined by Peter Mathews, whose son Kimble and fiancée, Nishiguchi Masako, perished in the crash. Concerned that their talks would lack impact if the students had no background knowledge of the crash, it was agreed that I would provide an introduction.

So it was that in early 2007 I began to research Japan Air Lines (JAL) flight JL123. I was struck not only by the number of webpages about the crash, but particularly the number and variation of videos on *YouTube* about the crash. What was also noticeable was that many of these had been uploaded around the time I was beginning my research, surprising as the crash had occurred nearly 22 years earlier in the pre-Internet age. Clearly some people were making a conscious decision to go back through old material on the crash and make it accessible. As I progressed in my research, I learned of more extensive photographic records that existed and Peter informed me that he had kept a diary during the time and kindly offered me access to it. Such resources are unusual yet invaluable to research. This accumulation of events left me with the feeling that it was not simply that I could do some additional research about the crash, but that I had the foundation of a book in English that told the story of this dramatic event.

Deciding to write a book about the JL123 crash was in the end a relatively easy decision to make. The key then was to identify the themes it would cover. Rather than a narrative about the crash itself, I decided to use this event to study broader aspects of Japanese society. I would start with the webpages and *YouTube* videos that had been partly responsible for initiating this research. With the wealth of additional resources I had been provided, I wanted to look at issues related to memorialisation of the crash and the behaviour and actions of the bereaved families (*izoku*), which would necessitate inclusion of Japanese attitudes to death and religion. But this was not enough; there was still missing something.

Having taught a course about the media in Japan, I was acutely aware of the lack of resources for students taking the course. This lack of literature may have been due to an underlying problem; what was there to write about that was original given that the underlying conclusion of studies of the Japanese media was overwhelmingly similar in its criticism: Japanese media is largely timid, serving as a mouthpiece for the government. The Japanese media did not fulfill the function of "watchdog," investigating the workings of companies, the bureaucracy and politicians to ensure that no wrong doing is taking place. The cosy relationship between government and journalists through the Press Clubs (*kisha kurabu*), whereby journalists were provided with space and press releases had been suggested as part of the basis for the conclusion. Scandals were likely to only be uncovered and reported on by foreign media, which had limited access to information, or by tabloid weekly publications, which often lacked credibility in the formalized structure of Japanese society. Cases such as the reporting of the Lockheed Scandal, first broken by foreign media, and then picked up by the Japanese media, although exceptional in themselves, seem to support this view of the Japanese media. Indeed, Seidenstecker's (1984) summary of the scandal cuts to the core of the concerns of Japanese media, when he offered that newspapers reported the original scandal in almost tiresome detail without pushing their efforts to the level of good investigative reporting. Such journalism

Reporting of the World's Biggest Single Plane Crash 135

was left to a monthly magazine, essentially making public what all journalists knew, but didn't render in print.

It became apparent as I studied the crash that through this research, I could test various assumptions about Japanese media that continued to exist. To this end, I decided to add an additional dimension to my study; local newspapers. Whilst the crash had made headlines internationally and a study of the national newspapers alone may have seemed sufficient for content coverage, as I gathered materials about the crash, differences between local versus national reporting became apparent. Over 80 books have been written in Japanese taking up the JL123 crash in some way. Among these books are two novels; *Shizumanu Taiyō* (*The Sun Does Not Set*) by Toyoko Yamasaki and *Kuraimāzu Hai* (*Climber's High*) by Hideo Yokoyama. The second takes up the story of a journalist who is put in charge of how his local newspaper covers the JL123 crash. The author was a journalist at a local newspaper and was one of those who covered the JL123. Although the novel may have been a work of fiction, it was likely to reflect at least some of the issues that faced a local newspaper in reporting this global story.

METHODOLOGY

I wanted my study of the reporting of the JL123 crash to cover both the process of getting the stories and also how the final product appears in the news, an interest for which print media is much more accessible. Furthermore, memorial events, which were a key part of my study, were reported on in greater depth in by the print media. Thus, whilst there was TV reporting of the crash, I decided to concentrate on newspapers.

In gaining an understanding about the process of gathering the news there was one resource that was particularly instructive. The editorial department of the *Asahi Shimbun*, one of the five main national newspapers, published a book, *Nikkō Janboki Tsuiraku: Asahi Shimbun no 24ji* (Asahi Shimbun Shakaibu, 2006), which focuses on its work during the first 24 hours of the crash. This was the first Japanese book that I read about the crash and it was instructive not only about the work of the journalists but also about the events that day. I also wanted to interview journalists who had covered the crash in 1985. Over 20 years had passed since the event and so memories about what happened would likely not be reliable, however, the processes about how information was obtained were likely to reflect practices of the time. Further, given the exceptionality of the circumstances, such recollections were less likely to be forgotten or be inaccurate. I already had some contacts in the Japanese media, and indeed one of these had even been involved with the events in 1985. Other key contacts were made in a less predictable fashion.

I first travelled to Ueno-mura, the village in which the crash site is located, for the anniversary of the crash in 2007. My primary aim was to observe the *izoku* and how the memorialization was done and also watch how these events were covered by the media. Not wanting to disturb them, I had no intention of interviewing any *izoku* myself. Should they approach me, I would explain my intentions and then, if they permitted, I would ask questions. I also had no intention of approaching any of the many journalists assembled there as I did not want to get in the way of them doing their work. Of course, what I had failed to take account of is the degree to which I would stick out from the crowd. Ueno-mura is a village of around 1,600 people, virtually all Japanese. Similarly in most years, almost all of the *izoku* and others who go to be part of the memorialization are Japanese. All of the journalists that I have ever seen there for the anniversary are either Japanese or Asian. I, in contrast, look neither. Consequently I was soon approached by inquisitive journalists keen to find out who I was and why I was there. Upon discovering that I spoke Japanese, it was not long before I was surrounded by journalists and interviewed by many of them. This experience has been repeated on each of the occasions that I have been to the anniversary events, often with the interviews effectively being repeated as journalists from any one organisation tend to vary from year to year in covering this story. The first time I initially found it a little frustrating to be interviewed as I saw it

Reporting of the World's Biggest Single Plane Crash 137

as hindering what I was trying to do, but then I realised that through this process I could get a better understanding of how the journalists operate. Furthermore, I could turn interviews around and ask the journalists about their work. As is common practice in Japan, there was also an exchange of name cards so I was able to contact these journalists at a later date to ask follow up questions or to ask for help in contacting journalists who had covered the crash in 1985 or otherwise ask for help in getting materials related to the JL123 crash and the coverage by their organisation.

A significant part of my study of the reporting was based on use of the newspapers themselves. Whilst it was possible to access some articles using an electronic database, the main problem with this approach was that in most cases I could not obtain a copy of the whole page of the newspaper, and therefore I was unable to get an overall impression of the coverage of the crash compared to coverage of other stories. It also did not give me adequate results in terms of what imagery, such as photographs, was used. Consequently I wanted to get hold of my own copies of the newspapers to read through.

There were, of course, two fundamental considerations regarding use of newspaper coverage of the crash; which newspapers to study and what time period to use. With the crash happening on August 12 and the first reports appearing in the newspapers of August 13, I decided that in terms of timing, a comparison of the coverage up to the end of August would be sufficient. In terms of the newspapers, it was natural that I would look at the five main national newspapers: the *Asahi Shimbun,* the *Mainichi Shimbun,* the *Nikkei Shimbun,* the *Sankei Shimbun* and the *Yomiuri Shimbun*. However, having been particularly alerted to the issue of local reporting by the novel *Kuraimāzu Hai*, I was keen to also study some local newspapers. Selecting the *Jōmō Shimbun,* which is based in Gunma Prefecture, where the crash occurred, and which is seen as the basis for the fictional *Kita-Kantō Shimbun* in *Kuraimāzu Hai*, was obvious. Although when travelling around Japan, I made a cursory study of a number of local newspapers in libraries, for my detailed research I wanted to use a local newspaper that had no significant connection with the crash. As there were no passengers and crew from Okayama on JL123, the *San'yō Shimbun,* published in Okayama, seemed appropriate for my needs. I was keen to use the libraries in the home city for the two local newspapers and for the *Sankei Shimbun* as I believed this would give me good access to all of the newspapers and allow for additional comparison with stories on other dates outside my main study as well as looking at contemporary papers to see if there had been any obvious change in style.

Analytical Points

In terms of looking at the similarities and differences between the various newspapers, there was a variety of ways to do this enabling me to consider the issues that concerned me. The studies I made were as follows:

Headline analysis: By looking at the wording of the headlines and whether JL123 was the main story or not on each day, it was possible to ascertain to what degree the story was of interest to a newspaper and also the degree to which newspapers used similar phraseology. It was expected, for example, that the *Nikkei Shimbun,* given its focus on business news, would not have as much coverage of JL123 as the other national newspapers. Additionally, for example, with the 40th anniversary of the end of World War II, which occurred just a few days after the crash, there was the possibility of seeing a variation in which story newspapers would cover. It was also expected that the *Jōmō Shimbun*'s coverage, being local to the crash site, would have greater coverage than the *San'yō Shimbun* and perhaps even some of the national newspapers.

Content analysis: I was particularly keen to test the idea that Japanese journalists are heavily reliant upon press releases for preparing stories and that this would lead to a degree of commonality of content between newspapers. I decided upon approaching the content analysis by looking at both what articles in relation to the crash included each day and also at the actual wording of the articles. Given the huge volume of articles written, I decided the best way in which to test this second point was to look at articles where the use of press releases for the basis of articles was inevitable. Announcements were made each day about the number of victims identified that day and who they were. Newspapers would get this information from the authorities rather than doing their own research; indeed, there would be no need to use resources doing their own research since it would be known that such information would be provided. Therefore, looking at whether the newspapers published such information and whether there were any variations provided a means to compare the newspapers over the period of my study. As these articles provided the basis for comparing the content of articles across the newspapers, the remainder of my content analysis concentrated primarily upon counting the number of articles written in relation to JL123, which section of the newspaper they appeared in and what the articles were primarily about (e.g. about the survivors, the cause of the crash, etc.).

Local versus National: Given that most purchasers of local newspapers also purchase national newspapers, I wanted to test whether the local newspapers do in fact avoid commentary on national news and prefer to focus on local issues. Correspondingly, I looked for signs of the newspapers trying to find a "local angle" to a national story. In the case of the *Jōmō Shimbun*, the local angle appeared obvious, but there was actually more than one; the crash site was in its territory, there was a passenger on board from Gunma and the Prime Minister at the time, Yasuhiro Nakasone, was also from Gunma.

Photographic analysis: Building on the previous analysis and having read in *Kuraimāzu Hai* about the concept that one way in which local newspapers can compete with the national newspapers is by doing things differently, in particular by including more photographs, I also analysed the variation in use of photographs (number, size and content) between the newspapers.

Additional Content Analysis: An example of additional content analysis came in the form of the details of the crew and passenger list and how the newspapers presented this. Although these lists were, in many cases, updated over the ensuing days, the way in which the list was presented in the first day's newspaper revealed the differences in resources available at each newspaper and, to at least some degree, an apparent difference in interests also. Further, while the main work of the content analysis focused on the crash itself, I also did some additional analysis of articles written about the anniversary each year. For this analysis, I was primarily concerned with (a) to what degree the level of coverage varied year-by-year and (b) to what degree there was a different level of coverage for the JL123 crash compared to other accidents. For the former, rather than study all newspapers, I used an electronic database to count the number of articles and their length, focussing on the *Asahi Shimbun* and the *Nikkei Shimbun*. As I was more concerned in this analysis about changes in coverage longitudinally rather than between newspapers, I considered the focus on the *Asahi Shimbun* as an example of the national newspapers to be sufficient, but also decided to study the *Nikkei Shimbun* as, given its focus on business, the inclusion of articles, particularly if their number or length increased, may highlight that additional analysis of the contents of the articles may have been needed. The same process was used when making a comparison with three other events; the China Airlines flight CI140 crash at Nagoya Airport in 1994, the Great Hanshin Earthquake of 1995, and the JR West Fukuchiyama Line train derailment in Amagasaki in 2005. Whilst each of these was different in nature and scale to JL123, I was looking to see whether there were any obvious patterns in the level of reporting.

The Crash and Its Memorialization

Japan Air Lines (JAL) flight JL123 took off from Tōkyō's Haneda airport at 18:12 bound for Itami Airport in Ōsaka. The plane itself was a specially adapted Boeing 747, designed specifically for the domestic market in that the seating capacity was over 530 rather than the more typical 300 to 350 that would be found on international routes around the world (JAL, 1985).

Reporting of the World's Biggest Single Plane Crash 141

The plane was almost full with 15 crew and 509 passengers on board. The passengers included many families as it was the middle of the school holidays and 12 August marks the start of Ōbon when businessmen find it easier to take holiday due to the widespread social expectation that many people will return to their ancestral home to see relations and pay respects to their ancestors in the local graveyard (Hood, 2011).

Twelve minutes into the flight, there was an explosion. Unknown to those on board, a large portion of the rear stabilizer had broken off. What the cockpit crew was aware of, however, was that there was an immediate loss of hydraulic fluid, making the plane almost impossible to fly. Indeed in communications with air traffic control, the Captain declared the plane to be "uncontrollable." At 18:56, some 32 minutes after the initial explosion, the plane crashed on a ridge of mountain in Ueno-mura, a remote village in central Japan. Today the official name of the crash site's location is Osutaka-no-One, "the ridge on Osutaka," which reflects the popular, yet inaccurate, belief that the mountain was Osutaka, as the site is colloquially referred to, rather than Mount Takamagahara (AAIC, 1987).

The search and rescue (SAR) activities started soon after the plane disappeared from radars, but due to problems in locating the crash, media helicopters were amongst the first to identify the site. The site was not finally confirmed until after 5:30 the following morning, some ten and a half hours after the crash. It took another five hours for SAR teams to reach the site, by which time some from the media were also on site. Despite the tardiness, four survivors were found, and the photographs and video footage of them being taken from the site, as well as some of the crash site itself, are amongst the most iconic and well-known images in Japanese journalism history. The media also covered the activities in Fujioka, the city some 60km from the crash site, where families gathered to identify their loved ones and their remains. The probable cause of the crash was deemed to be due to the faulty repair of the rear bulkhead of the plane following a previous accident in 1978 (AAIC, 1987). This was something that Boeing itself suggested and the accident investigation appeared happy to support this. There continue to be books written in Japanese about the crash and many of these have raised questions about the legitimacy of Boeing's claim and the findings of the official investigation, with some calling for a re-investigation.

Every year there are three main events concerning the memorialisation of the crash in a process which I call the "Osutaka Pilgrimage." The first of these takes place on the evening of August 11 and has been taking place every year since 1995. The ceremony is known as a *tōrōnagashi*, which is typically translated as "lantern festival," naming that does not capture the nuance of what takes place. Lanterns are laid out on the ground so that people can write messages on them. After some speeches and singing of songs, candles are lit inside the lanterns, which are then floated down the river in front of Ueno-mura village hall. On August 12, many families travel to the crash site and, as well as visiting the *bohyō* (marker posts) for their loved one(s), visit the collective memorials and attend a ceremony held in the morning. In the evening two back-to-back ceremonies are held at the Irei-no-Sono memorial in the centre of the village. The first of these includes laying flowers in front of the memorial towers, whilst the second has the lighting of candles and a minute's silence to coincide with the time of the crash. All of these events are covered by the media.

Due to the continued, and seemingly increasing interest in the crash, not only in Japan but globally, the various stories about what happened, the conspiracy theories and such like, I suggest that JL123 is Japan's and the aviation's world's equivalent to the sinking of the Titanic.

Results of My Research

Of the various areas of the reporting of the JL123 crash and its memorialisation, one of the first that had to be done by the newspapers was producing the passenger and crew list for publication on the morning of August 13. On the evening of August 12, the TV news had already

Reporting of the World's Biggest Single Plane Crash   143

announced the passenger list, but the newspapers attempted to include details such as having the names written in the correct *kanji* (the passenger list was initially provided in *katakana* format only), victims' ages, residences, home addresses, and reasons for being on the flight. The variation in results clearly reflected the varied priorities of the newspapers as well as the variation in resources at their disposal. The *Asahi Shimbun*, for example, assigned 30 people to the task (Asahi Shimbun Shakaibu, 2006), leading to the most complete of the lists. The *Asahi Shimbun*'s list started on page two and continued to page three, and had detailed information for 62%, with *katakana* for the remaining 38% listed separately. It also had all of the crew listed with facial photographs, presumably provided by JAL. The *Mainichi Shimbun*'s list was carried on page eight and included facial pictures for 36, with pictures of the crew included in an article on page 18. Unlike the *Asahi*, the *Mainichi* did not separate out those for whom additional information had not been found (about 55%). Also, unlike the *Asahi*, the *Mainichi*'s list of foreign passengers provided the names in Romanized letters rather than *katakana*. The *Yomiuri Shimbun*'s passenger list had details for only about 33% of passengers, but contained the most (89) photos. The *Sankei Shimbun* also managed to get 55 passenger photos and had details for about 33% of the passengers. As a business newspaper, the *Nikkei Shimbun* seemingly put no effort into getting details of the passengers, providing *kanji* for 19% of the Japanese passengers and the rest in *katakana*, together with brief details for one businessman. Moreover, whereas the other papers continued to update the passenger list over the following days, the *Nikkei* did not. As for local newspapers, no passenger or crew lists were carried on the first day, a sign that they did not have the resources for this task on that first night.

Considering the headlines of the newspapers, there was, as could be expected, a high degree of commonality on the first day. Three of the five national newspapers used exactly the same headline, and while all five used the term *tsuiraku,* meaning (plane) "crash," just four specifically mentioned that it was a JAL plane. However, the side-headline (*waki-no-midashi*) on the right-hand side of the paper revealed greater diversity.

All the papers also featured a picture of the crash site—three of them using the image taken by an SDF helicopter, whilst the *Asahi* and *Yomiuri* used images taken from their own helicopters. Looking at the local newspapers, the *Jōmō Shimbun*'s headline was different to that of the national newspapers, as it did not note the number of passengers, but added that the plane was a jumbo jet and noted that there was a fire. This last point was perhaps needed as it did not use a picture of the crash site unlike the national newspapers. But the main article also mentioned there being a local victim on the plane, clearly demonstrating that local newspapers look to find a local angle to any story. Other local newspapers' front pages more closely resembled those of the national newspapers, often using the same SDF picture of the crash site, indicative of their need to rely other agencies in the case of large scale events. Although the *Jōmō Shimbun* gave preference to Nagano over Gunma as being the location of the crash site, its accompanying map of the front page was a larger scale than those in the national newspapers as the local names would be familiar to readers.

On August 14, more variation in the headlines and stories on the front page was evident. Whilst one may expect to see stories about the survivors, this did not feature in any of the five national newspapers, probably due to the fact that it featured in the evening editions on August 13. As the recovery of part of the tail of the plane from Sagami Bay occurred late evening August 13, after the main evening television news, the newspapers may have considered this as being their best opportunity to provide a story which readers may have not been aware of. All five national papers included a headline or side headline about this, but for two the main story was the number of bodies that had been identified, with the *Yomiuri* saying 50 and the *Mainichi* 80. The focus of the local newspapers' morning editions on the same day, differing from the national papers, was on the fact that survivors had been found, most likely as local papers lacked evening editions. Having a local photographer on the scene also meant that the *Jōmō Shimbun* was able to include an independent photo, which accounted for about half of the page, to go with the story.

Reporting of the World's Biggest Single Plane Crash   145

The diversity in the articles increased over time. This may be due to a desire to continue to run with the JL123 story during what tends to be a relatively quiet time of the year for the media. But the lack of any significant developments in relation to the crash meant that newspapers had to go hunting for a story to feature. When a new story did break, commonality returned. Thus, by the third day of reporting (August 16), the *Nikkei*'s morning edition had dropped JL123 as its main story, turning instead to a business-related story, although a JL123-related story was on the front page. The *Yomiuri* also dropped JL123 as its main story, focussing instead on a possible increase in defense spending, but kept JL123 as a front-page item. *Asahi*'s main story was still JL123, whilst *Sankei* led with a story about survivors, and an assertion that had the SAR been faster, more would have lived. This article story was based on interviews with doctors in Fujioka conducting the identification process, and so it reflected investigative work by the journalists rather than merely relying upon press releases. The *Mainichi* had a surprising headline—that there was an initial explosion of the rear bulkhead; the story suggests that this subsequently damaged the tail of the plane. The story also questioned a link to a previous accident in 1978 at Itami Airport, when the plane had made a heavy landing. The content was based on comments from the Aircraft Accident Investigation Commission (AAIC) and Gunma police's investigation team, meaning that similar to the *Sankei*, the *Mainichi* engaged in a degree of investigative reporting.

Considering when newspapers stopped running JL123 stories on their front page, significant differences emerge. Not surprisingly, the *Nikkei* was the first stop carrying JL123 stories on its front page on August 21, having dropped JL123 as its main story on August 15. It did not run content again as its main story during the period that I was studying. The next to drop JL123 from the front page was the *Mainichi* on August 26. It had first dropped JL123 as its main story on August 21, after which is was the top story again the next day, before being dropped as the main story again on August 23. The *Asahi* first did not have a JL123 story on its front page on August 27, having dropped it first as it main story on

August 22 and then again on four more occasions. As above, the *Yomiuri* dropped JL123 as its main story on August 16, and it did not feature as the main story on five more occasions before the story was dropped from the front page on August 29. With its headquarters in Ōsaka, in the Kansai area of Japan and where many victims were from, it is not surprising that the *Sankei* had the latest drop date. Although crash content had been dropped as the main story starting on August 21, as of August 30, no JL123 content featured on its front page. Looking at the local newspapers, due to their desire to focus on local news, there was a higher tendency to both drop JL123 as the top story, on August 16 in most cases, and from its front page altogether, around August 27. Even the *Jōmō Shimbun* first dropped JL123 as its main story on August 17, when it focussed on the opening of the Kanetsu Expressway, although the crash returned to being the top story on subsequent days and remained on the front page until 31 August, later even than any of the national newspapers.

Despite this degree of diversity in the reporting of the JL123 crash, one area where I expected that there would be greater consistency was in the reporting of identification of remains. As journalists were not allowed in the morgues, I assumed that they would be reliant upon press releases for getting the information, and that this in turn would lead to similar reporting. This, in fact, was not the case. Looking at the papers on August 20, all of the newspapers included a list of those recently identified. However, the way they are presented and the order in which the names appear are different. The *Nikkei*, as may be expected, merely listed 33 names and ages while using the least space. The *Asahi* list included the city in which they were resident, but the names are not in the same order as the *Nikkei* list. The order of the *Mainichi* list was different again and it included full addresses and professions. The *Mainichi* was also the only paper to note the nationality of the Japan-resident-foreigner identified. The *Sankei* had full addresses for the victims and also provided employment details. Further, the name order was different and only 28 victims were listed. The *Yomiuri* list included 32 victims, together with age and city and prefecture of residence. So even with content that was almost

Reporting of the World's Biggest Single Plane Crash   147

certainly reliant upon an official press release, differences emerged due to the research the paper had been willing and able to do about victims. Looking at the local newspapers, while the *Jōmō Shimbun* listed victims' names, ages, addresses and employment, local newspapers tended to be particularly concerned with identification of local victims. Somewhat surprisingly, local newspapers also appeared to be more concerned than the national newspapers in reporting about the identification of, and the wakes and funerals of the famous victims, such as Sakamoto Kyū (singer/actor, born 1941).

Taking up the use of photographs in articles, on August 14, for example, newspapers carried a number of photos of the accident in addition to facial photos accompanying the list of victims and other file pictures, predominantly of the survivors and the rescue effort. The largest number of pictures was 11 in the *Mainichi*, whilst the *Asahi* had ten, the *Yomiuri* had nine, the *Sankei* had eight and the *Nikkei* just four. In most cases, the photos took up about one-third of page space. The relatively high use of photos demonstrates the scale and visual character of the event. The local newspaper *Jōmō Shimbun* carried significant coverage of the crash in its August 14 edition, including photos only on pages 4 and 5 together with a detailed map. The largest of these pictures, showing the search through wreckage, accounts for about three-quarters of the page. Ten days later, on August 24, the newspaper further demonstrated its photographic advantage by having a two-page spread of pictures with one picture representing each day in the "two week" period since the crash.

There are a few final observations I should add about my study of the newspaper reporting of the JL123 crash in 1985. Although the main comparisons were based on the morning editions of the five main national newspapers, as these have the highest circulation, I also looked at evening editions. Doing this led me to three conclusions. First, in order to get the full picture of an event, one would need to get both the morning and evening editions of papers as the morning edition of the next day does not necessarily contain information or articles that were contained in the evening edition on the previous day. Second, some of the articles in the evening editions appeared to be less conservative than the morning editions, with more articles critical of the SAR, for example. Third, the evening editions were much more visually based, with higher use of photographs (in some cases nearly a whole page is dedicated to one or more photographs) as well as graphs and other figures. Another observation relates to the reporting of local newspapers. Although I thought that the *San'yō Shimbun* met the criteria that I was looking for as a location with no passengers or crew among the victims, the reality was that even this paper carried a number of articles relating to "local victims" and the human-interest angle of "local survivors."

Turning to what I refer to as the Osutaka Pilgrimage, the media presence at the anniversary events each year is significant and appears to be disproportionately high compared to other transportation-related disasters. In part this may be due to the cocktail of issues, beyond the scope of this chapter, that make JL123 of interest. However, the relative lack of other political and business related news at this time of year may also be a contributing factor to what has been referred to as "August journalism" with its emphasis on memorialization (Satō, 2005, p. 129). By continuing to report about JL123, the media aided the aims of many of the *izoku* in ensuring the accident is not forgotten. This is an important point in terms of the legacy of those who have been lost but in also relation to the aim to promote aviation safety further. However, some of this happens at a rather superficial level for whilst articles may refer to the tragedy of 1985 and discuss the pain that families have felt as a consequence and these articles may lead readers to considering whether aviation could be made safer, the message is an implied one. There is a lack of articles which show that the newspaper has done additional investigations or analysis about aviation safety or the way in which accidents in Japan would be investigated, or whether there should even be a reinvestigation into the cause of the JL123 crash itself.

Reporting of the World's Biggest Single Plane Crash   149

One thing which is noticeable about a number of the interviews of the *izoku* conducted by the media was the level of co-operation between other media members. Perhaps out of a desire not to disturb the *izoku* any more than necessary, it is not uncommon to see one journalist interview the *izoku* and then turn round after the interview has finished and brief journalists from competitor organizations about what was said. This particularly happens at Osutaka-no-One, perhaps due to the limited space at the site. However, it should also be noted that in their need to find a story of interest many more *izoku* are interviewed whose story does not appear in print.

On August 12, the media are amongst the first to arrive at Osutaka-no-One. They effectively set up camp and prepare their computers and, those who have them, also set up their satellite-link technology for filing the stories. Most companies have between two or three reporters, one responsible for photographs and the other(s) are for interviewing. Those doing the interviewing may walk between the car park and the crash site several times during the day as they look for people to interview. They may also go with *izoku* to their loved one's *bohyō* or just walk around the site to try to find someone to interview.

The number of articles, and their length, covering the anniversary events in Ueno-mura in the *Asahi Shimbun*'s morning and evening editions has varied over the years (see Figure 2; Web Appendix). It is clear that the number of articles increase with particular anniversaries (the tenth, the twentieth and particularly the twenty-fifth). However, there are other media-specific reasons for some of the results. For example the drop in 2007 was caused by 13 August being a press holiday, so there was no morning edition of the *Asahi Shimbun*. In comparison to other disasters, I found that whilst media coverage of the Great Hanshin Earthquake is greater than that given to JL123, the coverage is greater than for the Fukuchiyama Line derailment and it is not unusual for there to be no articles at all for the coverage of the China Airlines flight CI140 crash anniversary.

Conclusions

Rausch (2012) has used newspapers to get a "window" on his local community in Japan. For Rausch, the broadness of issues it covers and how it covers them is key. For my study, the way in which a single story was covered by a variety of newspapers was key.

JL123 was very much a global story. The plane, a Boeing 747 jumbo jet, was the symbol of the jet-age, and the death toll was unprecedented in the case of a single aircraft. For the Japanese, there were additional factors on interest about the crash. All but 22 of the 520 victims were Japanese. The plane was operated by the national flag carrier, Japan Air Lines. Considering these factors, it was only natural that the Japanese media covered the story in such detail. But the reporting was uniform neither among national newspapers nor across national to local newspapers. Several national newspapers showed their true colors by turning attention to other stories even in the immediate aftermath of the crash. The headline of the right-leaning *Yomiuri Shimbun* on August 16, only the third morning edition after the crash, cited a possible rise in defense spending and a controversial Yasukuni Shrine visit by a serving Prime Minister. The *Nikkei Shimbun's* coverage was minimal due to its focus on business news as well as its expectation that readers likely would get in-depth news about the crash from another major newspaper.

Although a high-profile story, local newspaper coverage was not without significance. While covering the basics, local coverage also looked for a decidedly local angle. For the *Jōmō Shimbun* the local angle was geographic—the crash occurred locally— as well demographic—a victim was from the area travelling to Ōsaka to see the popular high school baseball tournament at Kōshien Stadium. This allowed the paper to connect the two stories whilst the local team remained in the tournament. For other local newspapers, where a local link was not apparent, the local newspapers either worked to identify some local connection or turned attention to coverage of the famous victims. Local newspapers clearly have fewer resources than the national newspapers, meaning that, in competition with the national newspapers, local papers are at a significant disadvantage. However, this research suggested that rather than being rivals, local newspapers can complement national newspapers. They can cover aspects of the story that the national newspapers would not be able to cover due to its local nature. But more than that, local newspapers appear also to be able to use more visuals. National newspapers lack the luxury of being able to give up space to large or numerous pictures. Thus, use of visuals is for local newspapers one area where they have a relative advantage.

In many respects the JL123 crash was unusual, but the reporting of it is likely to have followed the norms of reporting in Japan at the time. Whilst there is a perception of there being uniformity across the Japanese media, this chapter has shown that there is actually a significant degree of diversity. Although it may be that we cannot find high levels of investigative journalism in Japan, perhaps due to the use of *kisha kurabu* and reliance on high subscription rates which means that exclusives have little impact upon sales, the case of JL123 also reveals that the media are capable of doing investigative journalism if the conditions are right. The bigger question may be why are such articles, for example the ones that may be found in evening editions according to my research, not be developed further in morning editions and why is it that they can seemingly be ignored by politicians and society alike? The way in which reporting is done may have changed over the years, but the reporting of the Osutaka Pilgrimage can still tell us much about how Japanese media operates. The choice of articles, their headlines, where they are placed in the newspaper and what visuals are used can tell us much about the values of an individual newspaper. In turn the newspapers can tell us much about the values of Japanese society.

References

AAIC (Aircraft Accident Investigation Commission, Ministry of Transport). (1987). *Aircraft Accident Investigation Report: JA8119*. Japanese version available at http://jtsb.mlit.go.jp/jtsb/aircraft/download/pdf/62-2-JA8119.pdf accessed 1 February 2007. English version available at http://www.mlit.go.jp/jtsb/eng-air_report/JA8119.pdf accessed 1 February 2007.

Asahi Shimbun Shakaibu. (2006). *Nikkō Janboki Tsuiraku: Asahi Shimbun no 24jin* (17th edition, first published in 1990). Tōkyō: Asahi Shimbun.

Hood, C. (2001). *Education Reform in Japan: Nakasone's Legacy*. London: Routledge.

Hood, C. (2006). *Shinkansen: From Bullet Train to Symbol of Modern Japan*. London: Routledge.

Hood, C. (2011). *Dealing with Disaster in Japan: Responses to the Flight JL123 Crash*. Abingdon, Oxon: Routledge.

JAL. (1985). "747SR Background Data", a memo from JAL Tōkyō to JAL London.

Rausch, A. S. (2012). *Japan's Local Newspapers: Chihoshi and Revitalization Journalism*. London, U.K.: Routledge.

Satō, T. (2005). *Hachigatsu Jūgonichi-no Shinwa: Shūsen Kinenbi-no Mediagaku*. Tōkyō: Chikuma Shinsho.

Seidensticker, E. (1984). Far Eastern Economic Review, Vol. 124, 7 June 1984.

Yamazaki, T. (2001) *Shizumanu Taiyō* (5 volumes). Tōkyō: Shinchōsha.

Yokoyama, H. (2006) *Kuraimāzu Hai*. Tōkyō: Bungei Shunjū.

Chapter Seven

Japanese Journalistic Communities

Politics, the Newspaper and *Nico Nico Dōga*

Keizo Nanri

Introduction

Three videos were uploaded to Japan's second largest video-sharing website *Nico Nico Dōga* on the night before the general election held on 22 December 2012. Two of the three showed two former prime ministers, Abe Shinzō and Asō Tarō, presenting their speeches, and the other a scene after their speeches. Comments typed in directly onto the screen by viewers showed their enthusiastic support of the two politicians in the first two videos and enormous hatred of the mass media in the last one (*Kakkō*, 2012; Mitshashi Takaaki Jimusho, 2012a, 2012b). This third video showed a group of people, who had come to Akihabara to support the two politicians, shouting at the journalists around the area where Abe and Asō had made their speeches. Expletives such as *Gomi!* (rubbish or bullshit), *Kaere!* (Go back where you belong!), *Baikokudo!* (traitor), and *Gokiburi!* (roaches) were heard over and over again in this video. These Liberal Democratic Party (LDP) supporters clearly despised the "Established News Media" (hereafter ENeM), especially the "liberal" ENeM represented by the *Asahi Shimbun*, and had no reservations about publically showing it.

Nico Nico Dōga (NND) began as a website where users uploaded and shared videos, usually of such activities as their own singing, dancing, and video game-playing performances, as well as slide shows, and video clips from *anime* and TV shows. However, this once purely private-theme oriented website has recently transitioned into a more politically committed Internet website with a real-world presence as well. In October 2010, NND set up a political news department, sent reporters to press conferences held at government ministry offices, and broadcast some of the press conferences live. NND accepted Abe Shinzō's proposal to host and broadcast a debate by 11 party leaders prior to the 2012 general election, attracting 1.4 million viewers (*The Asahi Shimbun Dejitaru*, 2012). Abe and Asō had been quite popular among NND viewers, a fact made more significant with the outcome of the election, which ended in a landslide victory for the LDP and restored Abe, Asō and the LDP to power. As a result, this has come to create a situation where news disseminated by the ENeM is critically reviewed by Internet news consumers who are sympathetic to the ruling party.

Naturally, the "friendly" relationship between the ruling party and NND users is welcomed neither by the *Asahi* nor critics of the so-called "*netto uyoku*" (the Net far-Right). Commenting on the 2012 debate broadcast live by NND, an article in *Webronza* (run by the *Asahi*) quoted a foreign journalist as saying that the viewers' comments on the screen of the debate are nothing but toilet graffiti (*Webronza*, 2012). Yasuda et al. (2013), with experience of the Net far-Right's activities over the years, assert that Internet users such as NND users are an undereducated coterie who spread anti-Korean and anti-Chinese rumours, and who are obsessed with attacking the liberal news media. Putting aside the *Asahi's* sarcastic comment to focus on the more restrained comments by Yasuda et al., even this criticism is questionable, since it is based on the assumption that the ENeM disseminates reliable information whereas Internet users spread unreliable anti-China/Korea information, all without critically reviewing the information the ENeM and NND videos actually disseminate.

The purpose of this chapter is thus to critically assess whether the forgoing assertions, and assumptions, are valid or not. This will be done by analysing Japanese newspaper editorials and political videos popular among NND viewers from the viewpoint of the homogeneity and specificity of the information disseminated by those editorials and videos.

METHODOLOGY: EDITORIALS VERSUS VIDEOS

A newspaper editorial (*shasetsu*) is usually a short essay, normally around 1,000 characters long, written by a senior journalist, a *ronsetsu iin* (editorial board member), and is seen to represent the institutional viewpoint of the newspaper (Kim, 1981; Freeman, 2000). An analysis of editorials thus helps to identify what the management of the newspaper believes, or pretends to believe, to be true. These institutionalised essays have been said to be largely homogeneous across newspapers in Japan and virtually innocuous in their effect on public thought (Kim, 1981; Inagaki, 1996; Freeman, 2000). Homogeneity refers to similarity and uniformity; an innocuous editorial would be an editorial that reviews social issues but neither identifies who is responsible for causing those issues nor provides specific and implementable solutions to those issues. Indeed, Nanri's (2004, 2005, 2006) studies on Japanese editorials demonstrated their homogeneity and innocuousness through a discourse analysis of Japanese editorials commenting on the 9/11 attacks in the US in 2001. More than a decade has passed since 2001, yet, homogeneity and innocuousness still appear to characterize Japanese editorials. Further to the social effect of newspaper editorials, Mitsuhashi (2012a, 2012b) has asserted that the ENeM has functioned largely as a mouthpiece for the Finance Ministry and the Bank of Japan (BOJ) and unanimously criticises Abenomics.

Interestingly from a research standpoint, it is under these circumstances that NND has gained popularity among Internet users.

Methodology

To achieve the purpose of the chapter, three issues were selected as analytical themes, and data to be analysed was selected accordingly from newspapers and videos (and video clips) uploaded to NND. The three analytical themes examined were: (1) national/East Asian security in relation to Japan's territorial issue over the Senaku Islands with China; (2) quantitative easing in Abenomics (i.e., a set of economic policies proposed by Prime Minister Abe Shinzō); and (3) Japan's participation in the Trans-Pacific Partnership (TPP) negotiations.

Data Selection and Analysis

A total of 277 newspaper editorials and 41 NND videos were reviewed in the present study. The editorials, dated 1 to 30 April 2013, were posted on the homepages of 37 Japanese newspapers. The videos were selected from NND's top 100 political videos (updated daily) on 17 and 24 April and 1 May 2013. The videos were selected from the top monthly 100 (rather than top daily 100) lists because (1) by selecting video data from top monthly 100 lists, one should be able to identify political videos popular among NND viewers over time, and (2) this method of selecting data enables one to keep the amount of video data manageable.

Data Analysis

The following steps are taken to analyse the data:

> 1. Identification of the type of homogeneity (or diversity) in newspaper editorials by identifying any particular theory or theories employed by those editorials in explaining why a particular event (or events) under discussion has occurred.

2. Assessment as to whether NND viewers constitute an undereducated clique that criticizes the ENeM for no legitimate reasons by reviewing the substantive content of NND videos; and

3. Assessment as to whether or not the newspaper editorials under review are innocuous (or specific) in comparison with the information that NND viewers are exposed to.

First, I examined newspaper editorials and NND videos discussing or reporting on national/East Asian security, and then moved on to examination of the Abenomics data and finally to that of the TPP data in three subsections, each subsection taking the forgoing three steps.

References to the Data

For the research, each newspaper from which an editorial is taken is assigned an abbreviated name. Editorials are referred to by the abbreviated name of the newspaper, followed by the date of the issue of the newspaper in which the editorial under discussion appears. As an example, YOM401 refers to the 1 April editorial of the *Yomiuri Shimbun*. The complete list of reviewed editorials is provided in Table 1 (N=277; see Web Appendix). Videos are referred to by a Text Number. The complete list of reviewed videos, along with the topic(s) of each video, where EAS stands for East Asian security, AB for Abenomics, and TPP for Trans-Pacific Partnership, and other descriptive information for each video, is provided in Table 2 (N=41; see Web Appendix).

ANALYSIS OF THE ANALYTICAL THEMES

Analytical Theme 1: National/East Asian Security

The newspaper editorials commenting on national and East Asian security issues appear to exhibit diversity. However, this diversity is brought through connection to a single theory that interlocks the Yasukuni issue with the Senkaku issue. Each editorial may look unique, but these editorials are variants of combinations of two core arguments. As such, this "diversity" is little more than a mask for homogeneity. Regarding the video element, NND viewers take strong pro-Japan and strong anti-China/Korea stances, but stances based in issue details. Measured on the basis of the NND viewers then, none of the newspaper editorials can be seen as specific or critical, since they all avoid facing the comfort women issue and the Nanking Massacre. Therefore, all the editorials can be said to be innocuous.

The following content examines treatment of national/East Asian security, by focussing on editorials regarding the Yasukuni Shrine visits on 20 and 21 April by 168 lawmakers, including three cabinet ministers (hereafter: the Yasukuni visits), and intrusion into Japan's territorial waters around the Senkaku Islands by Chinese patrol boats on 23 April (hereafter: the Chinese intrusion). This is followed by examination of how the NND videos discuss or view national security.

Analytical Theme 1: Newspaper Editorials
For the sake of discussion, analysis of the editorials will follow three analytical viewpoints: (1) which country constitutes a threat to East Asia, Japan or China (referred to in the text as *viewpoint 1*); (2) why it is deemed a threat (referred to as *viewpoint 2*); and (3) whether any Yasukuni visits influenced the Chinese intrusion (referred to as *viewpoint 3*). Even though the analysis of editorials from these three viewpoints breaks down the 37 newspapers into eight groups (A1 and A2~G), all the editorials can be seen as variants of the combination of the following two arguments: (1) Japan is a threat to East Asian security, since it is drifting towards the Right, which is exemplified by its denial over its wartime responsibilities, e.g., attempts to revise the 1993 Kôno statement; and (2) China is a threat to Japan's security, since it has turned to expansionism, which is exemplified by its attempts to annex the Senkaku Islands. These two arguments form two extremes of a security-issue analytical scale, where all the editorials discussing national/East Asian security fall somewhere on this scale, as explained in detail below.

Group A1: Strong Anti-Japan and Pro-China

The argument of this group is characterised as follows: Japan is a threat to East Asia *(viewpoint 1)*. The basis of this view holds that that Japan denies any wartime responsibility for its colonial rule of the Korean Peninsula and aggression into Asian countries, the denial being exemplified by the Yasukuni visits *(viewpoint 2)*. This group maintains that Japan's nationalistic words and deeds provide China with some justification to intrude into Japan's territorial waters around the Senkaku Islands *(viewpoint 3)*. The newspapers of this group are the *Asahi, Hokkaidō,* and *Kōbe Shimbun*. Editorial ASA423, for instance, criticises Prime Minster Abe for allowing his three cabinet members to visit Yasukuni Shrine, which, the editorial argues, caused the foreign minister of South Korea to cancel his visit to Japan to resolve the issue of North Korea's missile testing. On this basis, ASA423 justifies the Chinese intrusion as a justifiable protest by China against Japan. Editorial ASA424 also interprets the Yasukuni visits as a denial of the 1993 Kōno Statement, which apologised for the Japanese military government's commitment to comfort women during World War II. This discursive strategy is also employed in six newspaper editorials in the *Mainichi Shimbun*, the *Hokkaido Shimbun* and the *Kobe Shimbun*, but with the following variations. Editorial KOB424 notes that the naturalisation of the Senkaku Islands by the Japanese government in September 2012 led to the intrusion of Chinese ships into Japan's territorial waters whereas HOK426 notes that it cannot be said that the Yasukuni visits have nothing to do with the Chinese intrusion.

Group A2: Strong Anti-Japan and Pro-China

The argument of this group is the same as that of Group A1, except for diversion regarding *viewpoint 3*. This group chooses not to refer to the Chinese intrusion, so the relationship between the Yasukuni and Senkaku issues is not clear *(viewpoint 3)*. The newspapers of this group are seven: the *Mainichi,* the *Shinano Mainichi,* the *Fukui, Gifu,* and *Chūgoku Shimbun,* the *Okinawa Taimusu,* and the *Ryūkyū Shimpō*. The difference is clear when viewed against a sample from Group A1. Editorial MAI423, for instance, criticises the Yasukuni visits as a callous act (*mushinkei na kōi*), where the Prime Minister's decision to allow his cabinet members to visit Yasukuni Shrine, has marred Japan's relations with China and South Korea. MAI424 describes the Yasukuni visits as an act of getting on neighbour's nerves (*ringoku no shinkei o sakanade suru*), implying that Japan has caused trouble in East Asia *(viewpoint 1)*. Editorial MAI424 urges Abe not to revise the 1993 Kōno Statement with respect to the comfort women issue, whereas MAI426 suspects that Abe wants to deny that the Sino-Japanese war was a war of aggression. Herein lies the difference between these two groups: Group A1 justifies the Chinese intrusion *(viewpoint 2)*, whereas Group A2 ignores it.

Group B: Weak Anti-Japan
This group believes that Japan has caused trouble to East Asia *(viewpoint 1)*, but not through Japan denying its wartime responsibilities, rather because Abe has mishandled the Yasukuni issue *(viewpoint 2)*, therefore exhibiting a weaker anti-Japan stance. None of the Group B editorials (except NII426) refer to the Chinese intrusion and the relationship between the Yasukini and Senkaku issues is not clearly stated *(viewpoint 3)*. The newspapers of this group are the *Nishinippon*, *Kōchi*, and *Minaminippon Shimbun*, the *Niigata Shimpō*, and the *Iwate Nippō*. Editorial NIS424, for instance, criticises Abe for allowing his cabinet members to visit Yasukuni Shrine, which generated strong protests from South Korea and China, leaving Japan isolated in East Asia, and meaning Japan caused trouble to East Asia *(viewpoint 1)*. But unlike Groups A1 and A2, the editorial criticizes Abe because he mishandled the issue due to a faulty historical perception *(viewpoint 2)*. The same discursive strategy is employed in editorials by the *Kōchi* and *Minaminippon Shimbun*, as well as the *Niigata Shimpō* and the *Iwate Nippō*.

Group C: Neutral
The argument of Group C is characterised by silence, as eighteen newspaper editorials refer neither to the Yasukuni visits nor to the Chinese

intrusion. These newspapers are the *Nayoro, Fukushima Min'yū, Ibaraki, Chūnichi, Shiga Hōchi, Kyōto, San'yō, Tokushima, Ehime, Saga,* and *Miyazaki Nichinichi Shimbun,* the *Akita Sakigake* and the *Kahoku, Niigata,* and *San'in Chūō Shimpō,* as well as the *Tōō* and *Chiba Nippō,* and the *Daily Tohoku.*

Group D: Anti-China
The only member of this group is the *Kumamoto Nichinichi Shimbun* (editorial KUM425) and the argument that China is a threat to Japan's security *(viewpoint 1),* justified because China has turned toward expansionism *(viewpoint 2),* exemplified in the Chinese intrusion and by the fact that China has territorial disputes with other countries such as the Philippines and Vietnam. This Chinese expansionism, however, has nothing to do with the Yasukuni visits *(viewpoint 3),* and Group D makes no reference to Japan's drift towards the Right.

Group E: Pro-Japan and Anti-China
This group, whose only member is the *Yomiuri Shimbun,* maintains that China is a threat to Japan's security *(viewpoint 1),* a view demonstrated by the Chinese intrusion representing the Chinese government's hardline stance to secure China's maritime interests *(viewpoint 2).* In this case, the Yasukuni visits and the Chinese intrusion are viewed as two separate issues *(viewpoint 3).* Editorial YOM424 admits that the Yasukuni visits worsened Japan-South Korea relations and thus criticises Abe. However, the editorial also supports the Japanese government stance that every country has a different position and that it should not affect bilateral diplomacy. Contradicting this, YOM425 argues that the Chinese intrusion should be seen as unacceptable, with YOM428 concluding that the intrusion represents the Chinese government's hard-line stance regarding maritime interests and dogmatic (*dokuzenteki*) expansionism *(viewpoint 2).* The Yasukuni and Senkaku issues are thus two separate issues *(viewpoint 3)* and no editorial refers to Japan's wartime responsibilities.

Group F: Strong Pro-Japan and Anti-China

The argument of this group, whose only member is the *Hokkoku Shimbun*, is that China is a threat to East Asia *(viewpoint 1)*. The rationale for this is that China has forced Japan to accept the Chinese interpretation of history and values (editorial HKO424), and China's expansionism, HKO330 suggests, should be held in check by Japan's signing of a Russo-Japan peace treaty *(viewpoint 2)*. The Senkaku issue has nothing to do with the Yasukini issue, since HKO424 notes that nothing is wrong with lawmakers' visits to Yasukuni Shrine *(viewpoint 3)*. No editorial of Group F refers to Japan's wartime responsibilities.

Group G: Strong pro-Japan and Strong anti-China

The argument of Group G, whose only newspaper is the *Sankei Shimbun*, is that China is a threat to Japan's security *(viewpoint 1)*. This reason for this is that China is aiming to take over Japan's territory *(viewpoint 2)* and the Yasukuni issue has nothing to do with the Senkaku issue *(viewpoint 3)*. Editorial SAN424 notes that China is able to mobilise as many as 3000 ships to the Senkaku Islands, whereas Japan's Coast Guard has only 117 boats for deployment, and also notes that the Chinese intrusion is a provocative act relative to Japan's territory *(viewpoint 2)*, concluding that Japan's sovereignty is being jeopardised *(viewpoint 1)*. Editorial SAN424 also praises Abe's remark that Yasukuni visits are a purely domestic issue, meaning that this group views the Yasukuni and Senkaku issues as separate*(viewpoint 3)*. As with Group E and F, no editorial of Group G refers to Japan's wartime responsibilities.

Analytical Theme 1: Newspaper Editorials Summary

When editorials above take a strong anti-Japan stance, they do so referring to Japan's militaristic past; when the issue of national security is reviewed from China's (or East Asia's) point of view, the argument is interlocked with the assumption that Japan, drifting towards the Right, is a threat to East Asia. In contrast, when an editorial takes a strong pro-Japan stance, it refers to China's expansionism and assumes that Japan is

Japanese Journalistic Communities 163

being threatened by China, while avoiding reference to Japan's wartime responsibilities. Starting from the strong anti-Japanese edge of the scale, as they becomes less and less anti-Japanese, editorials become less and less specific about the issue under discussion, avoiding reference to territorial issues and the issue of Japan's wartime responsibilities. Such editorials, then, enter a "neutral" zone, where the approach is omission. From there, as editorials trend toward becoming more and more pro-Japanese, they begin referring to China as a threat to national security. That all the editorials range on this scale between strong anti-Japan and strong pro-Japan is a given, as no newspaper can take both a pro-Japan and pro-China stance or take both an anti-Japan and anti-China stance.

Analytical Theme 1: Nico Nico Dōga Viewers
Looking at NND viewers in terms of their attitudes regarding Analytical Theme 1, East Asian Security, NND viewers take a strong anti-China/Korea stance with little issue or opinion diversity. However, judging from the information that they are exposed to, NND viewers should not be characterized as a uniformly undereducated group.

Strong Anti-China and Korea Stance
Twelve of the 41 NND videos deal with national security. Judging from viewers' comments on the screen accompanying the videos, three of these 12 appear to have been uploaded for the purpose of criticism. These three videos show three DPJ members, Okada Katsuya, Tsujimoto Kiyomi, and Tokunaga Eri, questioning Abe and his administrative staff members at the Lower House Budget Committee session on 7, 8 March, and 24 April. In the video labelled OKAD, Okada is accused (by Abe) for giving China excessive consideration (*kadono hairyo*) in dealing with Chinese ships in Japanese territorial waters around the Senkaku Islands when he was the deputy prime minister under the DPJ administration (see Table 2). In video TSUJ, Tsujimoto expresses strong objection to Abe's attempt to revise the 1993 Kōno Statement, going on criticise Abe by saying that his persistence in this has hurt Japan's diplomatic relations with the

EU and the US. In video TOKU, Tokunaga criticises the Yasukuni visits, asserting these caused South Korea's foreign minister to cancel a visit to Japan and generated objections by China. In what is a long sequence, she finally concludes that what really angered South Korea and China is the nationalistic character of the Abe Administration. All of these politicians, seen to take a decidedly pro-Korea and/or China stance, are harshly criticised by NND viewers, who use expletives such as *baikokudo* (traitor), *kokuzoku* (traitor), and *usotsuki* (liar). Incontrovertibly, these NND viewers take a strong anti-China/Korea stance.

The remaining nine videos of the 12 can be assessed as having been uploaded for the purpose of supporting LDP members. These videos are concerned with Chinese military build-up and threats, the Nanking Massacre, the comfort women issue, and Japan's colonial rule of the Korean Peninsula. Four LDP members refer to these four issues, and three of the four attempt to justify some part of Japan's militaristic past. In video ABES2, Abe Shinzō points out that Chinese military spending has quadrupled over the last few years, upsetting the military balance in Asia, thereby justifying Japan's military build-up. Similarly, Nishimura Shingo in video NISM quotes Zhu Chenghu, professor of China's National Defense University of the People's Liberation Army, as saying that a nuclear attack on Japan may resolve the issue of global population increase. Needless to say, NND viewers' comments on these LDP members are unanimously positive. But, most enthusiastically welcomed were Nishikawa (in video NISK) and Nakayama (in videos NAKA 2 and 3), who accuse the *Asahi* of the distortion of history.

Accusation 1: The Nanking Massacre
In video NISK, Nishikawa presents three pieces of "evidence" against the theory that there was a massacre in Nanking: The first are the recently discovered photos that were taken by reporters of *Asahi Gurafu* (affiliated with the *Asahi*) jointly with Japanese military camera men and citizens in Nanking during the period of the Nanking Massacre. According Nishikawa (in video NISK), none of these photos shows any

sign of the allegedly slaughtered 300,000 Chinese people. The second piece of evidence referred to in the video is the "fact" that no article in *The Times* and *The New York Times* (which were very critical about the Japanese army's movements) from 17 December 1937 to January 1938 referred to the massacre. Third is the fact that then-Chinese Foreign Minister Ku Wei-chün's "revelation" of the massacre was dismissed by the League of the Nations. Having pointed out these facts, Nishikawa maintains that what happened in Nanking was in fact no more and no less than normal battles and it was the *Asahi*'s campaign during the 1980s that upgraded those normal battles to the level of a massacre. *Asahi* editorials have not responded to this accusation yet.

Accusation 2: The Comfort Women Issue
In videos NAKA 2 and 3, Nakayama Nariaki talks on two issues: whether Japanese militaristic authorities procured comfort women or not, and whether the Japanese militaristic authorities exploited Koreans during Japan's colonial rule of the Korean Peninsula. In so doing, he accuses the *Asahi Shimbun* of distorting history and of inciting the comfort women issue. Nakayama's argument begins with the *Asahi*'s report on the comfort women issue on 11 January 1992 (NAKA2, NAKA3). This news report was the first revelation of a document that purportedly "proves" the Japanese Army's commitment to comfort women. But Nakayama argues that the document does not confirm the Japanese Army's commitment, but rather it raises alarm over the existence of unscrupulous labour contractors procuring comfort women, which, Nakayama maintains, demonstrates Japanese wartime authorities' attempts to crack down on the human trafficking abuses perpetrated by unscrupulous labour contractors.

Nakayama goes on to argue that the Japanese Army's commitment to comfort women was institutionally not possible as the colonial Korean government was, for all practical purpose, run by Koreans(NAKA2, NAKA3). Under such a system, Nakayama asserts, it would have been nearly impossible for the Japanese authorities to systematically take as many as 200,000 Korean women by force without causing any disputes.

Nakayama also states that Japan's colonial rule of the Korean Peninsula did not exploit the Korean people; rather, it helped them to build up their homeland, which is exemplified by Japan's construction of the railway system and universities.

No *Asahi* editorial in March and April 2013 responded to Nakayama. In addition, after being uploaded to *YouTube* on 8 March 2013, NHK requested that the video of Nakayama's session be deleted, which *YouTube* accepted (Kamei, 2013). As such, NHK rejected counter-argument, requesting deletion of the video instead.

Analytical Theme 1: National/East Asian Security Summary
As asserted, the newspaper editorials are variants of combinations of two core arguments; no editorial deviated from the variant production system. The editorials that criticize Japan in the most specific way are strong anti-Japan *Asahi Shimbun* editorials, which, as noted, refer to Japan's militaristic past. However, from the viewpoint of NND viewers, even these anti-Japan newspapers are not specific enough in criticizing the Abe Administration for the following reason: the *Asahi* (as well as the other newspapers) has not responded to two LDP members (in NAKAs 2 & 3 and NISK) who specifically accuse the *Asahi* of distorting history. This raises questions regarding the *Asahi Shimbun's* willingness to defend its anti-Japan editorials, a question which could be directed to all the other anti-Japan newspaper editorializing. From the analysis above, it is also clear that NND viewers take a strong anti-China/Korea and strong pro-Japan stance. But as far as the discussion of national/East Asian security is concerned, the analysis also suggests that it is unfair to regard NND viewers as undereducated and carried away by sentiments against anti-Japan news media.

Analytical Theme 2: Quantitative Easing
On 4 April 2013, the newly-appointed Governor of the Bank of Japan (BOJ), Kuroda Haruhiko, held a press conference and announced that "the Bank of Japan [would] conduct money market operations in such a

way that the monetary base [would] increase at an annual pace of about 60-70 trillion yen," and that under this guideline, the BOJ would purchase Japanese government bonds (JGB) such that the amount of outstanding JGBs would reach 190 trillion yen by the end of 2014 (Bank of Japan, 2013). The reaction of newspaper editorials was nearly unanimous in their opposition of monetary easing on the basis of a single economic theory. In contrast, NND viewers appeared to be better informed regarding the origin of this theory and what purposes it serves.

Analytical Theme 2: Newspaper Editorials
Out of the 37 newspapers, 31 referred to the issue of monetary easing. Of the 31, nine agreed with the monetary easing policy whereas 22 disagreed. Two of the newspapers that supported the policy and all 22 of the opposing newspapers employed the same theory to explain their views on monetary easing. Dissenters asserted that the theory holds that the BOJ's purchase of JGBs causes fiscal discipline to erode, which is followed by an over-issuance of such bonds. The market then loses confidence in those bonds, interpreting it as act of financing the government, and leading JGB prices to plummet. This plummeting in the value of JGBs in turn causes hyperinflation and then/or financial collapse. In order to ensure the clarity of the following analysis, I will refer to this theory simply as the "plummeting theory."

The following 22 newspapers employed the plummeting theory to oppose Abenomics in their editorials: the *Asahi, Mainichi, Hokkaidō, Shinano Mainichi, Gifu, Fukui, Kyōto, Kōbe, San'yō, Chūgoku, Tokushima, Kōchi, Saga, Kumamoto Nichinichi, Miyazaki Nichinichi,* and *Minimi Nippon Shimbun,* along with the *Daily Tōhoku,* the *Iwate Nippō,* the *Kahoku, San'in Chūō, Ryūkyū Shimpō,* and the *Okinawa Taimusu.* Only the *Yomiuri* and the *Ibaraki Shimbun* are positive about Abenomics, but still refer to the plummeting theory in their support. Examples of the sentiments expressed in these editorials are evident in the two following examples. Editorial FKU405, which opposes monetary easing, states:

> When the purchase [of JGBs] loses its ceiling, the purchase could be interpreted as an act of financing the Japanese government. The issue at stake is how to set up a new rule to assure the credibility of JGBs. (translation by author)

Editorial RYU407, also opposing quantitative easing, notes:

> The new Governor's stance is this: The purchase of JGBs by the BOJ is not an act of financing the government. But the moment the market has lost confidence in his remark, the long-term interest rate may rise immediately and JBG prices may plummet. A real estate bubble may also occur. (translation by author)

Two points need to be made here, the first about editorializing against a policy without offering an alternative and the second about being informed about the policy that is being editorialized. Regarding the first point, none of the foregoing 22 newspapers presented any alternative plan to revitalise Japan's economy. Regarding the second, none of the 37 newspapers revealed who exactly was advocating the plummeting theory and why.

Analytical Theme 2: Nico Nico Dōga Viewers

There are 13 videos concerning Abenomics in the data. Of these, videos JONE1 and YAMA in particular are worth noting (see Table 2). While these two videos offer clear support for quantitative easing, the point worth noting is that these videos clearly inform viewers regarding who opposes quantitative easing and why they oppose it, together with explanation of a theoretical discrepancy in the theory employed by those who do oppose it.

The Theory Opposing Abenomics

In video JONE1, economic commentator Jōnen Tsukasa reveals the names of high ranking bureaucrats who oppose quantitative easing and Abenomics. In addition to the BOJ governor introduced in RYU407, he also identifies Kinoshita Kōji, the then-Director of Budget Bureau of the Finance Ministry, as an influential opponent of Abenomics. Jōnen goes on to explain that these bureaucrats oppose quantitative easing because they believe that such an approach does not work to halt deflation; for them deflation in Japan is not an economic phenomenon which can be dealt with through monetary policies.

A Contradiction in the Plummeting Theory

Continuing with video JONE1, Jōnen says that those who oppose quantitative easing are the source of disseminating the plummeting theory to abort Abenomics. However, Jōnen (in JONE1), citing statements made by LDP member Yamamoto Kōzō and Abe Shinzō referring to the plummeting theory (in YAMA), points out the following: if a monetary policy such as quantitative easing does not halt deflation, then why would the plummeting of JGBs, which is supposed to be caused by the BOJ's purchase of JGBs, cause hyperinflation? According to Jōnen, the mass media employs the plummeting theory without noticing this theoretical discrepancy (JONE1).

Analytical Theme 2: Quantitative Easing Summary

Newspaper editorials commenting on monetary easing neither identifed who opposed this economic policy nor why they opposed it. Editorials negative about monetary easing simply criticise the policy approach and present no alternative plan to halt deflation. In contrast, NND videos inform viewers of the foregoing information regarding plummeting theory. One can conclude that NND viewers support monetary easing and Abenomics, presumably, not just because the policy was proposed by the Abe Administration, but because they are informed of what monetary easing is and what it does to Japan's economy. It is not the NND viewers but rather the newspaper editorials that could be characterized as an undereducated coterie carried away by unsubstantiated rhetoric.

Analytical Theme 3: Trans-Pacific Partnership

No issue has been treated more homogeneously and innocuously in newspaper editorials than that of Japan's participation in TPP. In contrast, NND viewers are split into three groups, with member seeming to be caught in a dilemma over the issue.

Analytical Theme 3: Newspaper Editorials

Japan's participation in TPP negotiations splits Japanese newspaper editorials into five groups: nine chose not to refer to this issue, while the remaining 28 newspapers reach four different conclusions based on the same three "facts."

On 12 April 2013, Minister of State for Economic Revitalization Amari Akira held a press conference to announce that preliminary consultations with the US prior to Japan's participation in TPP pact negotiations were concluded and the US Government approved Japan's entry into TPP negotiations. Disregarding the significance of this news, nine newspapers chose not refer to this announcement: the *Sankei*, *Fukushima Min'yū*, *Gifu*, *Shiga Hōchi*, and *Nishinippon Shimbun*, together with the *Kahoku Shimpō*, the *Chiba* and *Nagano Ninippō*, and the *Okinawa Taimusu*. The remaining 28 newspapers, on the other hand, managed to reach four different conclusions on the basis of the following three facts: the US will maintain its 2.5% import tariff on Japanese cars and its 25% tariff on Japanese trucks; Japan will not approve any new products of the insurance division of Japan Post, specifically *Kampo* Insurance; and the US government agreed that Japan has sensitive products in the agricultural sector. The 28 newspapers then summarised TTP negotiations as the management of opposition between the promotion of free trade and the protection of Japan's agriculture.

Of the 28 newspapers that offer editorials on TPP, five concluded that Japan must join TPP negotiations to promote free trade: the *Yomiuri*, the *Asahi*, the *Mainichi*, the *Chūnichi*, and the *Kokkou Shimbun*. Sixteen newspapers are caught in a dilemma between promotion and protection, unable to decide whether or not Japan should join TPP negotiations: the *Akita Sakigake*, the *Ibaraki*, *Shinano Mainichi*, *Fukui*, *Kyōto*, *Kōbe*, *San'yō*, *Tokushima*, *Ehime*, *Kōchi*, *Saga*, *Kumamoto Nichinichi*, and *Minaminippon Shimbun*, and the *Daily Tōhoku* together with the *Niigata* and *Ryūkyū Shimpō*. Four newspapers conclude that Japan should withdraw from TPP negotiations if Japan's sensitive products are not exempted from tariff elimination: the *Hokkaidō*, *Chūgoku*, and *Miyazaki Nichinichi Shimbun*, and the *Tōō Nippō*. And the remaining three conclude that Japan must not join TPP negotiations in order to protect Japan's agriculture: the *Nayoro Shimbun*, the *Iwate Nippō*, and the *San'in Chūō Shimpō*.

These editorials look alike except for their conclusions—conclusions that are based largely on two dominant themes: promotion of free trade versus protection of Japanese agriculture. They would look even more alike were one to recognize, for example, that there are as many as twenty-one fields of business practice that TPP negotiations are going to discuss, as will be pointed out in the next section.

Analytical Theme 3: Nico Nico Dōga Viewers

Eighteen NND videos take up the theme of TPP negotiations, categorised into three groups: pro-TPP (three videos), anti-TPP (nine videos), and reluctant pro-TPP groups (six videos) (see Table 2.) However, analysis of comments accompanying the videos reveal that the majority of NND viewers appear to be anti-TPP.

Pro-TPP Group

In video JONE 1 and 2, Jōnen supports Japan's participation in TPP negotiations, attracting general positive comments from the viewers. The same reaction occurs to the screening of Abe Shinzō's announcement of Japan's TPP participation at a press conference (ABES 4).

Anti-TPP Group

The anti-TPP group's negative reaction to eight of the videos reflects two important points regarding TPP. First, as already noted, there are as many as twenty-one fields of business that TPP negotiations are eventually going to discuss and come to agreement on. Second, TPP agreements include the issue of investor-state dispute settlement (ISDS). In videos MITS1-5, economic commentator Mitsuhashi Takaaki refers to the 21 fields. The protection of Japan's agriculture and promotion of free trade are just part of a big picture, which, Mitsuhashi says, is deliberately hidden from the public by the government and the news media. In the same video, Mitsuhashi then goes on to refer to mechanism to protect investors, i.e., ISDS. The ISDS is a mechanism that enables investors to sue foreign governments if those investors suffer any losses on their investments and if those losses are caused by governments' domestic legislation that breach TPP agreements. As explained and amplified in the MITS videos, this mechanism could easily change the entire legislative system in Japan; a concern emphasized by American liberal activist Lori Wallach in videos WALL1 and 2.

Reluctant Pro-TPP Group

The potential for negative influence in both the 21 business fields covered by TPP and the ISDS mechanism are intensively discussed in the videos of this group. However, unlike the other groups, this group reluctantly accepts Abe's decision to participate in TPP negotiations. LDP member Nishida Shōji (videos NISH 2 and 3) states that he has no other option but to trust the Abe administration's negotiation skills. Mizushima Satoru, managing director of *Channeru Sakura*, in videos MIZU 1-4 believes that Abe has no alternative but to accept Japan's TPP negotiations because the TPP is, he firmly believes, a conspiracy by the US to swallow Japan's economy to revitalise the American economy—a conspiracy, in this scenario, Japan is unable to counter.

Analytical Theme 3: Trans-Pacific Partnership Summary
The homogeneity of newspaper editorials in their treatment of the TPP issue is an unmistakable fact. Furthermore, managing to reach a conclusion based on just three facts is a clear indication of the innocuousness of the editorials of these Japanese newspapers. In contrast, NND viewers are exposed to specific information concerning TPP negotiations, e.g., the 21 fields of business practice to be reviewed during TPP negotiations and the specifics of the ISDS mechanisms. While some NND viewers appear to believe in the US conspiracy theory, these relatively uneducated viewers form just a part of the whole community of NND viewers.

CONCLUSION: EDITORIAL HOMOGENEITY AND INFORMED VIEWERS

This chapter has analyzed assertions that Japanese newspapers are homogenous and innocuous on the one hand, and that *Nico Nico Dōga* viewers are an uneducated coterie that is easily carried by emotional arguments on the other. The research first compared newspaper editorials commenting on national/East Asian security and *Nico Nico Dōga* videos commenting or reporting on the same issue. It is clearly evident that many editorials reflect the notion that Japan's national security undermines East Asia's security and vice versa. In contrast, *Nico Nico Dōga* viewers are informed of details of Japan's militaristic past, which form a core part of the argument presented by anti-Japan newspapers against, presumably, pro-Japan right-wingers, a group which includes *Nico Nico Dōga* viewers. These historical details have been presented by LDP lawmakers specifically against the editorializing of the *Asahi Shimbun*, but have been largely ignored by the established new media.

Taking up the issue of Abenomics and the question of quantitative easing, the editorials that oppose these policies seem to do so without fully understanding or recognizing the outcome of quantitative easing relative to Japan's economy. Some information that *Nico Nico Dōga* viewers are exposed to claims that such editorials reflect the interests of the Finance Ministry and the Bank of Japan, but as is the case with much macro-economic theorization, there is no telling which side can claim the truth based on economic fact. That noted, one thing is certain: twenty-one newspaper editorials employ the same theory, plummeting theory, to criticise Abenomics. Homogeneous editorializing is one issue here; offering alternatives along with criticism is another. In a similar manner, the editorials commenting on Japan's participation in TPP negotiations all refer to the same three facts, on the basis of which they manage to reach four differing conclusions. In contrast, *Nico Nico Dōga* viewers are informed of the fact that as many as 21 fields of business practices are going to be discussed through TPP negotiations and that the TPP agreements will include such far-reaching provisions as the investor-state dispute settlement provision, none of which is referred to in the editorials.

On the basis of this extensive analysis, there is sufficient evidence to conclude that Japanese newspaper editorials are, indeed, highly homogeneous and largely innocuous. Further, while questions regarding a community of news consumers drifting towards the Right in political ideology can, to some extent, be determined by the groups' political stance towards the "liberal" mass media as represented by anti-Japan editorials—meaning that *Nico Nico Dōga* viewers should rightly be labelled "right wingers"—this does not mean that *Nico Nico Dōga* viewers are, as a group, undereducated and emotionally carried away with anti-China/Korea sentiments. Ideology aside, at the very least, editorialists have no right to call them undereducated.

References

Asahi Shimbun Dejitaru. (2012, November 30). *Tōshu tōron@kikodō, sate saiten wa? 140man-nin ga shichō.* Retrieved from http://www.asahi.com/poliics/ intro/ TKY201211290697.html.

Bank of Japan. (2013, April 4). Introduction of the "Quantitative and Qualitative Monetary Easing. Retrieved from http://www.boj.or.jp/en/ announcements/ release_ 2013/k130404a.pdf.

Freeman, L. A. (2000) Closing the shop: information cartels and Japan's mass media. Princeton: Princeton University Press.

Inagaki, T. (1996). *Shimbun urayomi sakasayomi.* Tolyo: Shisōsha.

Kakkō. (2012, December 16). *Akihabara Abe sōsai gaitōenzetsukai shûryō chokugo, masukomi ni suramajii 'gomi' koru.* Retrieved from http://www. nicovideo. jp/watch/ sm19589691?ref=search_key_video.

Kim, Y. C. (1981). Japanese journalists and their world. Charlottesville: University of Virginia Press.

Kamei, A. (2013, April 8). *Hōsōhō dai 70 jō dai 2 kō no kitei ni motozuki shōnin o motomeru no ken.* Retrieved from http://akiko-kamei.home-p.info/20 13/04/ 08/ciaeueaeaiinnuaoi/.

Mitsuhashi, T. (2012a). *Nihon wa kokusai hatan shinai.* Tokyo: Jitsugyō no nihonsha.

Mitsuhashi, T. (2012b). *Shinsetsu nihon keizai.* Tokyo: KK Best sellers.

Mitsuhashi Takaaki Jimusho. (2012a, December 16). 2012.12.15 *Akihabara ekimae*

gaitō enzetsu (Asō moto-sōsai). Retrieved from http://www.nicovideo.jp/ watch/

sm19589198?Ref=search_key_video.

Mitsuhashi Takaaki Jimusho. (2012b, December 16). 2012.12.15 Akihabara ekimae gaitō enzetsu (Abe sōsai). Retrieved from http://www.nicovideo. jp/watch/sm19589774.

Nanri, K. (2004). An Anatomy of the Homogeneity and Innocuousness of Japanese Editorials. The Proceedings of the 15th Biennial Conference of the Asian Studies Association of Australia, Canberra, Australia.

Retrieved from http://www.google.co.jp/url?sa=t&rct=j&q=&esrc=s&frm=1&source=web&cd=1&ved=0CCkQFjAA&url=http%3A%2F%2Fwww.researchgate.net%2Fpublication%2F236247858_An_Anatomy_of_the_Homogeneity_and_Innocuousness_of_Japanese_Editorials%2Ffile%2F504635175e33a5c6a4.pdf&ei=mRQ8UvSiDu36iQf204FQ&usg=AFQjCNGylQ_2Alsc1D8CNaux-pX09sYrSw.

Nanri, K. (2005). The conundrum of Japanese editorials: polarizes, difersified and homogeneous. *Japanese Studies*, Vol.25, Number 2m pp.169-185.

Nanri, K. (2006). The rhetorical organization and identity of Japanese editorial writers. *Ilha Do Destrerro*, No.50, JAN/JUN 2006, pp.13-37.

WebRonza. (2012, December 7). Nico nico dōga to seiji no kiwadoi kankei. Retrieved from http://astand.asahi.come/magaine/wrpolitics/special/2012120600009.html.

Yasuda, K., Yamamoto, I., & Nakagawa, J. (2013). *Netto uyoku no mujun.* Tokyo: Takarajima shinsha.

SECTION THREE

JAPANESE JOURNALISM AND THE GREAT EAST JAPAN DISASTER

CHAPTER EIGHT

THE MEDIA, THE GOVERNMENT, AND THE TRIPARTITE DISASTER OF 2011

Mary M. McCarthy

INTRODUCTION

On March 11, 2011, the Tohoku region of Japan suffered a magnitude 9.0 earthquake and subsequent tsunami. This was followed by a nuclear crisis, as the natural disasters damaged nuclear power plants that were located in Fukushima prefecture. This chapter considers assessment of the government responses to the crises, which have been called the most profound that Japan has faced since the postwar period, and explores Japanese media coverage of those responses.

The media in Japan has been dismissed by its critics as a "lapdog" to government, as opposed to a "watchdog" for society; which is to say, some see the Japanese media as operating simply to relay to the public information regarding government policy without any independent, in-depth, or critical analysis. Others see a more nuanced process at work, as Krauss (2000) asserted that the Japanese media excels in what is often referred to being a "guide dog," vital in educating and informing the public. That said, it is the role of lapdog that drew attention following the tripartite tragedy of 2011, as charges were made that the media followed the government lead of disseminating empty assurances about safety without any explication.

Certainly, a time of crisis may engender quiescence among those in the media who would otherwise be critics, as the focus and function turns to creating unity and promoting stability. Still, a crisis that includes a dearth of political leadership and a plethora of both technical and political mistakes also presents an opportunity to the media, if not highlighting the responsibility of the media. Recent research has revealed changes in Japanese print media over the past two decades, as it has become more likely to be critical of government action and inaction on certain issues of public concern (McCarthy, 2003). Crisis demands leadership and there was no time of greater public concern and demand for leadership than in the aftermath of the 3.11 disaster of 2011. With this in mind, this chapter provides a case study exploring the question of how the media behaved in Japan's democracy at a time when the country was faced with a crisis of imminent panic and widening uncertainty, and where the leadership sought was not necessarily forthcoming.

The Role of the Media in a Time of Crisis

The major way in which the Japanese public gained information about the 2011 disaster was through the media. Although the tremors of the Great East Japan earthquake, according to the U.S. Geological Survey, were felt as far away as 1550 miles (2500 kilometers) from the epicenter, most of the Japanese population did not experience the full impact of the earthquake and tsunami. The full extent of the damage and the tragic consequences of the nuclear disaster only became clear with television and print media coverage and through the Internet. Earthquake and tsunami-related *YouTube* videos proliferated in the days and weeks after March 11, through which one could witness towns wash away with the force of the tsunami waves, ships tottering on the tops of buildings after the water had receded, and images of children crying amidst the rubble as the realization of lost towns and lost lives. The devastation was shocking and heart wrenching to those in Japan and around the world.

Assessments of official responses emerged in contrast with the expectations of what such a tragedy necessitated from government. Whether or not these expectations were being met was answered in part by the media as it assessed government actions and policies in its reporting to the public, but also through the experiences of individuals as these were related through the media. Although a relatively small portion of the Japanese public was directly affected by the initial tragedy, in the days and weeks that followed, the impact expanded. First, were the evacuations of residents from the communities surrounding the Fukushima nuclear power plant; then the impact was experienced on a wider scale, in the scheduled rolling blackouts enacted by the Tokyo Electric Power Company (TEPCO) to conserve electric power. Festivals, exhibits, and celebrations both annual and occasional were cancelled throughout Japan as a sign of *jishuku* (voluntary self-restraint), both reflecting and contributing to the depressed mood of the country. Concerns over environmental and food safety became a problem as anxiety and panic spread.

In the midst of this, the vast majority of the Japanese public criticized the government handling of the disaster. An *Asahi Shimbun* public opinion poll from March 18 revealed that 73% of those polled viewed the government's response to the crisis to be unsatisfactory. Two weeks later, a *Yomiuri Shimbun* public opinion poll yielded similar findings, with 70% indicating dissatisfaction with the prime minister's leadership in the crisis.

In such an environment of distress nd amidst widespread perception of lack of leadership there are various roles that the media can fulfill. On the one hand, the media can focus public attention on failings of the government, magnifying public dissatisfaction and leading to an increase of public awareness of the problems, as Flanagan (1996) discussed, with the potential of generating immediate and necessary changes in government response. On the other, the media can ally itself with the government, as Pharr (1996) has described, serving to help in prioritizing the government's objectives, primarily that of pacifying the public, promoting social stability and calm during an anxious time. In this role, the media usually emphasizes where the government is succeeding in its response as well as highlighting how it is adapting its response to match public needs, concerns and preferences. In some cases, the media can do both, promoting government policy in helping to reduce unease, while also illuminating the level of dissatisfaction among the public and identifying public preferences.

In this sense, the duties and responsibilities of media during a time of crisis are indispensible but also multi-faceted. Graber (2010) described three overlapping stages of crisis coverage by the media: being a source of information, creating an informed perspective and/or a coherent story of the crisis, and preparing people for the aftermath. As she related, "During crises, the public depends almost totally on the media for news and for vital messages from public and private authorities" (p. 114). With regard to the information function, it is not only the public that comes to utilize the media as a source; government officials can also gain valuable information from media reports. In fact, Prime Minister Naoto Kan reportedly first learned of the explosion at the Fukushima Daiichi Plant not from TEPCO or any branch of local government, but on television (Kaufman and Penciakova, 2011).

In the next stage, Graber specified how, "besides seeking information, the public looks to the media for interpretations of situations" (p. 115). When the topic is complex and evolves over time (such as nuclear power plants and radiation), the role of the media that lies not just in reporting information but in interpreting information—the mountains of facts and data—is even more important. This phenomenon has been analyzed by Schifferes and Coulter (2013) in the context of the global financial crisis. It is in this function that the eventual narrative of the event first takes shape. Finally, in its third stage of crisis coverage, the media "provide[s] emotional support for troubled communities" (Graber, p. 126) as they seek to rebuild or recover. It is here that there is an emphasis on looking towards the future.

In the case of 3.11, media observers noticed these stages of crisis reporting as well. Ichise (2011) recognized a shift in media terminology, from *jishuku* (voluntary self-restraint) to *fukko* (reconstruction), as "expressions of mourning of the victims [transitioned] to a national feeling to support...efforts toward future reconstruction." In his exploration of local newspaper coverage of the disaster and ongoing crisis, Rausch (2012) witnessed an evolution in coverage from the provision of information to a period that "can be described as 'coming to an understanding' of the event" to a focus on recovery efforts.

Throughout this process, it is important to note that the media is frequently in a position that is divergent from the norm. Although media is often touted as a check on government, in times of crisis it becomes "teammates of officialdom in attempts to restore public order, safety, and tranquility" (Graber, 2010, p. 126). According to Graber, "plans for covering natural disasters are generally predicated on the assumption that people tend to panic and that coverage must forestall this...Publicizing interviews with public officials and civic leaders who urge calm behavior and indicate that the situation is under control can soothe tempers" (pp. 121-122). Tkach-Kawasaki (2012) calls it "an intrinsic responsibility" of the media to help manage the crisis and not spark hysteria (p. 121). In fact, in exploring the case of the explosion of a chemical plant in the Netherlands in January 2011, van der Meer and Verhoeven (2013) found "that the news media have a soothing effect on public panic and speculation and therefore have potential to prevent crisis escalation" (p. 231).

Yet, not all analysts agree that such pacification should be the goal of the media, even in times of crisis. Kaufmann and Penciakova (2011) provided an interesting comparison between Fukushima and Chernobyl, where censorship and the lack of a free press in a time of crisis-driven fear and anxiety led to a public outcry. "Gorbachev himself has written that Chernobyl led to the collapse of the Soviet Union more so than the launch of perestroika (restructuring)," as public trust in government and media eroded through their mutual mishandling of the crisis. They argued that, in the case of Fukushima, transparency was the key. In their examination of the global financial crisis, Schifferes and Coulter (2013) observed that although some charged that, "the media coverage of the crisis had caused panic among the public and investors alike, worsening the crisis," others criticized the media for "abdicating its public responsibilities to investigate wrongdoing" (p. 229). These critics wanted to see the media do more to unearth the problems early on. This would apply to investigating mistakes as well, to find the truth behind a situation and to disseminate it to the public.

In the case of 3.11, there is much evidence that supports the idea that the media played the former role, that of "teammate of officialdom" and "pacifier of the public." Speaking to coverage of the Fukushima accident, Murai (2011) asserted critically that "mainstream media followed the government's example in withholding diverging opinions so as not to 'confuse' the public...There was a clear refrain from going beyond the plain reporting of officially released facts to offer multiple interpretations, let alone conjectures or criticism " (p. 116). Senju Hiroshi (2011), a traditional Japanese *Nihonga* painter, writing about his experiences of the crisis in *The Nation*, goes further in comparing Japanese television coverage and international assessments. "We were shocked at the gap between what we were being told [within Japan] and what we had just learned [from international sources]. In that moment, we lost our faith in the media. Those Japanese living in Japan seemed the calmest and the furthest from objective information" (p. 24). Kovalev (2011) also found evidence supporting this view, and claimed that the Japanese media promoted an incorrect, and dangerous, view that the Fukushima plant was safe.

Not all the blame can be delegated to the media, however. At the same time it was providing the information it had, the media itself was also clearly frustrated with the lack of information it was being provided. In an article titled, "Tepco [sic] versus the media," Fukase (2011) related the story of a press conference with TEPCO officials on March 16 and the cries from Japanese journalists: "Don't tell us things from your impression or thoughts, just tell us what's actually going on" and "We don't need your apology; some people are in critical danger. You should explain what's really going on there." Murai (2011) argued that media coverage did improve over time and that, perhaps, the watershed event in the transition was the March 28 issue of *AERA* (published by Asahi) with the cover headline reading "Nuclear radiation is coming." Although it was highly criticized as being sensationalistic and *AERA*'s editor-in-chief had to apologize for such dramatism, it loosened "the widespread practice of *jishuku* in the media. From the same week onward, a wider range of representations, including more-sensationalist pieces...began to appear in the popular media" (p. 118). Indeed, Samuels (2013) relates how Japanese media "across the ideological spectrum" began to severely criticize the Japanese government (particularly Prime Minister Kan) in late March and early April of 2011. While the *Asahi Shimbun* was "waiting to hear the voice of a great orator" and the *Yomiuri* sought "vital leadership," *Jiji Press*, a major Japanese wire service, had not heard a "sufficient explanation to dispel the people's fears" and the *Nihon Keizai Shimbun* only heard "criticism mounting" (pp. 100-101). Samuels vividly describes it as "a motif of leadership villainy" (p. 101) and "a tale of grossly incompetent leadership" (p. 102). By May 5, the *Yomiuri* was asking "Is Kan going to be the worst premier in history?" (p. 102).

Print Media Content Analysis

Research Design

In order to systematically explore media assessments of government responses to the tripartite tragedy of 2011, I conducted a content analysis of editorials in print media from March 11 – May 11 (translations by research assistant), during the height of the crises. I explored the degree to which the editorials were supportive or critical of the government, and if there were changes in the perspective of editorials over time, as some qualitative studies have suggested. To date, most of the scholarly analyses of the media and 3.11 have focused on the role of social media or on a comparison between Japanese and international coverage (Utz, Schultz, and Glocka, 2013). This is despite the fact that newspapers continue to be a significant source of information, framing, and interpretation of events in Japan.

Japan has the second highest percentage of newspaper readership in the world (after Iceland), with 92% of the population buying a daily paper (Ito, 2012). In this way, Japan can be seen as having resisted global trends that have readers moving towards other forms of media. According to the *Yomiuri Shimbun*, after 3.11, 86% of those polled responded that newspapers were their source of information about the disaster, whereas 85% looked to NHK for information, 71% to commercial television stations, and 59% to Internet web sites. The *Yomiuri* attributes this to the newspaper being seen as the "most credible media," with their polls indicating that 56% find the information provided by newspapers to be credible. What is notable in this response is the vast divide between newspapers and other media, as just 18% viewed television news sources as credible and 14% for the Internet. Other research confirms these views. Rausch's (2012) analysis supports this finding when he writes that people "looked to the newspaper for confirmation" of confusing or contradictory reports they heard on television. Kanayama Tsutomu, professor of media studies at Ritsumeikan University, identified the importance of sustained interactions between readers and their newspapers, stating that due to the long-term efforts of newspapers "to maintain a bond with their communities," survivors of 3.11 "flocked to newspapers and trusted their information in the aftermath of the disaster" (quoted in Ito (2012)).

While Japanese newspaper readers have a range of newspapers from which to choose, from local to regional and national, this study focuses on coverage in the *Yomiuri Shimbun*. The *Yomiuri* has the largest newspaper circulation in the world, with about 9 million readers. In addition, although the *Yomiuri* is ideologically conservative, I would argue that in the case of the disaster/tragedy of 2011 it was representative of mainstream print media coverage. In addition, the editorials that were chosen provide a view of the overall perspective of the newspaper and in what direction and through what themes they sought to influence the reading public. As Saft and Ohara (2006) wrote, "In Japan, editorials are seen to be representative of the views and stances of particular newspapers; they are regarded as the 'face of the newspapers' (*shimbun no kao* in Japanese)" (p. 85).

Research Findings

The findings of this research support, in part, the general impressions put forward by others that the media tended to support the government position in the days after the earthquake and tsunami, and as the nuclear crisis unfolded. However, my findings also show that the media assessments of the government were not uni-dimensional. The tripartite tragedy of 2011 was, obviously, extensively covered in the daily print media. This coverage included both news directly of the events and the government response, but also addressed issues relevant to this research, which is to say, assessments of government responses to the crisis. The content of this assessment was supportive at times, but could also be somewhat or even extremely critical. Furthermore, this criticism did not only begin in the later stages of the crisis, but could be detected early on in the emerging and escalating crisis.

Volume of Coverage and Coding of Content

Searching *Yomidasu Rekishikan,* under the keywords of *Higashi Nippon Daishinsai* or *Higashi Nippon Kyoudai Jishin* (Great East Japan Earthquake), I found that the *Yomiuri Shimbun* published 6,662 articles on these topics during the two-month period after the earthquake, from March 11- May 11. There was clearly a very high volume of coverage. As stated above, for the purpose of this analysis, I will focus on the editorials within this volume of coverage.

During the period of study, the *Yomiuri* published 90 editorials that took up themes related to the earthquake: 31 in the month of March, 50 in the month of April, and nine in the month of May (through May 11). The content of these editorials ranged from those that asserted how it would buoy the spirits of the victims if sumo were to be broadcast on television to those that criticized specific elements of local or national government response activities.

Within this broad spectrum of content, this study focuses on those editorials that directly assessed local and/or national government preparedness and responsiveness to the tripartite tragedy of 2011. Editorials on these topics totaled 54 (14 in March, 35 in April, five in May). All of these editorials were coded Critical, Generally Critical, Supportive, or Generally Supportive. Critical refers to a clear criticism of government action in response to the disaster, Generally Critical means that there is an area where more needs to be done regarding some disaster-related issue but does not explicitly say the government is at fault. On the other side, Generally Supportive editorials provide tepidly positive evaluations of government action and response, with Supportive editorials praising the actions of the government outright.

Regarding assessment of the national government, nine editorials were judged Critical, 31 Generally Critical, with nine judged to be Supportive. As for local governance, no editorials were deemed either Critical or Generally Supportive, with five judged Generally Critical and four Supportive. Of all editorials that contained government assessments, one editorial was Generally Critical of both national and local governance, two editorials were Generally Critical of the national government but Supportive of the local government, and one editorial was Generally Critical of the local government but Supportive of the national government. Overall, this means that although the vast majority of assessments focused on "more needing to be done" (62%), equal levels were "supportive" and "critical," 22% and 16% respectively (see Figure 3; Web Appendix).

Quantitative analysis can show broad trends in the editorials; qualitative analysis provides more depth of focus into the themes of the editorials. Through such an inquiry, four thematic motifs were identified: containing panic, calling for governmental leadership, chasing transparency and access to information, and encouraging political cooperation.

Containing Panic
Especially in the early days of the crisis, the *Yomiuri* clearly wanted to contain panic associated with the disaster, especially with regard to the Fukushima nuclear power plant. Language that reflected the information gap that was criticized by Senju for television coverage of the disaster was seen in the first relevant editorials in the *Yomiuri* as well. On March 13, after the first explosion at the Fukushima Daiichi Plant, the newspaper assured the public that it was the outermost building that had suffered the explosion, and that the nuclear reactor itself was safe. Crisis management and the provision of information were criticized in the editorial (as explored below), but the newspaper called for calm.

This was reinforced by editorials in the following days. On March 15, more detailed content was provided about the amount of radiation that had leaked from the reactor but the information seemed to rely solely on what had been provided by the government and TEPCO. In addition, the editorial warned of groundless rumors that were spreading on the Internet, and the reactions of the Japanese public in stocking up on daily necessities and the foreign public in cancelling trips to Japan were chided as "excessive responses." In these ways, the editorials represented what

Graber (2010), Tkach-Kawasaki (2011), and van der Meer and Verhoeven (2013) all recognize as the significant role for the media of calming the public during times of crisis, and acting in concert with government.

Still, this does not mean that containing panic was the only role that the *Yomiuri* editorials played in the first days after 3.11. In fact, the government's leadership, internal and external cooperation, and provision of information were all criticized even at these early stages and throughout the period of crisis. In fact, there were three editorials in March, five in April, and one in May that were directly critical of the national government in its dealing with the crisis.

Governmental Leadership

From the day after the earthquake, with its very first editorial on the topic, the *Yomiuri Shimbun* called on Prime Minister Kan to show leadership. In this first stage, this was not a criticism, but rather an appeal for what the newspaper saw as vitally necessary as Japan faced what Kan himself called the greatest challenge since the end of the Second World War.

As the crisis continued, this initial appeal transitioned into an outright criticism. In an April 2nd editorial, Kan's transmission of information was called vague and unreliable. Furthermore, the editorial criticized him for not taking reporter's questions, declaring that, "this type of guarded position gives the impression of hiding information from those both inside and outside the country." The public impression, generally and as illuminated clearly through public opinion polls, that the prime minister was failing to display strong leadership was also cited in an editorial two days later, on April 4.

Transparency and Access to Information

Prime Minister Kan was not the only member of the government criticized for lacking transparency and providing insufficient information. As early as March 13 (two days after the earthquake), the general way in which the government at large was providing information was questioned. The specific example that was cited in the editorial was the government announcement of the first explosion at the Fukushima Daiichi Plant on March 12. Chief Cabinet Secretary Yukio Edano, the face of the government during this crisis, held a press conference confirming the explosion a full two hours after it occurred. It took five hours for an announcement that there was no large radioactive leakage and that the containment unit had not exploded. The editorial questioned why there was such a delay for information that should have been obvious and available much earlier. It went on to find fault with the press conference itself for the lack of important instructions, such as details on public evacuation.

Political Cooperation

Another significant area of comment was that pertaining to cooperation within the political realm and with the professional realm. The *Yomiuri* consistently called for cooperation within government—cooperation among the majority and minority parties in parliament and cooperation between politicians and bureaucrats—as well as cooperation between the government and the professional/technical community of TEPCO.

Majority-Minority Parties

From its first editorial on the topic, the *Yomiuri* called on the political parties, both in and out of power, to put aside rivalries, call a "political truce," and work together in this time of crisis. In the editorials of the first couple of weeks after the earthquake and tsunami, the *Yomiuri* applauded the professed commitment of the minority parties to make every effort to work with the governing party to address the crisis. However, as time went on and politicking re-emerged, the appeals of the *Yomiuri* editorials became more specific, but also more frustrated. The newspaper began to call for a "Grand Coalition" of the governing Democratic Party of Japan (DPJ) and the minority Liberal Democratic Party (LDP)/Komeito coalition. They mentioned voices in support of the idea that there should be members of those minority parties in the Kan cabinet, particularly in areas pertaining to the crisis and recovery of the crisis.

This came at the same time frustration was growing at the failure of the parliament to pass an emergency supplementary budget with the speed and haste the newspaper felt was necessary. The *Yomiuri* editorials called on the DPJ to compromise with the opposition on proposals that the opposition had put forward. They asked the politicians to eliminate pork-barrel politics in this time of need. By April 8, they were criticizing "the government and all political parties [for] lagging behind in dealing with Japan's unprecedented series of crises." The *Yomiuri* argued that, even when the two houses of parliament are controlled by different parties, there must be a way for necessary legislation to pass quickly.

Political-Bureaucratic Relations
The *Yomiuri* editorials also called for cooperation between politicians and bureaucrats. They acknowledged that Kan had a deep-rooted mistrust of the bureaucracy—this from his time in the opposition—but noted that the bureaucracy has the skills that are needed in addressing this crisis. On April 2, a *Yomiuri* editorial asserted that "it is necessary to create a structure of bureaucrats and politicians wrestling with the crisis as one." They argued that to overcome the current crisis, "it will be necessary to revert to the time when a prime minister was able to use the bureaucracy." This was a reference to the long-time rule of the LDP, when it was perceived that (LDP) politicians and bureaucrats worked well together.

The *Yomiuri* was particularly dissatisfied with "political initiatives" that, by some views, were causing more harm than good. In the April 2nd editorial, an example was given of Prime Minister Kan inspecting the Fukushima power plant by helicopter the day after the crisis began to unfold. This was criticized by his political opposition as delaying the response of TEPCO to the crisis. The *Yomiuri* argued that it is in the bureaucracy where "practical business is well known" and this expertise should be fully utilized. Political initiatives should not take the place of well-considered policies implemented by those with practical experience.

Tokyo Electric Power Company (TEPCO)

Cooperation was not only sought within the government but between the government and those relevant bodies outside the government, particularly TEPCO. The relationship between the Japanese government and the nuclear industry is a complex one. Some have argued that the Kan administration was distrustful of TEPCO because of delays in provision of information, so it decided to elicit opinions from third parties who were nuclear power and crisis management specialists. Although the *Yomiuri* acknowledged this as understandable, it emphasized the importance of TEPCO being part of the conversation. In an April 2nd editorial it stated that, "The truth is that the Tokyo Electric Power Company is playing a central role in the accident management and, what is more, reconstructing a relationship of mutual trust with Tokyo Electric should be the first priority." Once again, the focus was on cooperating to best serve public needs.

Overall, cooperation was a key thread throughout the *Yomiuri* editorials. This was cooperation within government and between government and TEPCO. Tying leadership and cooperation together, the *Yomiuri* sought an overarching body to control the management of this crisis and ensure each agency worked efficiently and effectively. They recognized the delayed and, ultimately, unsatisfactory attempts at creating such a body as a fundamental problem with the government response to the crisis.

Conclusion

This chapter opened by noting that some have argued that the Japanese media tends to be quiescent, and that this was even more so with the tripartite tragedy of 2011, a time when the media could have been called on to step up and demand explicit information from government and technical sources. However, based on the content analysis of editorials in the *Yomiuri Shimbun,* I would argue that the truth is that the media response to the disaster was highly nuanced. Although the editorials in the *Yomiuri* did seek to encourage calm and may have reflected an overreliance on information provided by the government and TEPCO at times, they were not hesitant to point out and question such issues as lack of leadership, lack of political cooperation, and lack of transparency and access to relevant information. Moreover, this aggressive posture did not begin late in the crisis but as early as two days after the earthquake hit. As for what this analysis says about journalism and our assessments of journalism, the message may be to check our assumptions regarding cultural influences on social practices at the start of social science research. As in the present research, the combination of reality, response and reporting that make up the task of journalism often supersedes what we believe, or have been led to believe, about a particular culture or society.

References

Flanagan, S. C. (1996). Exposure and the Quality of Political Participation in Japan. In S. J. Pharr & E. S. Krauss (Ed.), *Media and Politics in Japan.* Honolulu: University of Hawaii Press.

Fukase, A. (March 16, 2011). Tepco versus the media. *Japan Real Time.* Retrieved from http://blogs.wsj.com/japanrealtime/2011/03/16/tepco-versus-the-media/

Graber, D. A. (2010). *Mass Media and American Politics.* (8th ed.). Washington, DC: CQ Press.

Ichise, A. (September 2011). Japan's Post-Disaster Vocabulary. *Frontline.* Retrieved from http://ipra.org/itl/09/2011/japan-s-post-disaster-vocabulary

Ito. S. (January 17, 2012). Newspapers in Japan defy West's media malaise. AFP. Retrieved from http://www.google.com/hostednews/afp/article/ALeqM5gaCXwhczczEvXcxFxct1RGORfeZA?docId=CNG.82d34fc4affe66dfee340b574d1077bb.4e1&hl=en

Kaufmann, D. & Penciakova, V. (March 16, 2011). Japan's Triple Disaster: Governance and the earthquake, tsunami and nuclear crises. Retrieved from www.brookings.edu/opinions/2011/0316_japan_disaster_kaufmann.aspx

Kovalev, V. (2011). Technologies of Deceit: Fukushima. *International Affairs (East View), 57*(1), 177-179.

Krauss, E. S. (2000). Japan: News and Politics in a Media-Saturated Democracy. In R. Gunther & A. Mughan. (Eds.), *Democracy and the Media: A Comparative Perspective.* Cambridge University Press, 266-30.

McCarthy, M. M. (2013). Government Stooge or Public Advocate? Japanese Newspaper Coverage of Government Policies Toward China. *Electronic Journal of Contemporary Japanese Studies. 13*(1). Retrieved from http://www.japanesestudies.org.uk/ejcjs/vol13/iss1/mccarthy.html

Murai, N. (2011). 'But is it not in Fact Leaking a Little?'. In J. Kingston (Ed.), *Tsunami: Japan's Post-Fukushima Future.* Foreign Policy. http://www.foreignpolicy.com/ebooks/tsunami_japans_post_fukushima_future

Pharr, S. J. (1996). Media as Trickster. In S. J. Pharr & E. S. Krauss (Eds.), *Media and Politics in Japan*. Honolulu: University of Hawaii Press, 1996.

Rausch, A. (2012). Framing a Catastrophe: Portrayal of the 3.11 Disaster by a Local Japanese Newspaper. *Electronic Journal of Contemporary Japanese Studies*. Retrieved from http://www.japanesestudies.org.uk/ejcjs/vol12/iss1/rausch.html

Saft, S. & Ohara, Y. (2006). The media and the pursuit of militarism in Japan: Newspaper editorials in the aftermath of 9/11. *Critical Discourse Studies. 3*(1), 81-101.

Samuels, R. J. (2013). Japan's Rhetoric of Crisis: Prospects for Change after 3.11. *The Journal of Japanese Studies, 39*(1), 97-120. doi: 10.1353/jjs.2013.0016

Schifferes, S. & Coulter S. (2013). Downloading disaster: BBC news online coverage of the global financial crisis. *Journalism, 14*(1), 228-252. doi: 10.1177/1464884912460171

Senju, H. (August 29/September 5, 2011). A Man-Made Disaster. *The Nation*.

Tkach-Kawasaki, L. M. (2012). March 11, 2011 Online: Comparing Japanese newspaper websites and international news websites. In J. Kingston (Ed.), *Natural Disaster and Nuclear Crisis in Japan: Response and Recovery After Japan's 3/11*.

New York: Routledge.

Utz, S., Schultz, F. & Glocka, S. (2013). Crisis communication online: How medium, crisis type and emotions affected public reactions in the Fukushima Daiichi nuclear disaster. *Public Relations Review. 39*, 40-46.

van der Meer, T. G. L. A. & Verhoeven, P. (2013). Public framing organizational crisis situations: Social media versus news media. *Public Relations Review. 39*, 229-231.

CHAPTER NINE

THE LOCAL PRESS IN JAPAN AND DISCOURSES OF NATIONAL SACRIFICE

Ann Sherif

INTRODUCTION

This chapter considers the use of the local newspaper in Japan as a source for researching public opinion in the twenty-first century media context. Local media is an important supplement to other means of ascertaining public opinion, such as surveys and interviews, as local newspapers play a key role in constructing knowledge, shaping citizens' attitudes, and reflecting those as public opinion. The research focused on a local newspaper, the *Chūgoku Shimbun*, as a means of gauging the character of discourses about the Fukushima area evacuees in the aftermath of the March 11, 2011 multiple disasters in the Tohoku and Fukushima area.

Researching National versus Local Views through the Media

Most research about Japanese media response to 3.11 focused on the role of national newspapers (*zenkokushi*). One survey of the early Japanese media coverage of the Fukushima disasters employed national newspapers and demonstrated the increasing independence of newspapers from the official government line in comparison with the initial reporting of the disasters (McNeill, 2013). Although analysis of national newspapers is essential, researchers should also take into account the influence of regional and local media, which offers the most detailed and constant coverage of the towns, cities, and rural areas that constitute the nation. In many cases, the local newspaper is more effective in capturing and disseminating the views of local stakeholders and residents. Steger reported that a local Iwate newspaper provided the crucial introductions to interviewees for her research on people displaced by the 2011 tsunami and nuclear disasters (Steger, 2013). The research of this chapter employed local newspaper coverage in order to ascertain issues of concerns to local residents, concerns which in turn became concerns of the nation at large, and show the respondent informational function.

3.11: Evacuees and the Discourse of Sacrifice

A nuclear power plant is unassuming: its low, geometric profile symbolizes a clean, nonthreatening presence. The buildings' simple design conveys a reassuring message about safety: undisturbed, such a modest facility generally delivers on its promise of safe, clean power for homes and families, economic opportunity for local communities, and a non-invasive presence among adjacent ecosystems. Yet, nuclear power comes with safety concerns: the by-product of uranium mining and the handling and storage of radioactive waste to name just two. In addition, no satisfactory solution has been offered should a power generation facility be breached by a large-scale disaster. In this, a nuclear power plant demands sacrifice

Discourses of National Sacrifice 199

on the part of nearby residents, not just for their own power, but for the economic fortune of the nation and the profit of the nuclear regime. Ultimately, Fukushima residents came to question the nation's promotion of nuclear energy versus their sacrifice, as they actively engaged with the goal of resilience in the context of complex ecological and political processes (Takahashi, 2012).

As the Fukushima multiple disasters of March 2011 fade into memory outside of—and even within—Japan, the media has come to provide less and less coverage of the nuclear evacuees. Only in some local newspapers can one find current news of the on-going challenges faced by the 150,000 people who are still displaced because of radioaction contamination. This chapter explores the dilemma of these evacuees, the former residents of the Miyakoji district of Tamura city, who grappled with shifting safety standards before being informed by the Japanese government, more than two years after evacuating, that it was safe for them to go home again, focusing on how the local media covered these contentious events.

ONE EVACUATED TOWN OUT OF MANY

Immediately after the disaster, the Japanese central government classified towns closest to the Fukushima plant as "restricted areas," permanently toxic and uninhabitable due to high radiation levels, while it assigned other communities within twenty kilometers of the plant to a temporary "caution" status; people living in these areas were ordered to evacuate. The line demarcating the evacuation zone ran right through the city of Tamura (population 39, 000); people living in the Miyakoji district of Tamura had to leave, while neighbors in other parts of the city were told they could stay.

The government's distinction between areas contaminated by radiation and other, uncontaminated, areas was somewhat random, in large part because radioactive fallout is random, traveling with the winds and in the rain, carried about at different levels of the earth's atmosphere, depending on the amount and height of radioactive discharge and climatic conditions. This yeilded a patch-work pattern of areas with varying degrees of contamination, some directly adjacent to the "no-return" zones. Accordingly, the government defined "restricted-residence zones" and "zones being prepared for the lifting of the evacuation order" on the basis of estimated annual radiation doses measured at periodic intervals, determined to be 20 millisieverts or less, and 20 to 50 mSv, respectively). Further confusion and controversy arose because the government failed to distinguish between safe dosages for adults and for children, even though children are more susceptible to radiation than are adults for anatomical and physiological reasons. The loose and often shifting interpretation of safety standards was symptomatic of the government and power company's approach to handling the long aftermath of the disaster.

The people of Miyakoji, of Tamura city, lived about twenty kilometers from the Pacific Ocean coast of Fukushima prefecture. Their homes had not been directly threatened by the giant tsunami caused by the earthquake, but because of their proximity to the Fukushima power plant, the radioactive fallout spewing from the heavily damaged nuclear facility rained down on their roofs, trees, farm fields, playgrounds, roads —onto every exposed surface in Miyakoji. The radioactive pollution immediately and profoundly disrupted the residents' lives as they were forced to immediately abandon their town. Then they waited, living in temporary housing, while the Japanese government scrubbed their rooftops and streets, and scraped off layers of soil from playgrounds and vegetable fields.

In June 2013, the national press covered in detail the interaction between the former residents of Miyakoji and the Japanese government, which had by this time reported that the decontamination of their neighborhood was complete. Officials from the Reconstruction Agency summoned the evacuees to a meeting hall and distributed handouts filled with data about the clean-up and post-contamination radiation levels around their

Discourses of National Sacrifice 201

houses, schools, and businesses. Then one of the officials announced, "It is now considered safe to return to your homes."

When the official concluded his presentation with such a rosy prognosis, the crowd sat in a stunned silence. Neighbor turned to neighbor, eyebrows raised, wondering how the Japanese government could have construed what appeared to be newly determined levels of radiation exposure—levels higher than those originally announced as the goal—as safe. And what exactly were they supposed to do with the state-of-the-art, high-tech dosimeters (devices that measure exposure to radiation) that the official provided them? The information session seemed designed solely to communicate the message that the government now viewed its job as complete, and it would be up to the residents to make their own decisions about the safety of living in their old town.

Over the more than two years of exile, the former residents of Miyakoji had grown more and more wary of pronouncements by government and the nuclear industry about fundamental issues such as the safety of food and water, and of their homes, workplaces, streets, and schools. The June 23 information session only served to aggravate already frustrated relations among the general public (whether displaced or not), the government, and TEPCO.

Evacuees from Miyakoji learned of the new policy on radiation levels and the lifting of evacuation around the very same time that Prime Minister Abe Shinzō announced his government's stance favoring the possible reopening of at least some of Japan's many nuclear power plants. Tellingly, while the Prime Minister admitted to nuclear power's "myth of safety," he defined, in the same breath, nuclear power as a core energy source for the nation's future. Indeed, the historical, economic, and political contexts of nuclear technology make it necessary for powerful interests to downplay the realities of radioactive waste and potential radiation fallout rendering ecosystems unsustainable, if not uninhabitable. That, however, is what has happened to the ocean, ground water, and rural and urban communities around the Fukushima Daiichi Nuclear

Power Station. The official's announcement that "it is now considered safe to return to your homes" communicated the message that the nation expected their community to sacrifice their health and livelihoods for the progress and energy needs of the nation.

After the information session, the people of Miyakoji did not, however, remain silent. They went to the local and national press and revealed the government's apparent eagerness to wash its hands of the whole affair. The Recovery Agency responded with a denial; they responded that they were not shifting the responsibility for radiation monitoring and protection against radiation exposure to local residents. Recordings of the meeting, however, confirm the evacuees' claims.

A New Realm of Knowledge

After March 11, people from Fukushima prefecture, and indeed, throughout eastern Honshu, whether evacuated or not, found themselves faced with the task of learning about the complex topic of radiation. Many Japanese are familiar with Hiroshima and Nagasaki atomic bomb survivors' exposure to radiation, largely through education about the 1945 bombings, public advocacy for survivors, and anti-nuclear weapons protests. Thus, in contrast to the level of general knowledge about *hibakusha* ("the bombed"), the notion of a cohort of people exposed to radiation from *non-bomb* nuclear technologies and uncontained waste, together with the means to measure that exposure and handle it, were new issues for Japanese. Nonetheless, a new league of "citizen scientists" who monitored radiation levels in their neighborhoods—along with those who travelled to Tohoku to lend post-disaster support—exemplified the spirit of social mobilization in the months after the disasters (Samuels, 2013).

Nuclear energy waste and fallout released into the atmosphere and water from accidents pollute ecosystems for long periods of time. After the initial radiation released in a nuclear bombing or nuclear energy plant accident, residual radiation in the environment can affect health of humans and nonhuman animals over the long term. Radiation lingering on the ground or human-made structures contribute to external exposure. In contrast, internal exposure occurs when people ingest radioactive particles through exposure to the rain or through the food chain, through consumption of food products such as grains or milk. The International Commission on Radiological Protection (ICRP, 2009) describes such radiation release circumstances as an "emergency exposure situation" and life in a disaster's aftermath as an "existing exposure situation."

While there were many domestic experts on nuclear technologies and exposure, the government, industry, and citizens also looked to international agencies such as the International Atomic Energy Agency (IAEA), World Health Organization (WHO), and the United Nations, all of which aim to ensure "the on-going protection of people and the environment from ionizing radiation following a nuclear emergency." Essential to that goal is dissemination to the public of "timely, clear, factually correct, objective and easily understandable information during a nuclear emergency on its potential consequences" (IAEA, 2011). Although the Government of Japan was first and foremost charged with providing such information, many specialists, local governments, and ordinary citizens also worked hard to develop a layperson's overview of unfamiliar concepts such as internal and external exposure, the units used to measure radioactive exposure and the controversial question of the biological effects of radiation (Pacchioli, 2013a). Such "new realms of knowledge" were essential to implementing effective evacuations and ensuring the cooperation of residents who lived both within and near the evacuation zones. The mechanisms of these social processes—a community's ability to share information, act collectively, and work within a social network—often determine the speed and success of recovery (Aldrich, 2012). Newspapers contributed significantly to the sharing of information in the region surrounding Fukushima.

In contrast to the most heavily polluted zones surrounding the disabled plant that will be uninhabitable for the foreseeable future—if not forever—

some less-toxic places were targeted for decontamination by the Japanese government. Authorities communicated with evacuees about plans to decontaminate, and explained the target radiation levels, which were close to pre-disaster levels (Cabinet Office, 2012). The success of these exchanges depended on citizen knowledge of the meaning of exposure and dosage, and the invisible dangers to health and ecosystems that prevented them from going home.

The Japanese government thus took responsibility for decontaminating eleven "caution list" towns with lower levels of radioactive pollution, after which they would be reclassified as one of the "areas to which evacuation orders are ready to be lifted" (METI, 2012). The government chose Miyakoji, the section of Tamura that happened to fall within the twenty-kilometer limit, as one of the first places to be decontaminated, and work began. In June 2013, the government announced completion of this decontamination, in spite of the fact that it had not achieved its stated goal of reducing radionuclide levels to doses below one milliSieverts (mSv) annually. The initial 1 millisievert (or "the lower part of the 1–20 mSv/year band") goal of exposure was based on safety levels established by the International Commission on Radiological Protection (ICRP, 2009).

In contradiction to its own previously articulated goals, the government now proposed that residents would be able to return to their homes once levels of twenty millisievert were achieved, since that is the number used for the *"hinanshiji kijun"* (standards for evacuation) (METI, 2012). As such, the government insisted Miyakoji was safe. In contrast, the ICRP acknowledges potential health hazards at any level of radiation exposure, even low ones:

The Commission recommends that reference levels, set in terms of individual annual effective residual dose (mSv/year), should be used in conjunction with the planning and implementation of the optimisation process for exposures in existing exposure situations . . . However, exposures below the reference level should not be ignored; they should also be assessed to ascertain whether protection is optimised or further protective actions.

With that information in hand, many people from Miyakoji requested that the government do the decontamination project again—and this time in accordance with the original goal of 1 mSv per year. The Reconstruction Agency pointed out the huge sums of money already spent on the decontamination, but stated that it planned to measure radiation levels again in the fall.

A History of Mistrust

The June 23 information session in Tamura was not the first time that the general public had reason to question the government's commitment and approach. Since the earliest days of the disaster in March 2011, both the central government and TEPCO had struggled to manage the disaster. The government initially determined mandatory evacuation orders based solely on distance from the Fukushima nuclear plant: at first, two kilometers; after the explosions at the plant, this was expanded to 20 kilometers; within 30 kilometers, people should stay inside. On April 22, the government started to employ actual radiation levels as a criterion for evacuation orders. The public grew increasingly suspicious as they learned through the national and local media, social media, and talking with their neighbors that the government measurements and those of experts and citizens sometimes differed considerably. The *Asahi Shinbun*, a widely distributed national newspaper, and others began to publish daily radiation levels.

Unlike the acute radiation exposure of Hiroshima and Nagasaki residents in an earlier age, the radioactive fallout in the case of Fukushima descended in lower concentrations onto areas surrounding the power plant, in patterns that depended on the winds and the weather. In March 2011, the government's statement about low-dosage exposure was reassuring, but unbelievable: it will have "no immediate effect" on health. Based on his research on the genetic and biological effects of radiation among Hiroshima survivors, Chernobyl residents, and, more recently, in the Fukushima area, Dr. Kamada Nanao (Research Institute for Nuclear Medicine and Biology, Hiroshima University) pointed out in a Hiroshima Peace Media Center-sponsored column series titled "Fukushima and Hiroshima," published in the *Chūgoku Shimbun,* that "It takes time for the effects of radiation to become apparent" (Hiroshima Peace Media Center, July 27, 2011). Most experts agree that the danger of long-term exposure to low-dosages lies in cumulative biological effects (such as cancer and leukemia) that may take years to manifest (Pacchioli, 2013b). Kamada also acknowledged the psychological and social aspects of radiation exposure, which at lower levels and over prolonged periods may affect some people but not others, making uncertainty a fact of life for those exposed.

Voluntary Evacuation

People outside of the 30-kilometer line were strongly encouraged to remain in their homes, rather than evacuate. However, with the government and TEPCO's slow response and less than transparent dissemination of information, many people even outside the mandatory evacuation area grew uneasy about the possibility of exposure. More than a third of the 105,000 people who had evacuated from Fukushima Prefecture between March 11 and 15, 2011 lived outside of the mandatory evacuation area, and decided to evacuate on their own. Such voluntary evacuation came with a huge set of economic, social, and psychological challenges (UNSCEAR, 2013 Press Release). Many people left their homes and jobs, without a secure destination or promise of employment, relocating as a family. Nor could these Fukushima residents outside the evacuation area look to the government for support.

The decision was based on stark facts: if the safety standards within the twenty to thirty kilometer zone changed over time depending on government views and aims—and the threshold itself varied even among physicians, scientists, and international agencies—then how were ordinary people supposed to judge whether it was safe for them to remain in their homes and workplaces? The complex question of the biological effects of low dosage over long periods was complicated by a general distrust in the government's capability, if not intention, to provide reliable information and manage the crisis effectively based on its poor record since the disaster started.

The debate over appropriate response in areas that had not been evacuated but showed elevated levels of radionuclides resulted in tensions within many communities. Concern over the danger of internal exposure prompted some parents to substitute lunches prepared at home for the school lunches that are an important part of the Japanese school routine. Parents with young children debated the wisdom of putting their children at risk by returning to areas that still may have "hot spots," areas of higher than natural levels of radioactivity. When 29-year-old Mr. Sakuma was informed by the government that he and his family could return to their home in Kawauchi, he decided that he would commute to his workplace, refusing to move the whole family back to live there. He explained in a *Chūgoku Shimbun* 'Fukushima to Hiroshima" column, "even doctors don't really know the effects of radiation on health . . . I can't take my daughter back there." (Hiroshima Peace Media Center, 12 March 2012). In the same column, Ms. Yamaki (28), of Koriyama, Fukushima, alluded to concerns about the acceptable limits for exposure set by the government, which were originally based on the ICRP's guidelines for adult doses in emergency situations (and thus much higher than for normal or non-critical situations), before the government redefined them as the new "safe" level for non-emergency times. She wondered whether the doses were low enough to ensure that her 5-year-old child would not be at increased risk for cancer.

This invisible radioactive pollution gave rise to considerable conflict in Fukushima communities. Because the Japanese government's post 3-11 standards for safety were unclear, if not unstable, the May 2011 'Fukushima and Hiroshima" column reported that some municipalities outside of the "no return" evacuation zones had taken the job of decontamination into their own hands. (Hiroshima Peace Media Center, 16

May 2011). At Ms. Yamaki's daughter's school, the kindergarten teachers explained their support for the Koriyama city government's decision to undertake cleanup, rather than rely solely on the national government's guidelines and decontamination program. The town scraped off surface soil in school playgrounds in order to lower radiation levels, even as it remained unsure of how to properly dispose of such waste. However, when parents in Iwaki town urged a school principal to keep the children indoors rather than let them play on a contaminated playground, one teacher testily responded, "Important people in the government say that it's safe for them to play outdoors, so it must be safe." School officials argued with parents because school policy followed the government's assertion that providing children with a stress-and worry-free environment was deemed a better way to protect their children's health than attempting to lower their exposure to radiation.

So tense did community relations become, according to Suginami Kaori, a lawyer and resident of Iwaki, that there seemed to be a taboo about even talking about radiation and safety. When concerned people mentioned the possible danger of radiation exposure, they were accused of being rude to people who chose to remain in borderline communities. Suginami and other lawyers and concerned citizens advocated for the "right to evacuate" and furthermore the "right to talk" and therefore exchange accurate information about radiation and safety (Kawasaki et. al., 2012). Historian Gabrielle Hecht noted that all "public debates about the world's nuclear and climate future" are "hyper-polarized." While nuclear power generation is among the many hazards of modern life, oversimplified statistics ("no one has died") should not "allow us to dismiss the social and health consequences of nuclear labor" and exposure of citizens, or to ignore the "complex social and physiological realities" faced by *hibakusha* (Hecht, 2013).

Powerful Interests

Extensive regulations and standards exist for nuclear power plants, but these were written on the assumption that the radioactive materials remain contained, inside the energy plants and waste dumps. The Liberal Democratic Party's victories at the polls since 2011 do not necessarily mean that the majority of voters support the party's specific agenda of reviving nuclear power. Indeed, many people have worked hard since to learn the facts about nuclear energy, safety, and waste. They are aware the level of controversy and complexity surrounding nuclear materials, and the folly of the simple label "safe." Rather than reducing the future of energy to a stark choice between nuclear energy and coal, these engaged citizens promote rethinking of high consumption life-styles and advocate devotion of resources to sustainable energy sources.

The government's 2013 announcement that Miyakoji was clean and safe enough seemed to have been precipitated by the realization of the enormous expense and time required for decontamination to levels that would satisfy international standards. A sixty-two year-old former resident of Miyakoji expressed astonishment that the government seemed willing to send people back to live in the area without specialized knowledge of the biological effects of nuclear exposure. "I used to work at the Fukushima power plant. Back then, TEPCO would never allow anyone who didn't have proper safety education to work there," he commented (Hiroshima Peace Media Center, undated). How, then, can the government think of encouraging Miyakoji residents to go home without instructing them about the necessary safety practices around radioactive hot spots and ground water?

Indeed, the approach of the Japanese government itself to managing contaminated areas around Fukushima failed to adhere to the IRCP's recommendation that

> The principle of optimisation of protection with a restriction on individual dose is central to the system of protection recommended by the Commission for existing exposure situations. Due to its judgmental nature, there is a strong need for transparency of the process. This transparency assumes that all relevant information is provided to the involved parties, and that the traceability of the

decision-making process is documented properly, aiming for an informed decision. (IRCP, 2009)

Japanese authorities clearly did not subscribe to the ICRP's recommendation that "the dissemination of a 'practical radiological protection culture' within all segments of the population" is necessary for successful protection of individuals from radiological exposure and that views of stakeholders are central to developing effective protection.

Tsuda Toshihide, Professor of Environmental Epidemiology at Okayama University, bemoans the erroneous information that has been disseminated by supposedly authoritative institutes such as the National Institute of Radiological Sciences (NIRS) in Chiba (*Chūnichi Shinbun,*11 July 2013). For a full year following the 3.11 disasters, the "Dose Scale" available by PDF on the NIRS website stated that there was "no excessive incidence of cancer" below the annual dose limit of 100 mSv. In 2012, the NIRS corrected the scale to read, "it has been found that the risk of cancer death will gradually increase with radiation dose" over 100 mSv. The "dose limit for nuclear and radiation workers" for five years is 100 mSv (natural and artificial radiation). The revised NIRS chart recommends 1 mSv as the "annual dose limit for the general public" and further notes that this limit is "not applicable to post-accident contamination." As Professor Tsuda points out, the 20 mSv dose determined by the Japanese government is one that applies in times of emergency, not in normal times. The cleanup of the Fukushima nuclear plants, furthermore, will result in "thousands of workers will be exposed annually to levels of radiation well in excess of 20 milliSieverts, the internationally recognized maximum limit for normal working conditions," despite nuclear proponents' claims that "the nuclear industry does not carry exceptional risks" (Hecht, 2013). According to Tsuda, internationally, scientists and physicians agree that there is no safe minimum dosage of radiation. He points out that misinformation tends to proliferate, even among experts. Tsuda also expressed concern about experts who publically downplay the possible biological consequences of exposure to ionizing radiation because such statements may put a damper on systematic and long-term research on the health of people exposed (*Chūnichi Shimbun*,11 July 2013).

As Sawada Shoji, emeritus professor of physics at Nagoya University, pointed out, the interests of "nuclear policy" and vested interests such as the power industry and Japanese government have long obscured research into the biological effects of radiation emitted by nuclear technologies. He noted, "Research into the effects of radiation exposure from the nuclear fallout of the Hiroshima and Nagasaki atomic bombs has been greatly distorted by U.S. nuclear policy and policies to promote nuclear power. Agencies such as the International Commission on Radiological Protection (ICRP), the International Atomic Energy Agency (IAEA), and the United Nations Scientific Committee on the Effects of Atomic Radiation (UNSCEAR) have also failed to fulfilled their original role due to their subordination to nuclear policy, with the result that the social responsibility of scientists to bring to light the truth about the effects of radiation has not been fulfilled" (Sawada, 2013). We can see this kind of partial reporting in the UNSCEAR's conclusion in 2013 that the Japanese people's exposure to radiation was low, or relatively low, due to prompt evacuation and sheltering. The UN report did not mention residual levels of radiation in areas outside of the evacuation zone, or in decontaminated areas.

Alternative Discourses: Cultures of Knowledge and Safety

Evacuees from the Fukushima have come away from the nuclear plant disaster with a new and independent perspective on Japan's complicated nuclear heritage. National discourses of nuclear allergy and peace advocacy have long roots in the Allies' use of atom bombs on Hiroshima and Nagasaki at the end of World War II, a notable and noteworthy deviation from the standard practice of air war with conventional weapons before 1945 and since. In tandem with widespread domestic resistance to nuclear discourses, the modern Japan-U.S. alliance meant that Japan (and other allies) came under the protection (?) of the American nuclear arsenal (described benignly as an "umbrella"). Powerful Japan-U.S. political and economic ties contributed to the development of a nuclear power industry in Japan from the 1950s, one that paralleled the rise of the peaceful atom in the U.S.A. Much of this was made possible through a skillful advertising/propaganda campaign waged by the Japanese government and much of the corporate media to win over a majority of Japanese consumers and local governments by convincingly evoking the safety, cost-effectiveness, and utopian promise of nuclear power. At the same time, parties with vested interests have tended to downplay the potential safety issues of power plants in an earthquake-prone, fault-riddled land, as well as the unsolved problem of nuclear waste disposal.

Fukushima does not fit comfortably into the longer narrative of Japan's "nuclear history." Connections between people in Fukushima and those tied to the historical nuclear events and sites have, however, evolved. The links between the Fukushima area and Hiroshima/Nagasaki have developed as evacuees and Fukushima residents look to Hiroshima for lessons about how to approach medical aspects of exposure, discrimination against radiation-exposed people, and what living with radiation can mean. Some evacuees chose to move to Hiroshima or Nagasaki because they hoped there would be less discrimination due to extensive "peace" education about *hibakusha* and radiation.

Conclusion: Discourse in Civil Society and Choice

Writing about civilian populations in proximity of the U.S. nuclear power plants, Iversen noted, "Many inescapable decisions have been forced upon us—decisions about nuclear weapons and nuclear energy that will have far-reaching consequences with sometimes dangerous and unintended results. To speak out or to remain silent is the first and most crucial decision we can make" (2013, p. 344).

More than a few evacuees from Fukushima used words such as "regret" and "betrayal" when speaking of their past support of nuclear power in general and the siting of the power plant locally in particular. When he served on town council, Mr. Yatsuda Mitsuharu (72) voted in favor of the building of new reactors at the Fukushima power plant. Now he has lost his home and farm, and cannot even visit his ancestors' graves. A former farmer, Mr. Amada Shiro speaks wistfully of the pear orchards that used to provide his livelihood in Namie. He describes the nuclear accident as his "worst fears" being realized, after worrying for decades about the safety of his harvest beneath the shadow of a nuclear power plant. One resident asserted that the government wants to erase memory of the accident by encouraging residents to return—as if it never happened" (Hiroshima Peace Media Center, undated).

Still other evacuees and returnees have focused on social activism and dedicated themselves to protesting against reliance on nuclear power and advocating for a safer future for younger generations. Since the Chernobyl disaster, Muto Ruiko had protested against nuclear power. She also rejected the dominant high-consumption life style by building her own home and business and living off the grid to the greatest extent possible (Yamaguchi and Muto, 2012). With the 3.11 disaster, she was forced to leave her Fukushima home, but was able to return. Muto is one of the more high-profile activists who demand that we question the way we live. She is an example of many Fukushima-area residents who have come to exercise political agency as a citizen by acting as a leader in grassroots environmental groups and exploring legal means of redress for those displaced by the nuclear disaster.

This chapter has highlighted on one hand the "discourse of sacrifice" that characterized the feelings of many of the evacuees early in the trajectory of the Fukushima tragedy. On the other, this chapter has also shown the discourse of knowledge that has emerged in response. What it has shown in terms of Japanese journalism is how the complex environment of informed comment and citizen sentiment that can be realized through the media is a vital view on events like disasters. Despite the complex media environment of the 21st century, local newspapers in print and electronic form remain a crucial part the social and political landscape. While it is important to take into account the increasing overlap, or "'mashup' of content flows through different information technologies and distribution platforms" that have the effect of blurring "the lines between social and mainstream media," scholars who employ local newspapers also need to consider the shifting roles of journalists and readings. Such blending and retransmission have the effect of transforming readers/users from a "passive consumer position" to one of actively "selecting content from mainstream media for retransmission and even editorializing about what counts as 'the news.'"(Slater et. al., 2012, p. 99).

The unassuming power plant on the shoreline did not live up to the promise made to the nation in the mid-twentieth century, and it stands in ruins, emitting toxic waste. For some evacuees from Fukushima, it will never be safe to go home; for many others, the safety of their communities and local ecosystems will long be a topic for debate. This chapter has shown the importance of the local newspaper in providing the content and context necessary for the public to participate in that debate.

References

Aldrich, D. (2012). Building Resilience: Social Capital in Post-Disaster Recovery. Chicago: University of Chicago Press.

McNeill, D. (2013). Them vs Us: Japanese and International Reporting of the Fukushima Nuclear Crisis, In T. Gill, D. Slater & B. Steger (Eds.), Japan Copes with Calamity Ethnographies of the Earthquake, Tsunami and Nuclear Disasters of March 2011 (pp. 127-150). New York: Peter Lang.

Ministry of Economy, Trade, and Industry. (2012). Practical operations for designating areas to which evacuation orders have been issued as newly designated areas. Retrieved from http://www.meti.go.jp/english/earthquake/nuclear/roadmap/pdf/20120330_01b.pdf

Cabinet Office, Japan, Support Team for Residents Affected by Nuclear Incidents. (23 July 2012). Designating and Arranging the Areas of Evacuation. Retrieved from http://www.meti.go.jp/english/earthquake/nuclear/roadmap/pdf/20120723_01.pdf

Hecht, G. (2013). Nuclear Janitors: Contract Workers at the Fukushima Reactors and Beyond. The Asia-Pacific Journal, 11(1-2). Retrieved from http://japanfocus.org/-Gabrielle-Hecht/3880#sthash.YleitPEg.dpuf

Hiroshima Peace Media Center. (2011-2012). Fukushima and Hiroshima. Chūgoku Shimbun. http://www.hiroshimapeacemedia.jp/mediacenter/index.php?topic=Fukushima_en&year=2011

International Atomic Energy Agency. (September 2011). IAEA Action Plan on Nuclear Safety. Retrieved from http://www.iaea.org/newscenter/focus/actionplan/reports/actionplanns130911.pdf

International Commission on Radiological Protection. (2009). Application of the Commission's Recommendations to the Protection of People Living in Long-term Contaminated Areas After a Nuclear Accident or a Radiation Emergency. ICRP Publication 111; ICRP 39 (3). Retrieved from http://www.icrp.org/publication.asp?id=ICRP%20Publication%20111

Iversen, K. (2013). Full Body Burden: Growing Up in the Nuclear Shadow of Rocky Flats. New York: Broadway Books.

Kawasaki, K., Suganami, K., Takeda M., & Fukuda K. (2012) Hinan suru kenri, sorezore no sentaku. Iwanami bukkuretto series. #839. Tokyo: Iwanami Shoten.

Pacchioli, D. (30 April 2013a) ABCs of Radioactivity: A Long and Winding Road to Achieve Stability, Oceanus. Retrieved from http://www.whoi.edu/oceanus/viewArticle.do?id=166969

Pacchioli, D. (8 May 2013b) Radiation Health Risks: How Can We Assess Impacts of Exposure? Oceanus. Retrieved from http://www.whoi.edu/oceanus/viewArticle.do?id=167749

Sawada, S. (10 June 2013) Scientists and Research on the Effects of Radiation Exposure: From Hiroshima to Fukushima. The Asia-Pacific Journal, 11(23). Retrieved from http://japanfocus.org/-Sawada-Shoji/3952'

Samuels, R. J. (2013). 3.11: Disaster and Change in Japan. Ithaca: Cornell University Press.

Slater, D., Nishimura K., & Love K. (2012). Social Media in Disaster Japan. In J. Kingston (Ed.) Natural Disaster and Nuclear Crisis in Japan: Response and Recovery after Japan's 3/11. (pp. 94-108). New York: Routledge.

Steger, B. (2013). Solidarity and Distinction through Practices of Cleanliness in Tsunami Evacuation Shelters in Yamada, Iwate Prefecture. In T. Gill, D. Slater and B. Steger (Eds.) Japan Copes with Calamity Ethnographies of the Earthquake, Tsunami and Nuclear Disasters of March 2011. (pp. 53-76). New York: Peter Lang.

Takahashi, T. (2012). Gisei no Shisutemu: Fukushima, Okinawa. Tokyo: Shueisha.

United Nations Scientific Committee on the Effects of Atomic Radiation (UNSCEAR). (31 May 2013). Press Release. Retrieved from http://www.unis.unvienna.org/unis/en/pressrels/2013/unisinf475.html

Yamaguchi, T. & Muto R. (2 July, 2012) Muto Ruiko and the Movement of Fukushima Residents to Pursue Criminal Charges against Tepco Executives and Government Officials. The Asia-Pacific Journal, 10(27-2). Retrieved from

CHAPTER TEN

LOCAL NEWSPAPERS AND THE POST-EARTHQUAKE AND TSUNAMI RECONSTRUCTION IN IWATE PREFECTURE

Shunichi Takekawa

INTRODUCTION

The media response to the Great East Japan Earthquake on March 11, 2011, the earthquake and tsunami and the Fukushima Nuclear Plant accident, attracted a great deal of attention, some positive and some negative. On the one hand, national newspapers and TV stations in Tokyo were severely criticized for their garbled coverage of the nuclear accidents, which created a high level of uncertainty and unease. On the other, prefectural and community newspapers were reported to have played crucial roles in tsunami-damaged coastal areas in Tohoku, such as Iwate and Miyagi prefectures. Despite working under extreme conditions and facing tremendous obstacles in both gathering information and publishing and delivering their newspapers, it was only the local and community newspapers that functioned to provide people in the tsunami-damaged areas with news during the days just after the disasters occurred (Yamada, 2013). One of the community newspapers in Miyagi Prefecture, *Ishinomaki Hibi Shimbun*, after their printing machine was destroyed by the tsunami, resorted to making and posting handwritten newspapers (*Ishinomaki Hibi Shimbun*, 2011). Moreover, due to the loss of electricity and telephone, only local newspapers could inform tsunami survivors of the state of their family members and relatives, disseminate vital information, and provide a wider picture of the disasters. Accordingly, newspaper people rediscovered the power of a print medium and their responsibility in ensuring its continuation (Iwate Nippōsha Henshūkyoku, 2012). The disaster clearly strengthened the consciousness of newspaper people in the Tohoku District.

The area along Iwate's coastline has a long history of tsunamis, evident in the extensive damage reported in the aftermath of the 1896 Sanriku Earhquake, the 1933 Sanriku Earthquake, and the 1960 Valdivia Earthquake. In this disaster, as well, it was the coastal areas that suffered: according to the Iwate prefectural government, 4,672 people died and 1,151 people are still missing; over 24,000 residential building were destroyed (Iwateken, 2013). In addition, the fisheries of the coastline, one of the major industries in the towns and villages that make up the area, were largely destroyed. However, due to the distinct geographical difference between Iwate's inland areas and its coastal areas, while coastline communities were severely damaged, the inland areas of the prefecture were only affected slightly by the earthquake shocks. Indeed, no one died in the inland area, with only approximately 100 reported injuries and light infrastructural damage.

Post-Earthquake and Tsunami Reconstruction 219

Reconstruction in the tsunami-damaged coastal areas has lagged, slower than the residents expected and government officials anticipated. Most of these areas have long suffered from depopulation and the lack of industry; now matters are worse. Newspaper people, well aware of this reality, now had to face this new and dramatic suffering on the part of the local population. The question of this chapter concerns what the newspapers, the journalists and editors offered as content during the recovery and reconstruction period. By studying the serialized content of local newspaper newspapers in Iwate prefecture, one of the most damaged-prefectures in Tohoku, this chapter ponders the multiple roles that newspapers play in such time.

In the field of Japanese media studies, national newspapers have gained considerable attention for their operational characteristics, ideological stances, and homogeneity in coverage and content. On the other hand, the local newspapers of Japan have been largely ignored. However, it should be noted that in many areas of Japan outside the major metropolitan centers of Tokyo and Osaka, the local newspaper is more popular than a national newspaper, so in fact the local newspaper may actually provide a more useful perspective to any study of a place within Japan. As such, this chapter also seeks to provide some basics to the study a local newspaper, thereby contributing to the undertaking of Japanese Studies.

OVERVIEW OF NEWSPAPERS IN JAPAN

Japan is seen as a media-saturated society, and rightfully so. One of the reasons for this is the size and significance of its newspaper industry. National newspapers are among the top newspapers in the world on the basis of daily circulation, with the newspaper industry itself second in size to the world's largest, the People's Republic of China, in terms of total newspaper circulation within a nation (Fujitake, 2012). Another important aspect of the Japanese newspaper industry is that its newspapers operate and provide coverage concurrently at different levels all over Japan. This national structure reflects a division between national and non-national newspapers; these non-national newspapers can then be categorized as regional, prefectural, and community. In any prefecture, it is possible to find that national newspapers, as well as regional and local newspapers, all compete with each other. In each of them, a reader can find international and national news coverage, as well as prefectural and municipal news stories. Both national and regional and local newspapers are published daily, many with both morning and evening editions. A majority of the local papers are integrated within the national frame of the newspaper industry and are members of the *Nihon Shimbun Kyōkai* (Japan Newspaper Publishers and Editors Association). At the lowest end of the scale are the community newspapers, local papers that specifically cover local news stories for the residents of the several municipalities that it covers. In addition, there are sport newspapers and specialized newspapers for industries and others.

Any understanding of the characteristics and importance of local newspapers is dependent on an understanding of how the national newspapers operate in Japan. First of all, the typical national newspaper has bureaus of staff reporters in all prefectural capital cities and other major cities in Japan, while also subscribing to wire services in order to fully cover international news. A national newspaper directly covers national political events taking place in Tokyo together with the economic news concerning Japan's major corporations located in Tokyo through its own staff reporters. As such, these national newspapers are called "*chūōshi*" (papers of the center) and are expected to deliver information from the center of Japan to places outside Tokyo; this is one of the major distinctions between national newspapers and local newspapers and one of the reasons why people in various prefectures subscribe to national newspapers.

Under such a national-centric large-scale system, a regional newspaper, referred to as a *block-shi* in Japanese, covers several prefectures as a geographical block. A regional newspaper usually has its headquarters in the largest city in the region, with its bureaus of staff reporters then disbursed to the major cities of the prefecture that it covers and sales both concentrated within the large cities and also sited across the rural areas of this block. A regional newspaper is more focused on local politics and the local economy, as well as local issues and local events, of its block of prefectures than is any national newspaper, while also publishing national and international news stories that mostly come from the Japanese wire services such as *Kyodo News* and *Jiji Press*. Examples of such block newspapers include the *Hokkaido Shimbun*, covering Sapporo city and Hokkaido prefecture, the *Kahoku Shimpō*, covering Sendai city and Miyagi prefecture, the *Chūnichi Shimbun*, covering Nagoya city and Aichi prefecture, the *Chūgoku Shimbun*, covering Hiroshima city and Hiroshima prefecture, and the *Nishi-Nihon Shimbun*, covering Fukuoka and Fukuoka prefecture.

A newspaper that focuses on one prefecture is referred to as *chihōshi* or *kenshi*. It naturally focuses attention on local news stories within a prefecture, specifically local politics and the local economy of the prefecture and municipalities while also relying on some content from wire services for national and international news stories. Its headquarters will be in the capital of the prefecture and it has bureaus and reporters throughout the prefecture. The reporters, editors, and staff of pefectural newspapers are likely from the prefecture and plan on living there through their career; this as opposed to national paper reporters, who reside in an area only for some years, based on the rotations and transfers common to national corporations in Japan. Accordingly, these local reporters have much stronger ties with local communities than reporters from national newspapers. Therefore, at a prefectural level, a local newspaper is major media outlet, and their reporters are much more knowledgeable about local events and issues than national newspaper reporters. In general, these prefectural papers have more subscribers than any national newspaper in its home prefecture. As of 2013, almost all prefectures have, at least, one prefectural newspaper, except for Osaka and Shiga prefectures (Fujitake, 2012).

In addition, there are community newspapers, or *chiikishi,* which cover a relatively large city and/or several neighboring municipalities, focusing almost exclusively on local issues and events. These newspapers intentionally choose not to publish national and international content, essentially relegating themselves as secondary newspapers. They assume that their paper will be read by local residents who also subscribe to a national or prefectural newspaper, and rather than compete with these other newspapers, they serve as a supplement to them (Shikata, 2013a; Yamada, 1985). Such a community newspaper usually has only 8 or 10 pages and may not publish everyday nor have evening editions. Although there is some instability in the *chiikishi* market, with newspapers emerging and going out of business, estimates put the number of such newspapers at around 200 in Japan (Nihon Chiiki Shimbun Kyōgikai, 2010).

Iwate Newspapers

Iwate is the second largest prefecture of Japan by area, with an 15,278 km^2 area, following Hokkaido, which dwarfs all prefectures with 83,456 km^2. Contrasting its size rank, Iwate's population is about 1.3 million, putting it 32nd amongst the 47 prefectures. These two demographics point to Iwate being one of the most thinly populated prefectures of present-day Japan. Geographically, Iwate faces the Pacific Ocean with a deeply indented 700-kilometer coastline, a fact that likely creates larger tsunami waves than more gently curved and sloping coastlines.

In Iwate prefecture, as outlined above, national and local newspapers coexist and complement with each other. In addition, there are also several community newspapers covering and serving highly local municipalities. Iwate's large area seems in fact to have yielded a rather complex multiple local newspaper market environment. Specifically, each of the five national newspapers has a local bureau with reporters in Iwate's prefectural capital, Morioka city. The daily circulations of the morning editions of these newspapers in Iwate range between 30,000 to 50,000 copies per day. In addition to these national papers selling, a larger regional newspaper, the *Kahoku Shimpō*, also covers Iwate. The *Kahoku Shimpō* headquarters are located in Sendai city, Miyagi prefecture, the largest city in six prefectural area of the Tohoku District, the *Kahoku* claims to be the newspaper of record for Tohoku. In Iwate, the *Kahoku Shimpō* has a main bureau in Morioka City and five other bureaus throughout Iwate in other major cities, publishing only morning editions. The *Kahoku Shimpō's* daily circulation in the six prefectures combined is about 580,000 copies (*Kahoku Shimpō*, 2013).

Despite the presence of both national newspapers and the Tohoku powerhouse, the *Kahoku*, the prefectural newspaper, the *Iwate Nippō*, is a major news media outlet which sells over 208,000 copies per day, based on a 24-page morning edition format (Nihon Shimbun Kyōkai, 2012). The *Iwate Nippō* was established in 1876, early in the Meiji period, and its headquarters are in Morioka city, the prefectural capital. The newspaper has five branch offices nationally, including offices in Tokyo and Osaka, and has fifteen bureaus for news coverage within the prefecture, with over one hundred editors and reporters (Nihon Shimbun Kyōkai, 2012). These prefectural bureaus are located in most major cities both the inland and in coastline areas, and from the north to the south of the prefecture. Iwate can claim another major newspaper, the *Iwate Nichi-nichi*, which was established in 1923 and has headquarters in Ichinoseki, a major city in the south side of Iwate prefecture, about 100 kilometers away from Morioka. The *Iwate Nichi-nichi* focuses coverage and sales concentration on the inland area of the south side of Iwate prefecture, yielding a circulation of about 50,000 copies per day in a 16-page morning edition format. The *Iwate Nichi-nichi* has nine bureaus in the inland areas of the south side for news coverage, and employs fifty editors and reporters (Nihon Shimbun Kyōkai, 2012). Accordingly, while the *Iwate Nichi-nichi* is clearly the second Iwate newspaper, it is sometimes categorized as a community newspaper (Nihon Chiiki Shimbun Kyōgikai, 2010). In addition, another regional newspaper, but one with less coverage than the *Kahoku Shimpō*, covers and sells in Iwate prefecture. The *Daily Tohoku*, originating in Hachinohe city of Aomori Prefecture, covers the north side of Iwate's coastline in news coverage and sales. The *Daily Tohoku* has bureaus for news gathering in Morioka, as well as Kuji and Ninohe, but sales are minimal.

The existence of these three different prefecture newspapers demonstrates Iwate's geographical and social diversity. The north and south ends of Iwate belonged to different feudal lords, Nanbu and Date, during the Edo period. Subsequently, they were administratively part of different prefectures as late as the early Meiji period. Even today, the northern and southern areas exhibit both vastly differing economies and cultural characteristics. This is very likely a primary reason why *Iwate Nichi-nichi* emerged and survived along with *Iwate Nippō*. Indeed, Shikata (2013b) argued that a community newspaper can emerge and survive along side a larger paper if it is located far enough away from the prefectural capital or if it serves an area that existed under a different feudal lord domain in the distant past; these conditions describe the case of the *Iwate Nichi-nichi*.

The complexity of Iwate's newspaper culture extends to include three community newspapers: the *Morioka Taimusu*, established in 1969 in Morioka city; the *Tankō Nichinichi*, established in 1946 in the inland city of Oshū; and the *Tōkai Shimpō*, established in 1958 in Ōfunato city, located in a coastline area. All three of these community newspapers publish morning editions. The *Morioka Taimusu*, unique in that it is the only community paper that publishes in a prefectural capital in Tohoku (Yamada, 1985), usually has 10 pages, and covers Morioka city and several surrounding municipalities. The *Tankō Nichinichi* and the *Tōkai Shimpō* have from 8 or 10 pages and publish about 22,000 and 17,000 copies per day, respectively (*Nihon Chiiki Shimbun Kyōgikai*, 2010). Like the *Morioka Taimusu*, each of these papers covers the areas surrounding their host communities: in the case of the *Tankō Nichinichi*, this means Oshū city and one other municipality. For the *Tōkai Shimpō*, the area of coverage is the Kesen region, made of Ōfunato and Rikuzentakata cities and Sumita town. Prior to the March 11 disaster, there was a community newspaper serving Kamaishi and Miyako cities, and Ōtsuchi and Yamada

Post-Earthquake and Tsunami Reconstruction 225

towns. The *Iwate Tōkai Shimbun*, established in 1948 in Kamaishi city and preceding the *Tokai Shimpō* in using local geographical referencing *(tokai:* eastern sea) as its namesake, was in fact shut down because of the damage caused by the tsunami. Prior to its closure, it published 14,000 copies per day (Nihon Chiiki Shimbun Kyōgikai, 2010). However, soon after this closure, former employees of the paper began a new newspaper, dubbed the *Kamaishi Fukkō Shimbun*. Established in June 2011 on the basis of subsidies from Kamaishi city, the *Kamaishi Fukkō Shimbun*, the name of which includes reference to revitalization with the term *fukkō*, publishes information from the Kamaishi city government as well as covering local news stories about Kamaishi residents.

ANALYSIS OF LOCAL AND COMMUNITY PAPERS IN IWATE

Basic Differences between *Iwate Nippō* and *Tōkai Shimpō*
Having established the complexity in Iwate's newspaper culture by outlining the different levels of newspapers in the prefecture, Iwate can be seen as being representative of a typical prefecture where national, regional, and prefectural newspapers compete on the one hand and where community newspapers complement this completion in different areas on the other. The analysis of this chapter focuses on a prefectural newspaper, the *Iwate Nippo*, and a community newspaper, the *Tokai Shimpō*, in order to highlight the different characteristics of those different levels of local newspapers. For purposes of this comparison, the crucible of the 3.11 disaster provides ample material. As the *Iwate Nippo* is the only prefectural newspaper that covers the tsunami-damaged coastline area and the *Tohkai Shimpō* is the only community newspaper that covers the tsunami-damaged area, these two newspapers will be the focus of the remainder of the chapter.

As above, in Iwate Prefecture, the *Iwate Nippō* dominates a competitive newspaper market that complements national, regional and prefectural newspapers. The *Iwate Nippō* covers about 40 percent of the market, followed by the *Yomiuri*, which covers nearly 10 percent (*Yomiuri Shimbun*, 2013). The *Iwate Nippō* publishes a 24-page morning paper everyday, with a sales area that extends throughout the prefecture. It is intuitive that the *Iwate Nippō* competes successfully with the other national and regional newspapers that publish in the area because, in addition to the prefectural and community news stories it publishes, it also provides a considerable number of national and international news stories, relying on the *Kyodo News* wire service. A copy of *Iwate Nippō* morning edition usually has three pages of general news section, which provide national and prefectural politics-related news stories, one-page of international news coverage, two-pages of business and economy news, and three pages of social affairs content, which cover legal trials, large accidents, significant social incidents, and some human interest stories. The paper also includes lifestyle, culture, and entertainment pages, in addition to a couple of pages of full-page ads. In this sense, the news organization of the *Iwate Nippō* is similar to that of a national or regional newspaper. However, the *Iwate Nippō* also dedicates three pages to high local news, in the form of a Morioka and Northern Prefectural Area page, a Southern Prefectural Area page, and a Coastline Area page. These local pages publish articles on local school and sport events, official announcements from municipal governments, and other local news and information. After the earthquake and tsunami, a bulletin board page of useful information for earthquake- and tsunami-survivors, such as legal consultations and health examinations, was established, along with a feature page focusing exclusively on the Great East Japan Earthquake, which published articles and included photos on earthquake- and tsunami-damaged areas and survivors.

The *Tōkai Shimpō* presents a valuable contrast, in that it covers inland areas that were not damaged by the tsunami on March 11, 2011. The *Tōkai Shimpō* can be seen as a very successful community paper: it claimed a daily circulation of about 17,000 copies in a town of 24,000 households prior to the earthquake and tsunami. Just after the earthquake and tsunami, however, the circulation fell to about 8,000 copies per day, only to recover and stabilize at around 14,000 copies by July 2012 (*Asahi Shimbun,* 2012 *Tōkai Shimpō,* n.d.). The paper usually publishes an 8-page morning paper from Tuesday to Sunday with almost all news copy focusing on the two cities and one town that it serves; there is no national, international, and prefectural news content included. The news covered in the *Tōkai Shimpō* is dominated by official announcements from the local governments, content related to the state of local businesses and the recovery of the local economy, as well as local cultural and sport events. While the spatial allocation of news content is neither clear nor consistent, small advertisements of local businesses are found at the bottom of each page.

Perspectives for Further Analysis
Ishizawa (1994) pointed out that, compared with American media outlets, Japanese media outlets are less aggressive toward and less critical of government authorities as news sources. Most observers have concurred, noting that the objective style of reportage in Japanese newspapers confirms this tendency. News articles in Japanese media outlets, especially newspapers, are overly factual and descriptive, often relying on authoritative news sources through mechanisms such as a press club, referred in Japanese as *kisha kurabu.* In this case, reporters are predominantly reactive, writing a news story based on information provided to them by authoritative informants in highly controlled and scripted environments. It is precisely for that reason that this chapter focuses on serialized articles, which reflect a different tendency

Serialized articles are often rendered in Japanese in terms that reflect continuity and planning, as *tsuzukimono* (serialization), *kikakumono* (project), or *rensai kikaku* (serialized project). These types of articles are not produced to present content about newsworthy events that just have taken place or informative remarks provided by authoritative informants. Rather, a single series of articles usually has from several to, in some cases, over hundreds of serialized articles, which are numbered to keep readers aware of the sequential character of the serialized content.

Serialized content usually emerges with reporters' active engagement in a newsworthy issue, outside the constraints of the press club setting. In order to bring out these issues, it is necessary for the reporters, and the editors, to study an issue and interview relevant and knowledgeable people so as to be able to present an issue from a variety of perspectives. Reporters want their readers to know, understand, and think about important issues, which is why such socially instructive content is usually presented not as news, but rather in serialized articles. In this sense, it is precisely through serialized content that it is possible for the reporter to identify the important themes and content regarding socially significant issues.

This serialization of content as reportage can also be seen as what can be termed "campaign journalism". This type of journalism is prevalent in Japan; not confined to reporters at ideologically driven newspapers, this format has been used by major news departments to bring about change in socially important issues. In this process, the newspaper, through an editor, publishes serialized articles on a particular topic, anti-pollution campaigns, for example, sometimes resulting in a change of policy by the government (Shimbun Hōdō Kenkyūkai, 1995). While campaign journalism can be seen as a characteristic of a Japanese style of public journalism, and something local newspapers use (Kitamura, 2009), campaign journalism has been viewed as questionable as reporters and newspaper companies can become co-opted as active actors in social and political movements. Moreover, campaigns conducted by national newspapers are often seen as more questionable than those by local newspapers because those emerging at the national level are often highly corrupted by political or ideological ends (Shimbun Hōdō Kenkyūkai, 1995). Examples of this can be seen in the *Yomiuri Shimbun's* campaign to revise the Japanese constitution and the *Sankei Shimbun's* campaign aiming at administrative reform, both largely seen as questionable in terms of journalistic practice.

Post-Earthquake and Tsunami Reconstruction   229

As noted above, local and community newspapers can be part of public journalism owing to their strong commitment to the residents of their host areas. Indeed, given the scale of such newspapers, such a function may be more important than any other role seen in contemporary journalism. Such public journalism takes on more importance in the extraordinary times after an event on the scale of an earthquake and tsunami. With that in mind, this section analyzes serialized articles in the *Iwate Nippō* and the *Tōkai Shimpō*, outlining categories and identifying the roles that these two newspapers played in the time of earthquake and tsunami reconstruction.

Serialized Content in the Iwate Nippō
From March 11, 2011, to March 11, 2013 the *Iwate Nippō* published twenty-four serialized articles, which in total constituted 803 articles, covering post earthquake and tsunami issues, the fate of victims and the state of survivors, and the reconstruction of the area. Those twenty-four series can be categorized into four groups: fact recording, collective memory creation, public policy relation, and human bond promotion (see Table 3; Web Appendix).

The category "fact recording" reflects a series in which reporters attempted to record objectively what had happened in disaster-affected municipalities and what the residents in those municipalities had done to survive the tsunami and reconstruct their lives, businesses, and local communities. This category includes eleven series of 421 individual articles out of the 803 total during the period (52%) and constituted the largest portion of the serialized articles in *Iwate Nippō*. Many of serialized articles in this category simply documented the disaster and the damage that resulted, whereas others reported on attempts to support those who were struggling to recover and manage their lives and businesses. In this sense, these "fact recording" series were an attempt to inform readers within the prefecture of what survivors in the tsunami-damaged area were experiencing and the character of their struggles. For example, a series titled, *"Asu e no ippo"* (A Step toward Tomorrow), documented what local business owners, farmers, fisherman, and other locals were doing in their efforts to recover their businesses. The series included sixty-one articles that ran from April to June in 2011. The longest series of this category was titled *"Moyai: hama ni ikieru"* (Anchoring: Life near the Seashore), and consisted of 120 articles carried from June to December in 2011. This series specifically focused on the lives of fishermen of the tsunami-damaged fishing ports. Although intended to be neutrally factual, the tone of both series of articles was positive, a reflection of reporting on the survivors' strenuous efforts to reconstruct their lives and businesses.

Content labeled "collective memory creation" functioned to commemorate the victims of the earthquake and tsunami, and included content related to those who had died or were missing as well as content that presented damaged structures and local scenery that had once been prominent in the area. This category consisted of three series totaling 27 articles (3%). An example is a series of seventeen articles titled *"Wasurenai"* (We Won't Forget) which published photos and stories of those who had died in the tsunami. The content was based on interviews with surviving family members or friends. This column specifically did not intend to introduce local heroes or highlight the fate of influential figures, but rather focused on ordinary residents who had perished in the disaster. According to Iwate Nippōsha Henshūkyoku (2012), nearly 3,000 victims were introduced through this series from March to October 2012. The other two series that constitute this category include articles introducing notable buildings and local scenery that had been destroyed or damaged by the tsunami.

Content under the "public policy relation" category is that which serves either to investigate the public policy needs in the damaged municipalities or to assess the reconstruction plans announced by prefectural and municipality governments. Nine series of 272 articles are included in this category, constituting the second largest component of the serialized articles in the *Iwate Nippō* and accounting for 34% percent of the total serialized articles. A prominent example of this category is the series *"Fukkō Seizensen"* (Front Line of Reconstruction), consisting of eighty articles, notable for outlining what needed to be done to reconstruct the tsunami-damaged municipalities and communities, covering a range of sectors, from public transportation systems, residential zones, and tsunami barriers, to community centers.

The last category identified was "human bond promotion," which reported how people in different places in the prefecture, such as survivors in the tsunami-damaged area and residents in the inland area, helped each other. There were two series in this category, comprised of 83 articles. In this content, it appeared that the *Iwate Nippō* was seeking to strengthen ties between the coastline and inland areas, which had considerably different experiences of the earthquake and tsunami in March 2011. A series consisting of sixteen articles titled *"Sasaeai"* (Mutual Support) focused on groups and organizations such as NPOs from outside of the tsunami-damaged area that aimed to help tsunami-survivors. Another series, consisting of 67 articles, titled *"Furusato o muneni, Nairiku kara no saiki"* (Restart in the Inland Area with the Homeland in One's Mind), introduced people from the tsunami-damaged area who had, post-disaster, moved to the inland areas of the prefecture.

Serialized Content in the Tōkai Shimpō
Over the same period, from March 11, 2011, to March 11, 2013, the *Tōkai Shimpō* published twenty-four series consisting of 566 individual articles covering similar content to that examined above. However, the content in the *Tōkai Shimpō* led to the necessity of an additional category: fact recording, collective memory creation, public policy relation, human bond promotion, and future and wishes (see Table 4; Web Appendix). As for the content of this additional category, the *Tōkai Shimpō* interviewed influential figures in affected municipalities and asked what they wanted to realize after the earthquake and tsunami, publishing the interviews at the beginning of 2012 and 2013. This content accounted for approximately four percent of the total serialization content.

The "fact recording" category in the *Tōkai Shimpō* consisted of six series of 162 articles, accounting for 29% of the total articles and constituting the second largest category in the *Tōkai Shimpō*. A notable series in this category was *"Teiten kansoku: Kesen no kiroku"* (Fixed-Point Observation: Record of Kesen), a series made of fifty-three articles and 106 photos. The format of the series was to choose a place damaged by the disaster and present a descriptive article accompanied by one photo taken just after the tsunami, followed by a photo of the same place somewhat recovered from the damage about one year after the tsunami. The series began in July 2012 and ended in March 2013. Another notable series was *"Fukkō ōen, Kasetsu tenpo mitearuki"* (Cheering on the Reconstruction: Checking in on Temporary Shops and Restaurants), consisting of forty-five articles describing the progress made in reestablishing such local businesses, carried from May 2012 to March 2013.

The category of "collective memory creation" was the largest in the *Tōkai Shimpō* data set. It included five series of 289 articles, covering 51% of the total serialized articles. This category includes four series of articles that featured photos of local scenery. Two of these series were carried under the same title, *"Kokoro no jōkei, Omoide shashinkan"* (Scenes in our Minds: Photo Studio of Memories), but were divided into two different periods, the first from July to December in 2011 and the second from January to May in 2012. The photos featured in the series were taken before the earthquake and tsunami, an effort by the newspaper to allow the residents to once again see the beautiful scenery of their hometowns. Interestingly, the second series of the two was started in part in response to requests on the part of local readers and in part in order to provide for volunteers a view of what these places destroyed by the disaster looked like in the past. Similarly, a series titled *"Kūchū sanpo"* (Flyover), carried from June to September in 2012, featured 24 photos taken by hung-gliding photo shooters showing the area before the tsunami struck. The final series of the four consisted of recollections of the area written by a range of local residents. This is perhaps what a small community paper is willing to do, letting non-reporters write and publish their notes in its media outlet.

The "public policy relation" content consisted of seven series of 58 articles, accounting for ten percent of the total articles. Two of these series, comprising thirty-four articles, introduced and outlined the reconstruction plans of Ōfunato and Rikuzentakata city governments. Another presented interviews with the two mayors of these cities. The "human bond creation" category had three series of 35 articles, accounting for six percent of the total serialized articles. The content of this category introduced voices of former residents of the municipalities, those who had left the region after the tsunami and were living either in Iwate's inland area or outside the area altogether.

Serialized Content in the *Iwate Nippō* and the *Tōkai Shimpō* Compared

In an odd coincidence, the two local newspapers each published 24 series, but the number of articles within these 24 in the *Iwate Nippō* came to over 800 individual articles, whereas in the *Tōkai Shimpō* the content appeared through 566 specific articles. This difference should not be surprising as the *Iwate Nippō* publishes a 24-page morning paper seven days a week, whereas the *Tōkai Shimpō* publishes just an 8-page morning paper six days per week. In this sense, the *Tōkai Shimpō* would seem to be more passionate for serialized articles than the *Iwate Nippō*, perhaps a reflection of the different trajectories as a prefectural newspaper versus a community newspaper.

The dynamics of competition between national and prefectural newspapers in outlying areas of Japan has been introduced. In the case of Iwate prefecture, the prefectural *Iwate Nippō* also faces competition from a regional newspaper, the *Kahoku Shimpō*. As such, the *Iwate Nippō* as a prefectural newspaper is obligated to circulate news stories to residents in a variety of places within Iwate and to provide news content relevant to policy-makers such as prefectural assembly members as well as prefectural government bureaucrats in Morioka, the prefectural capital of Iwate. On the other hand, a community newspaper operates with no intention of competing with newspapers operating at a higher level. Rather, a community newspaper focuses on its community without fear of market competitors. In this sense, the community newspaper can be seen as unconventional as a newspaper, in that it need not update news stories everyday. In this respect, the *Tōkai Shimpō* does not feel obligated to provide news either in a manner that would be relevant to prefectural assembly and prefectural government bureaucrats or to readers outside of its community host area. This reality may also explain why the *Tōkai Shimpō* could allocate space the publishing old photos of the damaged places for its reader residents. The *Iwate Nippō*, as a conventional newspaper, did not, and perhaps could not, publish such old photos. In a conventional way of news making, old photos do not make news of facts.

Looking at this on the basis of the quantitative distribution of series content, just four percent of content in the *Iwate Nippō* was related to "collective memory creation," whereas this category constituted over 50% in the *Tōkai Shimpō*. Quantitatively, this is explained by the *Tōkai Shimpō* publishing three different photo series consisting of 259 articles. This content featured photos of scenery of the tsunami damaged municipalities before the earthquake and tsunami. Similarly, over 50% of the serialized article content in the *Iwate Nippō* was categorized as "fact recording," whereas this constituted less than 30 percent in the *Tōkai Shimpō*. As noted above, whereas the *Tōkai Shimpō* concentrated on its own community, the *Iwate Nippō* provided factual coverage for residents in a variety of places in Iwate—including both coastal areas and areas inland—so a wide range of readers could update the status of survivors.

Finally, approximately 30% of the serialized content was relevant to policy in the *Iwate Nippō* whereas such content accounted for only ten percent in the *Tōkai Shimpō*. The *Iwate Nippō* is the prefectural-level newspaper, therefore, it is natural to assume that interested readers would look to it as a major source of information regarding what is going on in prefectural politics and policy. The *Iwate Nippō* is for them a media outlet to know what journalists think is important policy planning for the damaged coastal municipalities.

Conclusion

If journalism is assumed to include public journalism, there are multiple interpretations of how such public journalism emerges in reality. Takeuchi (1989) presented three roles inherent in community media: delivering relevant information regarding the community; presenting public issues of community concern for public consideration as well as offering different opinions regarding that issue; and helping community residents to form a sense of solidarity by introducing local traditional events and culture, and history. More recently, Rausch (2012) discussed revitalization journalism, identified on the basis of serialized articles in a prefectural newspaper of Aomori Prefecture. What Rausch presents seems a variation of public journalism; in a rural prefecture like Aomori, a prefectural newspaper seeks to revitalize its local society through its journalism practices. Having analyzed serialized articles in the *Iwate Nippō* and the *Tōkai Shimpō* in the aftermath of the 3.11 earthquake-tsunami disaster, this chapter re-categorized the roles that local newspapers, including both prefectural and community newspapers, tend to play in the period of reconstruction from the severe disaster-damages.

The previous section presented five different categories of serialized articles in the two local newspapers under examination. These categories were: fact recording, collective memory creation, public policy-relation, human bond promotion, and future and wishes. This chapter concludes by considering how these categories coincide with the roles outlined for newspapers in post-disaster areas. The fact recording category is included in Takeuchi's first role, that of information dissemination; however, it is also part of his third role and can also be regarded to be part of Rausch's notion of revitalization through journalism. The *Iwate Nippō* reported on those who were struggling in the damaged areas as a means of informing others in the prefecture of their plight. That is, this kind of reporting functioned to update the prefecture in general while also aiming to revitalize the damaged area. The collective memory creation category is somewhat new to newspaper analysis, but it does overlap with Takeuchi's third role, related to social solidarity. The photo series carried in the *Tōkai Shimpō* emerged out of an intention to share old images of the municipalities with those who had survived the tsunami. That sort of history sharing with residents within the affected municipalities amounts to solidarity building. The content of the third category, public policy-relation, is clearly part of Takeuchi's second role of the media, that of illumination of public issues. Following on this, the fourth category, human bond promotion, like collective memory creation, is close to Takeuchi's third role, solidarity. However, the content here is not related to the past, but rather highlights the present in an attempt to promote a sense of solidarity among the residents. The approach, interestingly, was practiced by the *Iwate Nippō* at the prefectural level and by the *Tōkai Shimpō* at the community level. Finally, the fifth category, found only in the *Tōkai Shimpō*, relates partially to Takuchi's second role, that of presenting public issues, as it is about wishes for the future policy-making.

In sum, the roles that local newspapers play in the reconstruction from severe-disaster damages are extensive and varied. These include the delivery of information based in and relevant to local communities as well as prefectural society in general, together with the presentation of public issues accompanied by different opinions, provided in some cases by residents, that can be brought to address these issues through policy-making by prefectural or municipality governments as well as efforts by communities and individuals. Newspapers play a role in creating and consolidating solidarity among community members at one level and prefectural residents at another through presentation of news stories that highlight local events and local places, as well as the commemoration of the people, the scenery, indeed the memories of a community that are now gone. Newspapers function in revitalizing destroyed communities, as well as in aiding the individuals of those communities through the reportage of those who make efforts to reconstruct their lives, businesses, and community. These are, needless to say, tentative roles; roles neither easily discernable nor managed; roles that emerge less by design that by response. Further studies are needed to understand local newspapers and the reconstruction from severe disaster damages.

References

Asahi Shimbun. (2012, October 26). Joho towa – hisaichi kara. *Asahi Shimbun* (morning edition), 17.

Fujitake, A. et al. (2012). *Zusetsu, Nihon no media*. Tokyo: NHK Shuppan.Ishinomaki

Hibi Shimbun (Ed.). (2011). *6-mai no kabe shimbun* (6 wallnewspapers). Tokyo: Kadokawa Magazines.

Ishizawa, Y. (1994). *Nichi-Bei kankei to masu media*. Tokyo: Maruzen.

Iwateken (2013). *Iwateken Higashinihon daishinsai tsunami no kiroku* (Iwate prefecture's record of the Great East Japan Earthquake and Tsunami). Iwateken. Retrieved from http://www.pref.iwate.jp/~bousai/kirokushi/2013kirokushi.html

Iwate Nippōsha Henshūkyoku. (2012). *Fūka to tatakau kishatachi*. Tokyo: Waseda Daigaku Shuppankyoku.

Kahoku Shimpō. (2013). Hakkō busū data. Retrieved from http://www.kahoku.co.jp/pub/media/hakkou/

Kitamura, Y. (2009). Chihōshi. In J. Hamada, et al. (Eds.) *Shinbungaku, shintei*. (pp. 50-60). Tokyo: Nihon Hyōronsha.

Nihon Chiiki Shinbun Kyōgikai (2010). *Nihon Chi'iki Shinbun Gaido 2010-2011*. Tokyo: Nihon Chi'iki Shinbun Kyōgikai.

Nihon Shimbun Kyōkai (2012). *Nihon Shinbun Nenkan 2013*. Tokyo: Nihon Shimbun Kyōkai.

Rausch, Anthony S. (2012). *Japan's local newspapers: chihōshi and revitalization journalism*. New York, NY: Routledge.

Shikata, H. (2013a). Kyodoshi: Chiiki jānarizumu kenkyū. *Liberal Time* 13(9), 52-54.

Shikata, H. (2013b). Kyodoshi: Chiiki jānarizumu kenkyū. *Liberal Time* 13(5), 72-75.

Shimbun Hōdō Kenkyūkai (1995). *Ima shinbun o kangaeru*. Tokyo: Nihon Shimbun Kyōkai.

Takeuchi, Toshiro (1989). *Chiiki media no shakai riron.* In T. Takeuchi & N. Tamura (Eds). *Chiiki Media, Shinban.* (pp. 3-16). Tokyo: Nihon Hyōronsha.

Tōkai Shimpō. (n.d.) *Tōkai Shimpō no Goannai.*

Yamada, H. (1985). Tohoku chihō ni okeru nikkan chi'ikishi no ricchi. *Tohoku Chiri* 37, 95-111.

Yamada, K. (2013). *3.11 to media* (3.11 and the media). Tokyo: Trans view.

Yomiuri Shimbun. (2013). Hanbai busū. *Yomiuri Shimbun Kōkoku Gaido.* Retrieved from http://adv.yomiuri.co.jp/yomiuri/busu/busu09.html

Chapter Eleven

From News to Memory Creation

Regional Newspaper Coverage of the Great East Japan Disaster, 2011

Anthony Rausch

Introduction

The Great East Japan Earthquake/Tsunami/Nuclear Power Facility Disaster of March 2011 (hereafter: the 3.11 disaster, or simply 3.11) may serve as an important transitional point in the trajectory of Japan's modern history. Based on a short-term media review, Samuels (2013) argues that, in the near term, the rhetoric of crisis that emerged with the 3.11 disaster yielded only the usual patterned response. This included political actors and policy entrepreneurs hurrying to explain what happened . . . and then assigning blame . . . and then pressing for their particular policy response–whether in terms of government policy or an outright rejection of nuclear power–to the public. In terms of outcome, he criticizes politicians for focusing solely on efforts at gaining advantage that frustrated both disaster response and meaningful change, the result being that the competing narratives meant that "stay the course" largely prevailed. However, Samuels also acknowledges, and applauds, the fact that policy entrepreneurs and citizen activists crafted and disseminated innovative ideas on a range of energy and social themes. Thus, he concludes that 3.11 leaves us with a paradox: it infused, if only termporarily, democratic politics and empowered new social actors, and aroused public interest, if not protest, in important policy questions and stimulated piecemeal reforms regarding nuclear energy policy. However, it has not yielded the game changing dynamics needed either for Japan specifically or the world at large to fully engage in the assessments and debates regarding nuclear power generation that many predicted. His conclusion regarding the disaster's place in Japan's historical trajectory: the master narrative for 3.11 and its meaning for Japan and the world is still a work in progress.

It is this "master narrative" that is the focus of this chapter—organized on the basis of a particular theoretical viewpoint with a specific research methodology, while looking at contrasting cases that emerged over a longer term view. This chapter frames the event in terms of long-term media coverage rather than immediate post-event rhetoric, looks at several disaster-area newspapers as well as a nationally syndicated column, and is based in a grounded research approach that uses news framing analysis and critical discourse analysis to assess appropriate and meaningful newspaper content for critical review. The research speaks to the transition from news of the disaster in the period directly after the event to narratives that emerged about the disaster over a longer period, using the notion of memory creation. The research speaks to journalism—particularly in terms of journalism's role in medium to long-term event coverage and the creation of social and public memory. The research also speaks to social sciences in a broader sense–particularly in terms of understanding how public memories emerge after significant events, particularly in the period before an event becomes history. Finally, the research speaks to Japanese studies, both with respect to particular Japanese patterns of journalism as well as in the more abstract realm of

Japan's relationship with its continually unfolding past—a reflection of Ben-Ari, Van Bremen and Hui's (2005) assertion of Japan's extensive and consistent preoccupation with the past and with memories of the past.

From Disaster Journalism to Memory Journalism

As Pantti et al. (2012) point out, for most people and for most disasters, the media provides our primary link to the event. The role of the media, in this case the print media in the form of the newspaper, in disaster reporting and coverage, is multi-dimensional, most usually seen in a social utility function, a post-disaster agenda setting function, and, a disaster response and mitigation and policy-education function, what could be termed "disaster journalism." Disaster journalism serves to provide information about a disaster itself—clearly a news function and usually in the period directly after the event—and, in a slightly longer term, to highlight specific aspects of the disaster in order to initiate changes in policy and social practice in response to disaster risks. Journalism and the newspaper also construct a social image of disaster events through the framing of its coverage, creating disaster images and narratives that survive after the event has passed. In this regard, a heretofore under-examined function can be added to these media functions: a role that serves to establish, develop and propagate a public memory about the disaster. The current research is found in such a social constructivist role, focusing on print media in the form of Japanese local newspapers, in the construction of a particularly local view of the disaster on the one hand, and in creation of a broader, even national, social and public memory construction of the disaster on the other. Through an examination of local newspaper coverage of the Great East Japan Earthquake of 11 March 2011, this chapter will examine this public memory creation function, what can be called "memory journalism," through the form of newspaper serial columns.

Regarding this intersection between journalism and memory, as Kitch (2008), Zelizer (2008) and Hume (2010) respectively detail, there is a significant, yet complex relationship at work, and one that is both under-explored and difficult to untangle. Kitch (2008) highlighted that such memory journalism works to construct memory across time and space as memory content is disseminated through various forms of journalistic form, genre and prose, but as content that is largely received by audiences as news. Zelizer (2008) offered that while journalism has long been seen as providing the first draft of history, particular forms of journalism and journalistic agendas require more intensive and/or extensive memory content. Thus, disaster journalism can come to operate in a manner to meet myriad societal expectations associated with disaster events, not just commemorative, but also informational, political and policy oriented. The role of journalism in the realm of memory construction relative to disasters necessitates consideration of what constitutes disaster memory and the accordant processes as they relate to journalism.

As for the process of memory creation, Neiger, Meyers and Zandberg (2011) outline the following media memory premises:

1. Collective memory is a socio-political construct – it is a socially-constructed version of the past;

2. Collective memory construction is a continuous, multi-directional process beginning with the event and followed by connection with frames of past reference to guide understanding of the event;

3. Collective memory has function–the act of remembering and under-standing that what is remembered serves some purpose; the question is what?

4. Collective memory must be concretized – it demands physical structure and cultural artifact;

5. Collective memory is narrational – memory must be structured with a familiar pattern.

Luthje (2009) conceptualized an operationalization of memory construction, identified in the interconnected agents, among them media, which create the collective and public memory of a disaster. The research identified two memory careers that yield remembrance of the event: discovery and awareness. While discovery is remembrance whereby a previously unimportant event is re-discovered through ascription of relevance at some point after the event, awareness, defined as a continuous assignment of relevance by media to an event, begins with the event itself and continues through the event's total memory career, which ends when the media ceases to focus on the event. Luthje cites Eulmann and Stadelmaier (2009) in outlining the specific media processes involved in the creation of such memory careers, which include knowledge and public opinion creation and dissemination, and initiation and impetus for some resulting action. As media and audience interact in the construction of memories, memory careers for the event are created and sustained, which initiate follow-up actions in various social settings, whether these be conversations in social groups, memory commemoration activities by interested parties, and informed mitigation, response and adaptation strategies by government (Welzer, 2001). Also taking the view of journalism as an agent of prospective memory, (Tenenboim-Weinblatt, 2011) identifies agenda setting as the primary way that the media shapes present concerns and near-future action. This is a function of quantitative and qualitative characteristics of coverage—the amount and prominence of coverage and the emphasis given to particular attributes in coverage—and takes place in the windows of opportunity in real time (i.e. in the near-term after the event) for event and time-based cases.

The literature on journalism in response to disasters thus identifies a journalism that can be termed "disaster journalism," which, over time and in combination with processes that can be labeled "memory journalism" contributes to memory formation, whether identified as social, collective, public, communicative or cultural, constituting a "disaster-memory journalism." The focus of the present research is on one form through which these disaster memories are created.

The Disaster and the Japanese Journalistic Response

The Great East Japan Earthquake/Disaster of 2011 is now history and the details are well known. The earthquake occurred off the eastern coast of northern Japan at 14.46 JST on Friday, March 11, 2011 and was one of the five most powerful earthquakes in modern history. The earthquake triggered enormously destructive tsunami waves, which, in addition to the loss of life and destruction of infrastructure, caused a meltdown at three reactors in the Fukushima Nuclear Power Plant complex, necessitating the establishment of evacuation zones affecting hundreds of thousands of residents. The Japanese National Police Agency has confirmed 15,882 deaths, 6,142 injuries, and 2,668 people missing across eighteen prefectures, but concentrated on the three coastal prefectures of Fukushima, Miyagi and Iwate, which, along with three other prefectures (Aomori, Akita and Yamagata) constitute the Tohoku Region of East Japan (National Police Agency of Japan, n.d). The earthquake and tsunami destroyed hundreds of thousands of structures, large and small, commercial and residential, and caused massive wide-scale damage to coastal municipalities, roads, railways and other infrastructure. Early estimates place insured losses from the earthquake alone at US$14.5 to $34.6 billion (Hennessy-Fiske, 2011). The nuclear plant catastrophe led to the evacuation of a large area surrounding the power plant site itself and resulting in radiation release into the nearby Pacific Ocean and into the air. This generated concerns in the short-term about direct exposure and in the longer term about area agricultural products. Rebuilding of destroyed coastal areas has been slow as difficulty in disposal of waste material has been problematic. Nuclear power generation has been in lock-down nationally (with a few exceptions) as various social agents—the government, power companies, activist groups and academics—try to formulate policy, weigh in with information, protest both nuclear-based power generation and the resulting increases in the cost of power.

There have been other views of the media response and coverage of 3.11. The most notable "newspaper story" is that of the six reporters of the *Ishinomaki Hibi Shimbun,* their facility destroyed in the disaster, diligently posting hand-copied issues of the newspaper at sites where residents gathered for six days after the disaster. A short examination of Japan's post-disaster vocabulary showing that the Japanese terms for "self-restraint" and "reconstruction-recovery" both reached their peak appearance in five main Japanese newspapers in the first week of April 2011, after having increased over the four-week period directly after the earthquake (Ichise, 2011). After this peak, the frequency of references to self-restraint fell off sharply, while reconstruction- recovery continued to be used by the media in a consistent pattern through to the end of the examination period in mid July 2011. Ichise makes an elite agenda-setting interpretation in attributing this to the media adopting various positions espoused by political leaders in the immediate aftermath on the one hand, even though the symbolic importance of respectful restraint as espoused by these media elites contradicted the economic need for recovery activities as offered by others. On the other hand, she also sees a cultural influence at work, contending that in the use of the "restraint" vocabulary, the media was reflecting persistent Japanese ethic characteristics which both called for conformity, in the form of restraint, along with the unspoken specter of condemnation should one ignore the calls for restraint. As for broader newspaper related research, Rausch (2012a) looked at the six-month coverage by one local newspaper, identifying the news-oriented trajectory of the disaster coverage. However, virtually no research has examined local newspaper coverage over a long-term post-event period, for a period exceeding a year, and with the viewpoint of a specific social outcome in mind.

Research Methodology

It has been shown that mass media cover disasters for shorter periods of time than they do other issues and that the focus is largely on the current impact of disasters rather than on any longer term themes (Houston, Pfefferbaum, and Rosenholtz, 2012), yielding limited research on the role of journalism in memory creation. Therefore, an important but heretofore under-recognized characteristic of disaster journalism research is the value of a long-term multi-dimensional view, a view that identifies transitions to coverage through frames and discourses that create and propagate a public memory of the event. Such a long-term view requires consideration of coverage of the event on the order of months, if not years, and demands a more holistic approach to viewing the media presentation of the event. Such a view makes possible identification of the transformation from established themes and issues into new themes and issues through reframing, largely through the emergence of emphasis frames, those that offer qualitatively different yet equally relevant viewpoints that influence how readers view an issue (Chong and Druckman, 2007). Recognition of this reframing is made possible by identification of multiple modes of presentation with a single medium: in the case herein, in the form of long-running thematic columns, the *rensai*, within newspapers that differ qualitatively from traditional newspaper articles. Such serial columns have a clear thematic element that is evident in critical discourse analysis of the themes that defines the content over the episodic period that any particular column is carried. As such, these columns exhibit theme and content focus, theme and content continuity, and theme and content consistency—the essential elements of an influential long-term frame—often over several months and tens of sequential individual columns within a single broader column theme. It is in this combination of thematic focus, continuity and consistency that the newspaper column as an element of disaster journalism functions in the construction of public memory of the event.

The present research focuses on the reporting and representation of the Great East Japan Earthquake by three prefectural newspapers of the disaster area. These three newspapers—the *Fukushima Minpō* of Fukushima Prefecture, the *Kahoku Shimpō* of Miyagi Prefecture, and the *Tōōnippō* of Aomori Prefecture—can be expected to reveal a contrast of views, as much of the tsunami damage associated with the earthquake was on the coastal areas of Miyagi whereas the nuclear power facility disaster played out primarily in Fukushima. Contrasting these two highly affected areas, Aomori was minimally affected by the triple disaster, and as such, can provide a viewpoint that is regional and local (i.e. not national or in another district of Japan), yet not immediate to the earthquake, tsunami or nuclear accident.

The research adopts a multi-faceted approach, starting with a numerical "one-year keyword trend" based on the *Tōōnippō* newspaper database, a review of the frequency of keyword associations showing news theme trends, before turning to the frames found in the disaster-themed columns of the three newspapers along with a nationally-syndicated column. In a methodology that followed that of Miles and Morse (2007) and Barnes et al (2008), the Japanese term *higashi nihon daishinsai* (Great East Japan Disaster) was used searched in the *Tōōnippō* newspaper database (registration required; Japanese only), with various terms added to identify the range and strength of certain combinative notions. The added terms included aid (*shien*), recovery (*fukkō*), damage (*higai*), economy (*keizai*), lifestyle (*seikatsu*), tourism (*kankō*) and policy (*seisaku*). An overall time period (12 March 2011 to 31 March 2012; 385 days) was used to establish a baseline for the frequency of keywords, which is contrasted by frequencies over the initial 12 March to 31 March period followed by frequencies for each month.

The second component of the research methodology was a focus on the framing of the event on the basis of newspaper columns that focused directly on the earthquake carried by the three newspapers at periodic points after the disaster. News framing analysis, as outlined by Nisbet (2010), suggests that media frames—modes of presentation that serve to organize abundant or complex content—both resonate with the existing schema that readers use and while also generating new schema, thereby strengthening existing connections and creating new connections between current events and broader underlying concepts (Scheufele, 1999; Scheufele and Tewksbury, 2007). The methodology of Van Gorp (2010) outlines how examination of source material can identify frames on the basis of mode presentation, schema presentation, and specific content presentation, an approach used by Rausch (2011, 2012b) to identify localized "revitalization journalism" through long-running, thematic columns in the Aomori Prefectural *Tōōnippō* newspaper. "Columns" in this research represent a specific type of presentation mode, defined and identified on the basis of being a long-running column of content organized on an identified theme, evident through critical discourse analysis (Richardson, 2007). A "column" as viewed for this research is essentially a series of individual columns within a thematic title that identifies the general content of the overall column, with each separate individual column in the sequence, usually numbered, carrying a specific sub-theme related to the larger theme. For example, a column title related to 3.11 is *Aomori Thinks about the 3.11 Disaster—Lessons from Fukushima*, within which there are six sub-sections, each with its own sub-title and consisting of multiple columns. Most columns are one-sixth of a news page, have an eye-catching logo, and are carried at regular intervals for a set period-of-time (e.g. everyday for one week; every Tuesday for two months) in the same place within the newspaper (e.g. upper left corner of page 18). Most of the columns are written by newspaper staff; in other cases, an unaffiliated group may prepare the content. In the present research, the unit of analysis is the newspaper columns that emerged after the disaster event constituting the presentation mode, with the schema reflected in the thematic title and content of any single column series constituting the interpretive frame as in the methodology of critical discourse analysis. The titles of the column subsections—the framing of the specific columns—can be viewed as a significant element in the social construction of the post-disaster consciousness surrounding the event.

The One-Year Keyword Trends

First of all, the primary term Great East Japan Disaster *(higashi nihon daishinsai)* yielded 5200 hits for the *Tōōnippō* newspaper over the period 12 March 2011 to 31 March 2012. This translates into an overall average of approximately 14 references to the disaster per daily newspaper for the entire period. For the immediate post-earthquake period, from March 12 to the end of that month, 765 "Great East Japan Disaster" references emerged, equaling 38 references per day (Rausch, 2014, p. 285). By April, this had fallen to 26, by May and June to around 18, by July and August around 11 and by September to nine references per newspaper day. The one-year anniversary (March 2012) saw the daily references rise to 12 per day. Over time, two broad trends emerged. First, the crossover points at which references went from being above the average for the year-long period versus being below occurred across June, July and August. What this indicates is that, as a news item, the event was above its average trend for the year for April, May, June, July and August, after which the number of references declined to be below the average for the research term. As will be shown, this five-month post-disaster period is the point at which many of the newspaper columns dedicated to the event introduced in the next section were begun. The second trend concerns the themes that were associated with the disaster, with a high frequency combination being associated with "aid," at 4.5 references per day overall, followed by relatively high associations with "recovery" (3.9 references per day) and "damage" (3.4 references per day) overall. Naturally, the levels for aid and damage were higher than recovery during the period directly after the disaster itself (14 and 13 references/day versus 5.4 for March, with a similar pattern for April), after which aid and recovery were generally higher for each monthly period thereafter. While terminological—and thus thematic—overlap is inherent in this assessment, this one-year view serves to identify the trends and the content of the coverage of the disaster as news.

LOCAL FRAMING IN LOCAL NEWSPAPER COLUMNS: THE THREE TOHOKU NEWSPAPERS

As an example of newspaper columns specifically in the framing of the 3.11 disaster, the *Kobe Shimbun* provides a non-disaster area example.

Motivated by its own experience with the Great Hanshin Earthquake (or Kobe Earthquake) of January 1995, the *Kobe Newspaper* has devoted notable space to content related to the Great East Japan Earthquake. As shown in Table 5, from March/April to September of 2011, 16 thematic columns were carried by the newspaper, with a total of 152 individual columns within these themes. The themes were varied, from "rebirth" and "revival" to "life in the disaster area" along with specific themes related to victims, children and volunteers. While only one column (consisting of nine columns) was carried in 2012, 2013 has seen three separate column themes: supporters, the state of recovery and life in the disaster area (the latter Part Five of a column series titled "Life"). The Kobe Shimbun columns are instructive in identifying thematic groups for analysis of the Tohoku papers. As indicated in Table 5 (see Web Appendix), there were five columns related to the "Disaster Event" itself (labeled DE in Table 5), six columns related to post-event "Human Interest" aspects of the disaster (HI), and three columns related to "Economic Recovery" (RE) and one to "Evacuees" (EV). In addition, there was a five-part column that encompassed 39 separate columns focusing on a single Sanriku disaster-affected town.

As for the disaster-related columns of the three newspapers of the disaster area—the *Fukushima Minpō* of Fukushima Prefecture, the *Kahoku Shimpō* of Miyagi Prefecture, and the *Tōōnippō* of Aomori Prefecture—the framing that emerged in the serial columns mirrored the groupings of the Kobe newspaper on the one hand, while also presenting, understandably, three very different views of the disaster (Rausch, 2014). In the case of the *Fukushima Minpō*, based on review of the newspaper homepage, there have been 16 column titles related to the disaster. Of the 16 columns, eight focused specifically on the nuclear reactor failure and the aftermath directly as evidenced by the column title and contents, with these accounting numerically for just over 70 percent of the total number of columns. However, this 70 percent portion reflected one column comprising just under 80 percent of the columns on the reactor disaster (*The Accident at the Fukushima First Plant*; 1684 columns). In addition, while there were two Human Interest-related columns, the nature of the Fukushima disaster necessitated Informational columns and also provided an example of a Time View column, the "post-seven months" column, the "post-eight months" column, and so on.

For the *Kahoku Shimpō* of Miyagi Prefecture, while the number of column titles was just one-third of the *Fukushima Minpō*, the number of columns was more evenly spread across a broad range of themes. Indeed, the framing for the *Kahoku Shimpō,* by percentage of the total number of columns, was divided over three major themes: Human Interest, Recovery and Economy and Disaster Event. However, the makeup of this distribution is highly informative of the potential of columns to influence the view of the disaster. While the Disaster Event focus emerged in the form of one column, *Testimony–Focus: The 3.11 Disaster,* which accounted for 327 columns, the Human Interest element emerged in 358 individual columns over seven column titles, of which one column theme (*Living from now with the Disaster*) accounted for 11 sub-titles and 79 individual columns. In a similar manner, the Recovery and Economy element emerged in 218 individual columns over 12 column titles, where 72 columns were carried in five series under the title *Course of Recovery.* These examples constitute frames within a frame structure, contributing to a powerful continuity and consistency of theme within which tremendous and highly specific detail is provided. A final element was the degree to which both individuals were used as sources for columns, seen in 29 interviews in the case of the *Hometown Recovery* column, and the fates of towns was followed through the one-year period, as in the *Course of Recovery* columns.

Finally, in the case of the *Tōonippō* of Aomori Prefecture, there notably fewer columns focusing specifically on the disaster, but these were clearly focused on policy and the way forward for nuclear energy. According to the *Tōonippō* website, there were four columns related specifically to the 3.11 disaster: *Thinking of Aomori and 3.11: Views of Heart and Life* (14 columns), *3.11 Lessons for Hachinohe (City)* (six columns), *The Fragile*

254   JAPANESE JOURNALISM AND THE JAPANESE NEWSPAPER

Lifeline (six columns), and *Aomori One Year On* (nine columns). However, beginning with a column run from July 2011, there was a more extensive column dedicated to questions relevant to Aomori that emerged out of the Fukushima nuclear power facility disaster: *Aomori Thinks about the 3.11 Disaster—Lessons from Fukushima*. The column consisted of the six sub-sections, with from three to eight columns for each. What emerges from analysis of the contents of these six sections was a picture of a column transitioning from the "reality" of the catastrophe, to framings of "policy," "technology" and "governance," constituting a highly analytical and forward-looking treatment of the event—essentially coming to speak to the issues relevant to policy development.

NATIONAL FRAMING IN A NEWSPAPER COLUMN: *NEW JAPAN HAPPINESS*

Contrasting these three local treatments of the disaster, there were three other series columns carried in the Aomori newspaper but which were representative of non-place based themes: *New Japan Happiness* (*Shin-Nippon no Kōfuku*; six sections: 5 January 2012 to 5 December 2012), *Disaster and Literature* (51 columns, completed 6 August 2012), and *Earthquakes and Comics* (four columns, 13-17 September 2012). The latter two, while less prominent than former, reveal a framing which connects the event to other influential social frames, namely literature and manga. More prominent, however, in terms of both volume (the number of columns) and breadth (the range of issues taken up), was the *New Japan Happiness* column.

The series is attributed to *Kyodo News Service* and, according to a *Kyodo* spokesperson, is carried in from 20 to 30 newspapers nationally. The six sections that have been published have been authored by six different journalists, with place associations reflecting disaster site areas such as Miyagi, Iwate and Fukushima Prefectures, as well as one section that makes connections to Kobe on the basis of the Hanshin-Awaji Earthquake of 1995 and various sites to which disaster site residents have evacuated. As shown, the disaster-related themes seem to have little to do with "new happiness," covering, in order: (1) *ijitachi*, the orphaning of children that accompanied the tsunami fatalities (20 columns); (2) *kokyō yo*, the places that were destroyed by the tsunami and left without residents due to the nuclear power plant disaster (15 columns); (3) *hibaku fuan*, the fear regarding radiation that accompanied the plant disaster (23 columns); (4) *ikyō kara*, the realities of evacuation from the disaster areas for the evacuees residing elsewhere (13 columns); (5) *kizuato*, the longer-term and continuing effects of the disaster, in a column section titled "scars" (22 columns); and (6) *machi to genpatsu*, the new reality of local towns and nuclear power generation (12 columns).

Capturing the content of the six column themes and the 105 columns is difficult. The "voices" reflect the thematic frame, and are thus predominantly family, usually parents but also sons and daughters, or residents, whether portrayed simply as residents or as farmers, fishermen, or the aged. The list of "who" also includes evacuees, civic leaders, volunteers, and those who lost someone to the disaster. The circumstance or change that is presented is most difficult to capture, but the general theme is one of change, whether this is framed as through the loss of someone or one's hometown, the temporary character of life as an evacuee or the recognition that the life that was will never be the same again. As for the message or the meaning, there are messages of loneliness and despair, descriptions of the difficulty of working out a future, lamentations of the daily burden of adapting to a totally changed circumstance, and recognition of the importance of human connection in times of difficulty (see Table 6; Web Appendix).

Discussion: A Disaster, Japanese Journalism and Public Memory

The research herein has looked at local newspaper coverage over a two-year period following the Great East Japan Earthquake of March 2011, examining long-running disaster-related newspaper columns of three disaster-area local newspapers. The research focuses specifically on serial columns (*rensai*) as a newspaper journalism style and the long-term treatment of the disaster through such columns, highlighting first, the transition of newspaper coverage from treating the disaster as "news" to coverage in the form of serial columns, and second focusing on the specific content of these "post-news" serial columns.

The implications regarding social sciences, journalism in general, and disaster journalism specifically have largely to do with timing and transition. Suffice it to say, the timing of the transition from news to column reflects the reality of news: any event or issue eventually becomes sufficiently covered as news, while new events and new issues emerge that demand the news space allocated to the original issue and coverage of the issue fades. However, in the present case, the transition to newspaper coverage of the earthquake disaster through newspaper columns is significant not just because it happens, but rather on the basis of the explicit signaling of the transition from news to something "post news" which is created by this framing through columns. The columns signaled disaster-related content through the series column titles, with the themes ultimately accommodating a wide range of views about the disaster that were not "news" but constituted content about the disaster event, human-interest aspects and concerns about recovery and the economy. The use of the column as a primary mode of framing also ensured continuity and consistency in the presentation of these specific themes. The characteristics of continuity and consistency inherent in journalistic framing are evident in the number of individual columns carried within a particular column title (most in the "tens" of columns per column title, in the hundreds for several of the *Fukushima Minpō* columns and 150-plus separate columns in just two column titles of the *Kahoku Shimpō*).

The range of thematic coverage revealed in the various newspaper columns highlights the multiple geographic, social and thematic spaces that make up post-disaster journalistic coverage. What is seen in the

From News to Memory Creation 257

newspaper coverage through the rensai columns on one level is a Kansai newspaper responding across a geographic divide—due to its own experience with an earthquake disaster—together with two local newspapers responding within their geographic exclusivity, the case for Fukushima and Miyagi. The former is however, constrained thematically to the implications of its "nuclear disaster" while the Miyagi newspaper reflects a multi-thematic reality: loss of life, widespread damage, survivors, economic recovery, and so on. At another level, the newspaper coverage by the Aomori newspaper, while geographically removed from the event (and therefore spared "direct thematic" implications related to the earthquake), takes up the nuclear aspect of the disaster due to its own nuclear power profile. And finally, the *Kyodo News Service's* treatment of the events incorporates the geographic and thematic elements into a universally approachable Japanese social treatment, one that is directed to a national Japanese audience, irrespective of geographical or thematic closeness to the actual event itself. This outlines a new understanding of disaster journalism in general—in the form of columns over the longer-term view that reflect themes related to "human-interest" and "recovery and the economy." This is an example of where Japanese studies-based research can contribute to general social sciences—a view of how journalism simultaneously reflects and transcends geography based on the demands of a particular theme.

The value of the research in term of Japanese Studies in general speaks to the value of reading several newspapers, among them a local newspaper, and making note of the geographic scale that is constructed in the thematic discourse within. While it is understandable that the *Fukushima Minpō* and the *Kahoku Shimpō* would concentrate on themes relevant to their specific post-disaster circumstance, the *Tōōnippō* presents a different case through two different columns. Although being relatively unaffected by the earthquake or nuclear disaster, the *Tōōnippō* was host to a detailed assessment of the future of the nuclear power industry, in the form of the *Lessons from Fukushima* column. Building on the idea of serial columns as signaling content that is not news *per se*, the *Lessons from*

Fukushima columns served as policy-related informational-educational content for residents of Aomori Prefecture, home to three nuclear power related facilities—two nuclear energy power plants and a nuclear waste reprocessing facility. Finally, that a column taking up such tragic issues as the circumstance of post-disaster orphans, the general unease over radiation exposure, the realities of resident evacuation and the long-lasting effects of such a such a disaster should have as its moniker *New Japan Happiness* is revealing in its framing and, presumably, indicative a new interpretation to serial columns in their treatment of the 3.11 disaster. Such optimistic framing over such a long term — six column themes totaling over 100 separate columns carried by approximately 20-30 papers across Japan (according to a spokesperson for Kyodo News) — speaks to the potential for column framing in the process of public memory creation, in the form of the awareness component of the 3.11 memory career.

Further to the value of this research in relation to Japanese Studies, as Ben-Ari, Van Bremen and Hui (2005) offer in an edited work on social memory in Japan, there is an extensive and consistent preoccupation with the past and with memories from the past among Japanese people. This they contend is a result of cultural experiences with large-scale crisis, a search for a distinctive cultural identity, the economic success that make such preoccupation possible, a desire to avoid loss of memory as living memories fade over time, and the importance of place in Japanese consciousness. Saaler and Schwentker (2008) also take up memory in modern Japan, pointing out that Japanese research has concentrated on "remembrance" and "memory" guided by such approaches as the "invention of tradition" and "imagined communities," before concluding that Japan has yet to develop a body of systematic research on the Japanese "realms of memory." Taking up disasters specifically, a work included in the Ben-Ari, Van Bremen and Hui book examines preservation of the memories of the January 1995 Hanshin (Kobe) Earthquake, in the form of "memory volunteers," who orally recount the event and add subjective moral lessons (Thang 2005). While not written to reflect on media processes, the work highlights the de-politicization of the event that takes place through such oral memories, whereby references to the scale of the disaster being the result of a government not equipped to deal with such a catastrophe are replaced with lessons of hope that can be taken from the event—the disaster resulted in the emergence of unprecedented numbers of individual volunteers and the systemization of the non-profit sector in Japan. That noted, this construct of public memory (what they term "social memory") manifests itself principally in commemoration, but, as was pointed out earlier in this chapter, commemorations are often based in narratives created and disseminated by a variety of memory agents, among them journalists and newspapers. It is here that the distinction of newspaper columns less as commemoration than memory is meaningful.

What is outlined in the present research presents a new and distinct view of memory in Japan and its emergence in journalism. The practice of columns as described in this present research could be surmised to be a part of the work of journalism as memory agents, in a form that initially establishes and thereafter sustains event awareness. The general columns, those carried by the local papers and taking up the specific local issues that emerged out of the disaster, represent the first step of a public memory career for the event at the local level. In the case of the *New Japan Happiness* column, the influence is not only wider, both in terms of content and geographical extent, but also in terms of establishing such a tragic event as a starting point for "new Japan happiness." While the research herein has focused on the transition in the journalistic treatment of Japan's 3.11 disaster from news item to serial columns and the character and content of such columns, a question that begs more research concerns the long-term function, manifest and latent, of these columns. I have offered a longer-term view, a view that extends beyond immediate post-event "news coverage," together with the topic range and flexibility together with thematic consistency and continuity as the manifest characteristics of columns that mark them as distinct from news articles. In addition to this, I propose a latent function in the establishment and near-term development of the 3.11 public memory through these disaster-related columns. At present—spring, 2013—the number of columns have decreased and 3.11 is now generating from as few as three mentions per day. The everyday reporting on the status and future of nuclear power generation that emerged out of the disaster now only rarely includes reference to the disaster itself. Thus, I conclude by allowing that the first wave of 3.11 memory journalism is over—the manifest function has run its course. As to what will follow and when regarding the outcome of the latent function of this first wave, only will tell what memories are lost and what are kept . . . ultimately becoming the public memories of 3.11.

REFERENCES

Barnes, M. D., Hanson, C. L., Novilla, L. B., Meacham, A. T., McIntyre, E. & Erickson, B. C. (2008). Analysis of Media Agenda Setting During and After Hurricane Katrina: Implications for Emergency Preparedness, Disaster Response, and Disaster Policy, *American Journal of Public Health,* 98(4), 604-610.

Ben-Ari, E., Bremen, J. V. & Hui, T. Y. (2005). Memory, Scholarship and the Study of Japan. In T. Y. Hui, J. V. Bremen & E. Ben-Ari (Eds.), *Perspectives on Social Memory in Japan,* (1-19). Kent, United Kingdom: Global Oriental.

Chong, D. & Druckman, J. N. (2007). Framing Theory, *Annual Review of Political Science 10,* 103-126.

Eulmann, M. J. & Stadelmeier, M. (Eds.). (2009). *Media Governance and Medienregulierung.* Berlin: Vorwarts.

Hennessy-Fiske, M. (2011). Japan Earthquake: Insurance Cost for Quake alone Pegged at $35 Billion, AIR Says. *Los Angeles Times* (13 March 2011). Available online: http://articles.latimes.com/2011/mar/13/world/la-fgw-japan-quake-insurance-20110314.

Houston, J. B, Pfefferbaum, B. & Rosenholtz, C. E. (2012). Disaster News: Framing and Frame Changing in Coverage of Major U.S. Natural Disasters, 2000-2010, *Journalism and Mass Communication Quarterly 89*(4), 606-623.

Hume, J. (2010). Memory Matters: The Evolution of Scholarship in Collective Memory and Mass Communication, *The Review of Communication 10*(3), 181-196.

Ichise, A. (2011). Japan's Post-Disaster Vocabulary. *Frontline* (September 2011), Article ID 2226. Available Online: www.ipra.org/print.asp?articleid=2226. Accessed 10 October 2011.

Kitch, C. (2008). Placing Journalism inside Memory—and Memory Studies, *Memory Studies 1*(3), 311-320.

Luthje, C. (2009). Conceptualizing the interconnected agents of collective memory: The transforming perception of a regional geohazard between mediated discourse and conversation. Paper presented to

ECREA Philosophy of Communication Conference, 9-11 December. Available Online: www.wiso.uni-hamburg.de/fileadmin/sowi/journalistik/PDFs/CLuethje-London-02 1209.pdf

Miles, B. & Morse, S. (2007). The Role of News Media in Natural Disaster Risk and Recovery, *Ecological Economics 63*, 365-373.

National Police Agency of Japan. (n.d). Damage Situation and Police Countermeasures. Emergency Disaster Countermeasures Headquarters. Available online: www.npa.go.jp/archive/keibi/biki/higaijokyo_e.pdf

Neiger, M, Meyers, O. & Zandberg, E. (2011). On Media Memory: Editor's Introduction. In M. Neiger, O. Meyers & E. Zandberg (Eds.). *On Media Memory: Collective Memory in a New Media Age*, (1-24). New York: Palgrave Macmillan.

Nisbet, M. C. (2010). Knowledge into Action: Framing the Debates over Climate Change and Poverty. In P. D'Angelo & J. A. Kuypers (Eds.). *Doing News Framing Analysis: Empirical and Theoretical Perspectives*, (43-83). New York: Routledge.

Pantti, M., Wahl-Jorgensen, K. & Cottle, S. (2012). *Disasters and the Media*. New York: Peter Lang.

Rausch, A. S. (2011). Revitalization Journalism in Rural Japanese Newspapers: A Case Study of the Tōōnippō Newspaper and Aomori Prefecture, *Journal of International and Advanced Japanese Studies 3*, 1-14.

Rausch, A. S. (2012a). Framing a Catastrophe: Portrayal of the 3.11 Disaster by a Local Japanese Newspaper, *electronic journal of contemporary japanese studies*. Available online: www.japanesestudies.org.uk/discussionpapers/2012/Rausch.html

Rausch, A. S. (2012b). *Japan's Local Newspapers: Chihoshi and Revitalization Journalism*. London, U.K.: Routledge.

Rausch, A. S. 2013. The Regional Newspaper in Post-Disaster Coverage: Trends and Frames of the Great East Japan Disaster, 2011, *Keio Communication Review, 35*, 35-50.

Rausch, A. S. (2014). The Great East Japan Disaster, 2011 and the Regional Newspaper: Transitions from News to Newspaper Columns and the Creation of Public Memory, *International Journal of Mass Emergencies and Disasters, 32*(2), 275-296.

Richardson, J. (2007). *Analysing Newspapers: An Approach from Critical Discourse Analysis.* London, U.K.: Palgrave Macmillan.

Saaler, S. & Schwentker, W. (2008). Introduction: The Realms of Memory: Japan and Beyond. In S. Saaler and W. Schwentker (Eds.). *The Power of Memory in Modern Japan,* (1-14). Kent, UK: Global Oriental.

Samuels, R. J. (2013). Japan's Rhetoric of Crisis: Prospects for Change after 3.11, *Journal of Japanese Studies 39*(1), 97- 120.

Scheufele, D. A. (1999). Framing as a Theory of Media Effects, *Journal of Communication 49*(1), 103-122.

Scheufele, D. A. & Tewksbury, D. (2007). Framing, Agenda-setting, and Priming: The Evolution of Three Media Effect Models, *Journal of Communication 57*, 9-20.

Tenenboim-Weinblatt, K. (2011). Journalism as an Agent of Prospective Memory. In M. Neiger, O. Meyers & E. Zandberg (Eds.). *On Collective Memory: Collective Memory in a New Media Age,* (213-225). New York: Palgrave Macmillan.

Thang, L. L. (2005). Preserving the Memories of Terror: Kobe Earthquake Survivors as 'Memory Volunteers'. In T. Y. Hui, J. V. Bremen & E. Ben-Ari (Eds.), *Perspectives on Social Memory in Japan,* (191-203). Kent, United Kingdom: Global Oriental

Van Gorp, B. (2010). Strategies to Take Subjectivity out of Framing Analysis. In In P. D'Angelo & J. A. Kuypers (Eds.). *Doing News Framing Analysis: Empirical and Theoretical Perspectives,* (84-109). New York: Routledge.

Welzer, H. (2001). Das soziale Gedachtnis. In H. Welzer (Ed.). *Das soziale Gedachtnis,* (9-21). Hamburg: Geschichte, Erinnerung, Tradierung.

Zelizer, B. (2008). Why Memory's Work on Journalism does not Reflect Journalism's Work on Memory, *Memory Studies 1*(1), 79-87.

Conclusion

In an edited work such as this, one seeks the sum that ultimately emerges from the many respective chapters. In this work, each chapter presented a different and highly specific view of Japanese journalism: some were historical, others contemporary; some were empirical, others ethnographic; most focused on domestic elements, several considered regional implications; many were primarily descriptive, a number clearly critical.

Combinative and Connecting Themes

While individual readers will find combinations and connections that fit their disciplinary background, theoretical viewpoint and research objectives, there are four broad themes that seem to emerge from the chapters herein.

First, there is the notion of "place" in local journalism and local newspapers and the reality and significance of local, regional and national in Japan and Japanese Studies. While Kanzaki's chapter focuses exclusively on shifts and tensions related to journalism and place, first in the historical development of newspapers across the divide of Kansai versus Kanto, and second in the potential for digital newspapers to prioritize local over national, other chapters speak to place as well. Hood's chapter regarding news coverage of the 1985 JAL airline disaster also takes note of "place," both in the sense of an event that captures national attention, but one that is bounded by constraints of place in its occurrence and in the representation of that event in different regional newspapers that reflect different operational realities and content priorities. The chapters by Takekawa and Rausch both privilege place in the form of local newspapers and their representations of the 3.11 disaster: in the former in a comparison of newspaper coverage by the newspapers of two affected areas and in the later in a view that covers both a broader geographical scale and a longer time period. In this sense, these chapters highlight Japanese journalism's relation to place as well as what a careful "place-based" approach to viewing Japanese newspapers can offer to a wide range of Japanese Studies research themes.

The second summary theme concerns the role of journalism and the newspaper in contemporary society and its effect on social discourse. There is a wealth of content in the work of this book that speaks to the broad practice, function, influence and effect of journalism in Japanese society and the implications this has for Japanese Studies. Han provides an Asian-wide view of how journalism arbitrates, if not manipulates, history, creating functional but also political memories out of the ambiguity of historical events. Lee likewise provides an examination that reveals how newspaper editorials in Japan have influenced the trajectory of history beyond Japan, showing that newspapers influence not only social discourse, but through this discourse, government policy. Nanri's chapter points to the implications inherent in accessing different news venues, outlining in abundant detail how news is produced according to differing templates that construct background, provide context and offer alternatives, thereby yielding different reader impressions of the same events; Nanri's work speaks to how media acts to create specific and distinct communities of news consumers.

The 3.11 disaster has been the basis of much recent research, some on response and recovery, some on the changes it has forced, and some on the ethnographies of the disaster. Specifically with regard to journalism, the 3.11 disaster provided the basis for McCarthy, Sherif, Takekawa and Rausch to consider how reportage of the event as a function of journalistic views and formulaic framing yield differing interpretations of the same

Conclusion 267

event, noting in particular how similar newspapers can focus on and emphasize different points of reference. McCarthy's chapter in particular, along with the chapters by Ogawa and Nanri, speak to assertions regarding the Japanese journalism community of being quiescent to power versus acting as a watchdog of government and the private sector on one set of analytical criteria and homogeneous and innocuous versus diverse and meaningful on another. Sherif's chapter points also to the influences of the newspaper on social discourse, in this case with regard to safety as a contested arena of scientific reasoning versus government statements, where journalistic reporting takes on the added burden of triangulating the two sides of any issue with the descriptions of reality as experienced by citizens. As above, Takekawa and Rausch both focus on local newspapers and their representations of the 3.11 disaster, in both cases considering the extensive meaning production that the newspaper column allows for.

Finally, research methodology constitutes an important theme of several of the chapters in combination and connection. Chapters by Maeshima and Kanzaki herein point to the rich historical trajectories of journalism as both newspaper and magazine, offering the development of these mediums as windows onto Japanese society in the past. Maeshima's chapter in particular provides cautionary notes for such research: beware of simple extension of present-day interpretations of media to the past, not solely regarding the characterization and categorization of different media, but also in terms of the complex relationships between media and other institutions of society and the implications thereof. Han's work also provides methodological insights through use of critical discourse analysis along with recognition of, as above, the creation of memories for specific agendas. Research methodology is also a main point of Ogawa's chapter, where he posits that digital news sources provide researchers with the opportunity to bypass the institutional bias inherent in news production, offering the researcher unfiltered sources they can access independently. Instructive research dichotomies emerge as methodological hints from other contributors: Hood points out that the same event can yield areas of content that are largely homogenous, along with other areas that reveal diversity. McCarthy sees in journalism's reporting of a disaster both quiescence as well as independence, concluding that often a single medium will offer contrasting, viewpoints yielding contradictory outcomes to reporting on the same event. Rausch stresses the importance of both near-term and long-term views in using journalism in social scientific research, pointing out that the newspaper is often the most stable media resource for gaining such often divergent viewpoints.

Journalism and the Newspaper in Japanese Studies: Going Forward

Chris Hedges (2010), in his treatise *Death of the Liberal Class*, had much to say about the importance of journalism and newspapers in modern society. He asserted that the demise (if not death) of the liberal class in American society has been accompanied by a shift from a print-based culture to one where image dominates. He offered that the demise of newspapers (together with the degradation of the education) "has created a culture in which verifiable fact, which is rooted in complexity and discipline of print, no longer forms the basis of public discourse or our collective memory" (207). The loss of the distinguishability and traceability that is inherent in print has provided for a culture of emotionally driven narratives in which facts and opinion are now interchangeable.

Hedge's work is offered not to spark a debate about liberalism and a liberal class in Japan or journalism's influence in maintaining such an ideology or social class, but rather to point to one opinion arguing the importance of journalism and newspaper reading in the trajectory of modern societies; journalism and print media as a vital part of healthy contemporary societies. In this sense, research on Japanese journalism is important not just in terms of what it says about Japanese journalism *per se*, but as importantly, as a measure of the state of Japanese political and social society. One need only look at three recent trends that will influence the future of Japanese journalism to see this vital connection:

Japanese journalism's self view, Japan's fall in the 2013 World Press Freedom Index and passage of the State Secrets Law in December 2013.

First there are the findings from an Institute of Journalism & Media Studies survey showing that Japanese journalists increasingly see their role as being "watchdogs on government," "arousing public opinion," and "setting an agenda on social issues" as opposed to simply "education and enlightenment" and "creation of social consensus" (Oi, et al., 2012). The problem, as the IJMS data also shows, is that Japanese journalists themselves admit that they are not very successful at "investigating claims made by government." Indeed, the IJMS data shows that about six out of ten Japanese news professionals view the relationship between journalists and government sources as cooperative, rather than antagonistic. It is with this in mind that Yamawaki (2012), in an essay titled *Reinvigorating National Newspapers in Japan*, pointed to professional development, multi-sourced reporting, and editorial independence as the pillars of new journalistic practice in Japan.

Second, as reported on the *Global Journalist* webpage (2014), Japan's Press Freedom Index ranking fell from 22nd in 2012 to 53rd in 2013, largely a reflection of Japan's lack of transparency and respect for access to information regarding issues related to the March 2011 Fukushima disaster. In this regard, see the work of Ogawa, McCarthy and Sherif herein. As troubling as this trend is, the intentionality of the State Secrets Law is more chilling. As widely reported, the State Secrets Law give government agency heads discretionary power to classify as a state secret 23 types of information in four categories (Kurtenback, 2013; *The Yomiuri Shimbun,* 2013; Traywick, 2013). The law stiffens penalties for leaks by government officials as well as for journalists who seek such information, disregarding objections that such a law could be used to hide government errors and abuses on the one hand, and suppress civil liberties and independence of the press on the other. Worries abound that the law may be used to hinder public disclosure, punish whistle-blowers, and, as journalists can be jailed for seeking information that they may not know has been classified as secret, muzzle the media. The degree to which conditions at the disabled 3.11 nuclear power station, for example, constitute "state secrets" will, along with assessments of other information related to defense, diplomacy, counterintelligence and counterterrorism, be contentious for some time. As Traywick reports, while the measure may be seen as part of a larger effort by Prime Minister Abe to move away from Japan's pacifist constitution and establish stronger military and defense ties with the United States, critics argue that virtually any matter of national significance could be deemed a "state secret," including cases showing government culpability in areas of public health and safety.

While the State Secrets Law as a current issue is framed in terms of the functioning of Japanese political society, the larger point of this book is that journalism provides an illuminating view onto and into Japanese society. Journalism allows the researcher to see both specific historical events as they unfolded as well as the broader historical trends of history: the first draft of history as well as the continually and often contested emerging drafts (plural) of history. Journalism illuminates the reality of regionalism and the differing concerns of different places, both national concerns as they unfold in local places and local issues as they influence national discourses. Journalism provides insight into the connections between professional editorials, informed opinions, broad social discourses, and ultimately, governmental policy, public and diplomatic. The study of journalism allows researchers to see the opinions, and the basis of the opinions of the populace. In short and to conclude, journalism, in the form of the daily newspaper or the monthly magazine, provides a view of our topic that is edited, but dynamic; accessible, but stable; informative, but illuminating. For the researcher, it is a window onto the world.

REFERENCES

Hedges, C. (2010). *Death of the Liberal Class.* New York: Nation Books.

Kurtenback. E. (2013, December 6). The Big Story: Japan parliament approves contentious secrets law. *Associated Press.* Retrieved from http://bigstory.ap.org/article/japan-parliament-approves-contentious-secrets-law.

Oi, S., Fukuda, M. & Sako, S. (2012). The Japanese Journalist in Transition: Continuity and Change. In D. Weaver & L. Wilnat (Eds.). *The Global Journalist in the 21st Century* (pp. 52-65). London: Routlege.

The Yomiuri Shimbun. (2013, December 9). Issues remain over implementation of Japan's secrets law. *Asia News Network.* Retrieved from http://www.asianewsnet.net/Issues-remain-over-implementation-of-Japans-secret-54800.html.

Traywick, C. (2013, December 6). In Japan's State Secrets Law, Shades of Red, While and Blue. *Foreign Policy.* Retrieved from http://complex.foreignpolicy.com/posts/2013/12/05/in_japan_s_state_secrets_law_shades_of_red_white_and_blue.

Yamawaki, T. (2012). Reinvigorating National Newspapers in Japan. *EastAsiaForum.* www.eastasiaforum.org/2012/11/24/reinvigorating-national-newspapers/ (November 24, 2012; accessed December, 2013).

Web Appendix

An electronic appendix for this book with figures and tables is available from the book website. Please visit http://www.teneopress.com/books/9781934844700.cfm for more information.

Index

analysis, xiv–xv, xviii–xix, 50, 135, 138–140, 186, 194, 198, 236, 242, 248–250, 252, 265, 267
anti-nuclear, xvii, 56–64, 66, 202

centralisation, xvi, 32, 50
chirashi, xiii
circulation, xii, xiv, 3–4, 13, 15, 17, 19, 21, 33–34, 42–43, 46, 50, 147, 187, 219, 223, 226
columns, xx, 10, 16, 94, 98, 110, 243, 248–260
Content Analysis, xviii, 138–140, 186, 194
cooperation, xviii–xix, 42, 189–194, 203
crisis, xviii, 42, 180, 182–184, 191–194, 206–207, 258
Critical Discourse Analysis, xvii, 77, 86, 242, 248, 250, 267

demographic, xiii, 150
desu/masu, 8
digital, xv–xvii, 31, 44–49, 55–57, 61, 63, 66, 68–69, 72–73, 265–267
discourse, xvii, 75, 77, 79, 85–87, 91–92, 95, 97, 105, 107–110, 112, 114, 116, 118–119, 121–122, 125–126, 155, 198, 212–213, 242, 248, 250, 257, 266–268
diversification, xvi, 7–8, 10, 50

editorial, 4, 10, 15, 21, 93–97, 106–107, 113, 117–119, 121–123,
editorial (*continued*), 135, 155, 157, 159–162, 166–168, 173, 189–193, 269
Established News Media, 154
evacuees, 197–202, 204, 211–214, 252, 255

foreign policy, xvii, 107–111, 113, 118–121, 123, 125–126
framing, xvii, 186, 242–243, 249–254, 256, 258, 266
Fukushima, 56–61, 64–68, 73, 161, 170, 179, 181–182, 184–185, 189, 191–192, 197–203, 205–207, 209–214, 217, 246, 248–250, 252–254, 256–258, 269

gender, 7–9, 11, 15, 21, 68
Great East Japan Disaster, xv, xviii–xx, 177, 180, 188, 217–218, 226, 241, 243, 246, 248–252, 255

historical trajectory, 242
homogeneity, 155–158, 173, 219

Independent Web Journal (IWJ), 55, 58–61, 63–64, 66–67, 69, 72
Interwar, xvi, 3–5, 9, 12–13, 15, 17–21
Iwate, xv, xix, 160, 167, 171, 198, 217–219, 222–226, 229, 233–235, 254

Japan Airlines, xv, 132
journalism, ix–xii, xv–xix, 3–4,

journalism (*continued*), 18–22, 35,
  37–41, 50–51, 55–57, 61, 67,
  69–73, 75, 78, 80, 83–86, 98,
  115, 118, 124, 131, 134, 141, 148,
  151, 177, 194, 213, 228–229, 235,
  242–245, 248, 250, 255–257,
  259–260, 265–270
 and social memory, 78
 disaster journalism, 243–245, 248,
  256–257
 independent journalism, xvi, 55–56,
  73
 Japanese journalism, ix, xii, xv,
  xvii–xviii, 22, 35, 38–39, 41,
  72–73, 75, 118, 141, 177, 213,
  255, 265–269
 memory journalism, 243–245, 260
 memory site, 79, 82–84, 86, 88, 91,
  97–98
 new journalism, xvi, 3, 20–21, 55
 periodical journalism, 18
 revitalization journalism, 235, 250

Kamaishi Fukkō Shimbun, 225
Kansai newspapers, xvi, 31
keyword trend, 249
kisha kurabu, 41, 134, 151, 227
Kobe Shimbun, 42–44, 48–49, 159,
  251
Kyodo News, 49, 58, 70, 226, 254,
  257
Kyoto Shimbun, 42–44

leadership, xviii–xix, 63, 96, 120,
  180–182, 185, 189–190, 193–194

magazines, 3–22, 32, 44–45, 57,
  109–110
commercialization, 11, 13, 19
content, x–xi, xiv–xv, xviii–xix,

content (*continued*), 6–11, 14, 16,
  18, 20, 32, 37–38, 41, 43, 46–50,
  55–56, 67, 80, 119, 131, 135,
  138–140, 145–146, 157–158,
  186–189, 194, 214, 219, 221–222,
  226–231, 233–234, 236, 242, 244,
  248–252, 255–259, 266–267
 gender, 7–9, 11, 15, 21, 68
 innovations, 9, 16
 readership, xiii–xiv, 10, 15–17, 21,
  97, 131, 186
 research, vii, ix, xiv–xviii, xx, 5, 44,
  55–58, 61, 63–64, 66–67, 72–73,
  79–80, 85–86, 91, 108, 133–135,
  137, 139, 142, 147, 151, 156–157,
  173, 180, 186–187, 194, 197–198,
  205–206, 211, 242–243, 245,
  247–251, 255–259, 265–268
 sociocultural, 86
 master narrative, 242
 media role, 108
 memory, xvii, xix–xx, 77–92,
  97–98, 229–232, 234–236,
  242–245, 248, 255, 258–260, 268
 memorialization, 136, 140, 148

News Framing Analysis, 242, 249
newspaper circulation, 187, 219
newspaper editorials, xvii, 117–119,
  121, 155–160, 162, 166–167,
  169–170, 173–174, 266
newspaper overview, 56, 203, 219
newspaper revenue, xii
newspapers, ix–x, xiv–xx, 33–43,
  47–51, 58, 89, 96, 118–119,
  121–122, 135, 137–138, 140,
  143, 147–148, 150, 157, 163, 166,
  173–174, 183, 187, 197–198, 205,
  214, 217–226, 228, 232–236, 241,
  243, 247, 251, 254–257, 265–267,
  270

Index

Nico Nico Dōga, xviii, 67–69, 153–154, 173–174
North Korea, xvii, 105–108, 110, 112–126, 159

Osaka journalism, 35, 37–40, 51
Our Planet TV, 67–69

panic, xviii, 180–181, 183–184, 189–190
place, xi, 84, 95, 97, 109, 117, 125, 134, 142, 193, 219–220, 227, 232, 242, 245–246, 250, 254, 258–259, 265–266
politics, x, xviii, 22, 33, 38, 41, 63–66, 77, 80–81, 86, 90, 92–93, 96–97, 106, 111, 116, 121–122, 153, 192, 221, 226, 235, 242
post news, 256
press club, xv, 41, 56, 58, 61, 70–73, 227–228

quantitative easing, 156, 166, 168–169, 173

radiation, xix, 59–60, 183, 185, 189, 199–208, 210–212, 246, 255, 258
readership, xiii–xiv, 10, 15–17, 21, 97, 131, 186
reconstruction, xix, 85, 98, 183, 200, 205, 217, 219, 229–233, 235–237, 247
representation, 40, 78, 80–81, 83, 87, 110, 248, 265
revitalization journalism, 235, 250

sacrifice, xix, 197–199, 202, 213
security, xviii, 15, 92, 106–108, 112–118, 123, 125, 156–158, 161–163, 166, 173
serialization, xix, 6, 10, 14, 16, 219, 227–235
social discourse, xvii, 75, 85–87, 97, 105, 107–110, 112, 118–119, 122, 125–126, 155, 213–214, 242, 250, 266–268
socio-cultural background, 17–18
State Secrets Law, 73, 269

threat, 38, 106, 114, 125, 158–159, 161–163
Tohoku newspapers, 251
Tokyo, xvi, 31–34, 40–41, 46, 50, 223
transparency, xviii–xix, 184, 189–190, 194, 209, 269
Trans-Pacific Partnership, 156–157, 170, 173

videos, xviii, 133–134, 153–158, 163–165, 168–169, 171–173, 181
viewers, 110–111, 153–158, 163–164, 166–171, 173–174

women's magazines, 3–21
World Press Freedom Index, 73, 269
writing style, 7–9

Yasukuni Shrine, xv, xvii, 79, 88–93, 95–96, 150, 158–160, 162

Contributors

Choonghee Han is an assistant professor in the Department of Communication at Hope College. He is a former broadcaster and journalist turned academic with an interest in journalism as a cultural practice, collective and cultural memory, and digital film production. His recent research has focused on the politics of memory in East Asia and public service broadcasting in a rapidly changing political and technological climate.

Christopher Hood is a Reader in Japanese Studies at Cardiff University. Dr. Hood's publications include: *Japan: The Basics* (2014), *Osutaka: A Chronicle of Loss In the World's Largest Single Plane Crash* (2014), *Dealing with Disaster in Japan: Responses to the Flight JL123 Crash* (2011), *Shinkansen: From Bullet Train to Symbol of Modern Japan* (2006), and *Education Reform in Japan: Nakasone's Legacy* (2001). Homepage: www.hood-online.co.uk; Twitter: @HoodCP

Sachiyo Kanzaki received her Ph.D. in anthropology from the Université de Montréal, with a thesis on Kansai regionalism. Lecturer at the UdeM since 2007, she has been affiliated with the Osaka City University and University of Saskatchewan. She focuses her research on regional development, social mobilization and social change. She is currently working on the municipal management of communities hosting nuclear power and green power stations.

Seung Hyok Lee is an adjunct assistant professor in the East Asian Studies, Renison University College, at the University of Waterloo in Canada. He was previously a visiting scholar affiliated with the Asian Institute in the Munk School of Global Affairs and the Department of Political Science at the University of Toronto. He is also program coordinator of Japan Futures Initiative (JFI).

Shiho Maeshima is Associate Professor at the University of Tokyo. Academically trained in Japan, the US, and Canada, Dr. Maeshima has been conducting research on the comparative historical study of the democratization/popularization of print and reading culture in modern Japan and the discursive formation of everyday modernity through Japanese interwar mass media.

Mary M. McCarthy is an associate professor of politics and international relations at Drake University in Des Moines, Iowa. Dr. McCarthy specializes in Japan's domestic and foreign policies. She has written on topics including the Japanese media, cooperation and conflict between Japan and China in the East China Sea, and the historical legacies of the Asia-Pacific War on Japan's foreign relations. She is also a 2014 Japan Studies Fellow at the East-West Center in Washington.

Keizo Nanri. PhD in Linguistics, University of Sydney. Convenor of the Oita Text Forum. He is interested in the process of text generation, in particular the relationship between culture, personality, and text structure. He is currently investigating argument patterns of Hashimoto Toru, the mayor of the city of Osaka, and the way of resenting product information by Japanese fashion magazines.

Akihiro Ogawa is a professor of Japanese studies at Stockholm University, Sweden. He completed a Ph.D. in anthropology in 2004 at Cornell University, followed by postdoctoral work at Harvard University's Program on US-Japan Relations and Department of Anthropology. His major research interest is contemporary Japanese society, focusing on civil society. He is the author of the award-winning book *The Failure of Civil Society?: The Third Sector and the State in Contemporary Japan* (SUNY Press, 2009) and extensive writings on politics, social movements, peace, and education.

Anthony Rausch is professor in the English Department of Hirosaki University, Japan. He completed a Ph.D. in Japanese Studies at Monash University in 2007. His research interests focus on rural Japan and he has published on volunteerism, media, cultural commodities and the cultural

Contributors

economy and the Heisei Mergers, including *Cultural Commodities in Japanese Rural Revitalization* (Brill, 2010) and *Japan's Local Newspapers* (Routledge, 2012).

Ann Sherif teaches in the East Asian Studies Program at Oberlin College, Ohio, USA. Her current research interests focus on networks of literary writers, independent publishers, and journalists in 20th century Japan.

Shunichi Takekawa is Associate Professor at Ritsumeikan Asia Pacific University (Beppu-city, Oita Prefecture, Japan) where he teaches journalism and media studies. His research interests include the Japanese press and nationalism, and popular culture and identity in Japan. His works appeared in *Social Science Japan Journal, Asia-Pacific Journal: Japan Focus,* and *Journal of Mass Communication Studies*, among others.

CPSIA information can be obtained
at www.ICGtesting.com
Printed in the USA
BVHW041301070719
552799BV00010B/28/P